COOPERSTOWN CORNER

Columns from The Sporting News
1962-1969

By Lee Allen

A SABR Publication

Cover Design by Pati Ingold.
Cover Photography by David Kennedy.
Lee Allen Photograph Courtesy of the
National Baseball Library.

COOPERSTOWN CORNER, COLUMNS FROM THE SPORTING NEWS
by Lee Allen (ISBN 0-910137-41-2). Published by the Society for American
Baseball Research, Inc., P.O. Box 93183, Cleveland, OH 44101. Postage paid
at Pittsburgh, PA 15233. All rights reserved. Published through an agreement
with The Sporting News, A Times Mirror Company, St. Louis, MO. Printed by
Mathews Printing, Pittsburgh, PA.

INTRODUCTION

By Steven P. Gietschier
Director of Historical Records, The Sporting News

ALMOST EVERY BASEBALL ANTHOLOGY WORTH ITS SALT contains a piece by Lee Allen. You can look it up. When the best baseball writing is collected and published, Lee Allen is wont to be there. The first "Fireside Book of Baseball," for example, includes an Allen essay on players' nicknames. The second and third Fireside volumes follow suit. "The Armchair Book of Baseball" and the fourth Fireside both reprint "A Study in Suet," Allen's deft and humorous look at the game's heaviest (and lightest) players.

There's a good reason why editors frequently turn to Allen. Class tells, and Allen wrote with such flair that anthologists have been hard pressed to keep him out. Indeed, Charles Einstein, the Fireside compiler, confessed to the other problem, the seeming impossibility of selecting one of Allen's pieces above all the others. "I should have liked," Einstein wrote, "to include the entire contents of Lee Allen's book 'The Hot Stove League.'"

At the time of his death in 1969, Allen had for ten years been the historian at the Hall of Fame's National Baseball Library. He was widely celebrated for his encyclopedic recall of persons famous and obscure, events large and small. "I care very little for statistics as such," he always said. "My concern is the players. Who are these men? What are they? What problems have they faced? Where are they now?" Allen dedicated his life to asking these questions and then to answering them. He demonstrated his knowledge on radio programs and television shows and was a prolific writer whose books and articles marked him as baseball's foremost historical expert.

Some boys dream of a life in the circus; others, like Lee Allen, dream of a life in baseball. Born in 1915, he was the son of a Cincinnati attorney who served three terms in Congress. Having seen his first Reds game while still in knee pants, Allen was a regular at Redland Field (later Crosley Field) by the time he entered Hughes High School. Whether he cajoled the principal into letting him escape from class early, as some romantic accounts have it, or whether the school day ended before the late afternoon games began, Allen got to the ball park every day in time for the first pitch.

Paying his way into the grandstand, he positioned himself in the upper deck near the press box where he one day hoped to work.

Readers of the Cincinnati Enquirer soon noticed that Jack Ryder's "Notes of the Game" column often included an exact tally of how many balls and strikes each pitcher had thrown. Ryder was a good reporter, but these data were supplied by Allen who charted every pitch while munching on a steady supply of food from the concession stand. Later he earned seventy-five cents a game for telephoning out-of-town scores from the Western Union ticker in the press box to the scoreboard. "I lost money on that deal," Allen remembered. "I used to spend about a $1.50 a day for ice cream, soda, and peanuts."

After graduation, Allen matriculated in psychology at Kenyon College in the same class as Bill Veeck. He covered baseball for the campus daily but in truth didn't know what occupation to pursue. In 1935 he somehow managed to tour the Soviet Union with newsman H.V. Kaltenborn and was far out of touch with baseball until reaching Moscow where ambassador William Bullitt let him read back copies of The New York Times.

After Kenyon, Allen enrolled in the Columbia University School of Journalism. But after little more than one semester, he was invited to join the Reds as a paid assistant to Gabe Paul, then the team's publicity director and road secretary. Allen stayed with the Reds as they won consecutive National League pennants in 1939 and 1940. When the United States entered World War II, Allen was rejected for military service because of high blood pressure. In 1942, he took a civilian post with the navy and shipped out of Seattle to work as a laborer on Kodiak Island, Alaska. After a year or so, he returned to Cincinnati to replace Paul, himself called to the service.

All the while, Allen was accumulating the foundation of an outstanding collection of baseball books, manuscripts, and notes. In fact as he recalled later, "a book — 'The Baseball Cyclopedia' by Ernest J. Lanigan — got me started. I always loved baseball, but I wasn't very good at playing the game. I wasn't fast enough. But I still wanted to be a part of it and this was a way I could do it." He began to build a variegated career as a baseball researcher, putting in stints for two Cincinnati newspapers, appearing on radio and later television, and even working a year for The Sporting News. "It was my observation of Taylor Spink," he said, "that taught me the only real happiness is in one's work."

Still, as many baseball researchers have learned, breaking into print for profit requires not only talent but luck. "You just can't get out of college and say, 'I'm a writer; hire me,'" he once reminisced. While working with the Reds he saw that G.P. Putnam had begun publishing its series of club histories. He wrote to them cold, "and a fellow wrote back saying they didn't know anything about me as a writer and that they hadn't decided who they would assign the Reds book to." Putnam told him to take a stab at it. "I wrote the book, they accepted it, and it got me started."

That first book, "The Cincinnati Reds" (1948), led in turn to "100 Years of Baseball" (1950) and "The Hot Stove League" (1955), an absolutely marvelous collection of unusual research and anecdotes that would eventually attract the anthologists. Just as important, these books established Allen as a recognized expert who could make a living from his passion. On Cincinnati's radio station WSAI, for example, he once challenged listeners to write in — this was before talk shows — giving the names of former players for him to identify. On May 23, 1952, while working in Philadelphia, Allen and Phillies manager Eddie Sawyer engaged in a Baseball Talkathon from 11:15 p.m. to 5:00 a.m. on KYW. The pair answered questions telephoned to several operators and forwarded to moderator Jean Shepherd.

In early 1959, the National Baseball Hall of Fame announced that Allen would replace his "start," retiring Ernest J. Lanigan, as historian. It was a propitious appointment for both the Hall and Allen who brought with him to Cooperstown not only his knowledge and research skills, but a vast baseball library. The mover who trucked the books from Cincinnati said they filled fifty-five cartons and weighed 5000 pounds. Allen, who began his new job with no advance instructions, had a firm idea of how he would proceed. "I hope to make the office of Historian of the Hall a place where anyone may write for information about almost any phase of baseball history and receive accurate replies."

The Allen family — for Lee had married the former Adele Felix the previous August — settled into Cooperstown just a few months before the birth of twins Randall and Roxann in October, 1959. The new father nevertheless dove into his work with a great deal of gusto. Ensconced in the old library on the second floor of the museum, Allen established a daily routine that included meeting a steady stream of visitors, answering mail as soon as it arrived, and chipping away at the long-range research projects he set for himself. His workdays soon stretched to twelve hours and his weeks to seven days.

One of these assignments involved uncovering the date and place of death for nineteenth century National Leaguers. Another had him breaking down the number of games outfielders had played in left, center, and right fields. "No one has ever separated outfields before," Allen told Sports Illustrated shortly after he began. "When Zack Wheat is inducted into the Hall of Fame this summer, I'll be able to tell him how many games he played in each field."

Allen's major effort, though, was to collect biographical data on the 11,000 men he estimated had played in the major leagues to that point. In this mammoth task that would grow into the first edition of The Baseball Encyclopedia, he labored with other pioneers in baseball research, including John Tattersall, S.C. Thompson, Frank Marcellus, Karl Wingler, Harry Simmons, Allen Lewis, Joseph Overfield, Clifford Kachline, and Paul Rickart.

After a while, the Allens decided to spend the summers in Cooperstown but the winters in Boca Raton, Florida. Allen used the trips back and forth as opportunities for extended research odysseys. He would visit one remote hamlet after another, prowl through graveyards and courthouse records, and gently pump as many townspeople as necessary for the information he was seeking.

Allen did not sit on his research. He turned it into a long list of articles, innumerable speeches to dozens of groups, and a series of books renowned for their original insights. In "The National League: The Official History" (1961), for example, he used his unprecedented access to league documents and correspondence to throw new light on pivotal events such as Fred Merkle's boner and Hal Chase's involvement in fixing games.

In the companion volume, "The American League Story" (1962), Allen related how president Ban Johnson moved the Milwaukee franchise to St. Louis, home of The Sporting News, and how in 1903, type for the peace agreement between the leagues was set in that newspaper's composing room.

Basking in the success of these books, Allen accepted an additional commission, a column in The Sporting News called "Cooperstown Corner." Simultaneously, other books appeared: a joint history of the Giants and the Dodgers, a collection of biographical sketches written with Tom Meany, lives of Babe Ruth and Dizzy Dean, and a history of the World Series published in 1969 as professional baseball observed its hundredth anniversary.

Surely, Allen must have looked forward to this centennial. For one thing, he now went to work in the new National Baseball Library, opened in 1968 as a separate building from the Hall of Fame. For another, the celebration commemorated events in his native city. He contributed a special essay on the Red Stockings of 1969 to The Sporting News and journeyed back to his hometown in May for a ceremony honoring Cincinnati players. After presenting a silver plate to Edd Roush as the greatest Red of all time and participating in the attendant festivities, Allen climbed into his car for the long drive back to Cooperstown.

When he reached Syracuse early on the morning of May 20, he stopped and called a cab, complaining of chest pains. Two hours later, at St. Joseph's Hospital, he was dead of a massive heart attack. If the truth be told, Allen had not been a well man. Undoubtedly, he worked far too long and too hard, ate, drank, and smoked too much, and had probably suffered an earlier heart attack several years before. Still, his death was both untimely and a shock to the baseball world that had come to treasure him.

This present volume collects for the first time the columns Lee Allen wrote for The Sporting News while he was employed at the Hall of Fame. "Cooperstown Corner," as it was called, ran from April 4, 1962, to May 31, 1969, a total of 133 times. It began as a biweekly feature whose regular appearance was sometimes delayed for lack of space. After August 24, 1963, it was printed much more sporadically: twice during the rest of that year, nine times in 1964, six in 1965, and not at all in 1966. In June, 1967, the column resumed a biweekly schedule. It proved to be so popular that it became a weekly feature in February, 1968, and remained so until Allen's death. The last two columns appeared posthumously.

Taken together, the "Cooperstown Corner" pieces display the same traits that marked all of their author's work. The research, of course, is impeccable as Allen believed he had no higher calling than to lay out the truth and debunk the phony. Moreover, the reader can follow Allen's yearly treks from New York to Florida and back, enjoying his forays into small towns along the way. But what most distinguishes the columns is their style, the flawless writing, the sparkling connections between a person here and an event there, and the inspired wit. Lee Allen was a unique individual with a mind that incessantly soaked up information and a pen that dispensed it gracefully. Two decades after his death, those who care about baseball history are still the richer for his efforts.

FOREWORD

By Paul D. Adomites
Publications Director, SABR

IN READING THROUGH THESE WONDERFUL LEE ALLEN masterpieces, one thought becomes very clear: before there was a SABR, Lee Allen was a SABR member. As you read here, you can almost hear him, through the smoke of a late night session at a National Convention, holding forth on the births and deaths of 19th century stars, describing players who died in plane crashes, relishing stories of fat pitchers, elucidating his all-Lithuanian team. He thought about the game the way we think about the game: as a source of constant richness and joy.

Not all of his "Cooperstown Corner" columns are included here. Most of those not reprinted are simply out of date — "Will Mickey break the Babe's run total?" Others are more travelogs than baseball pieces, descriptions of cemeteries and newspaper offices he had visited in his ongoing search for facts about players' births and deaths.

But there is no doubt, this tour of the mind of one of the game's great historical thinkers is a pleasure extraordinaire. Enjoy.

And a special thanks to Greg Wiley and The Sporting News for their cooperation.

SPRING TRAINING DAYS

APRIL 4, 1962. YOU HEAD NORTH FROM THE FLORIDA TRAIN-
ing camps, seeing in reverse the roadside signs that a month or so before
screamed at you like a carnival barker, in a lush invitation to orange juice,
cocoanut pralines, foot-long hot dogs, alligator bags, kosher salami, sunglasses and ice water. But now you see only their backs, and the lettered
messages merely shout, "Come again!"

The palm trees are behind you now, but live oaks nod a sleepy welcome
to South Carolina, and the air is still and the sun hot over the pineywoods.
You try to gather your thoughts as another training camp season comes to a
close. Baseball has entered the motel age, and gone are the sleepy lobbies of
mid-Victorian hotels. Deep in the past are the snipe hunts and badger games,
the rookie with a straw suitcase, and the horseplay of an unsophisticated age.

The mass training idea, introduced by Branch Rickey at Vero Beach after
World War II, has changed the face of the game. The process by which a high
school shortstop has been hardened into a major leaguer has been speeded
enormously by barracks life, with its mimeographed daily schedules, time
clock efficiency, specialized coaching, mechanical pitchers, sliding pits and
calisthenics.

Spring training is mostly hard work, demanding as much of the aching
veteran as the scared bonus boy.

Arizona has emerged as a serious rival, but 14 of the 20 major league clubs
prepared for the season in Florida this year, prolonging an annual custom
that has its roots deep in the previous century. The Washington Senators of
1888, a National League entry, were the first team to visit Florida, pitching
camp at Jacksonville. Among the players in that camp was a young catcher
named Connie Mack, and later in life he used to recall an event of his train
ride to the base that year that illustrated the cruel humor typical of the time.

"Our manager in 1888 was Ted Sullivan, a great pioneer of the game who
established many minor leagues," Mr. Mack once said. "There were many
stops on the ride to camp, and we ate many meals in station restaurants.
Sullivan carried a silver dollar, and at the start of a meal he would lay it on
the table. The waiter, eyeing a larger tip than he had ever received, would
provide us with double portions and the best service you ever saw. But at the
end of the meal Ted would put the silver dollar back in his pocket and stroll
out."

Both the state of Florida and the game of baseball have undergone
extraordinary growth since 1888, and the process of change is still going on.
There is an intensity to training today that did not exist in the leisurely past.

Stan Musial, preparing for his twenty-first season and a further assault on the record book, was explaining the changes he has seen in his time.

"I came into camp this year weighing 184, four pounds lighter than a year ago," the Nestor of the Cardinals said. "And believe me, those four pounds make a difference. It used to be that a player would purposely report overweight, intending to play his way into shape. A player who would try that today would find himself out of the running. The competition now is fierce!"

Exactly 20 years ago, Stan the Man attended his first camp at St. Petersburg, rooming with Ray Sanders, the first baseman. A torrid debut with the Redbirds the previous September had apparently assured him of a place as a regular, but Musial now thinks he came close to being shunted back to the minors.

"They were patient with me in the spring of 1942," he told Bob Broeg, "probably because of the way I broke in the September before.

"But after getting a couple of hits in the first exhibition against the Yankees, I didn't do much of anything. I was really the lemon of the Grapefruit League.

"I think there is a tendency to overrate pitchers and underrate hitters down here," Stan went on. "In most of the parks, the background for a hitter is terrible, and you really notice the difference when you get home and see those double-decked stands."

Musial's awareness of the game's growing intensity reminds you of something Joe Garagiola said. The former National League catcher who now sparkles on television is supposed to be a comic, and there is no denying that his glib wit is a conspicuous feature of his personality. But glibness is often a patina that covers insecurity, and there is a serious streak in Garagiola's makeup born of his knowledge that the life of a ball player can contain heartbreak, and he knows the agony and the ecstasy of the game.

"Players have hurts and fears and anxieties," Garagiola said one morning on the sidelines at Al Lang Field. "As an announcer, I'm strictly for the underdog."

He was that way in his book, too. "Baseball Is A Funny Game" contains plenty of good humor, but it is possible that the title is ironic.

So you head home, and you have the same feeling of suppressed excitement that you always have in April. The bell is about to ring, and after all the instruction and all the practice, new names are about to spill out on the pages of the game's continuing story. New names, and some old, familiar ones, too.

MEMORIES OF THE METS

APRIL 18. 1962. ONE OF THE HAPPIEST EVENTS OF THE TOD-dling season has been the revival of the Mets, a team bearing a name once important to the game and a club from which future grandeur can be expected. The warriors of George Weiss and Casey Stengel carry with them in their appointed rounds the best wishes of millions, and whatever they do this year, their most significant achievement will have been to restore National League baseball in New York City.

The original Metropolitans, or Mets, were not National League members, but struggled in the American Association, which was then a major league, from 1883 through 1887. It has thus been 75 years since the Mets were in the field.

That last Met team, the 1887 aggregation, was not particularly memo-rable, finishing seventh in a field of eight, but it was certainly not without interest. The club was owned by Erastus Wiman and played its home games on Staten Island, occasionally battling in Sunday contests at Weehawken, N.J., near the heights where Alexander Hamilton and Aaron Burr staged their celebrated duel.

Because Wiman was a Tammany chieftain, the Mets were also called the Indians.

Staten Island was then, and still is, the least populous of the areas which now make up the five boroughs of New York, but the Mets played there because Wiman had a financial interest in the Staten Island ferry, which, with the exception of swimming or rowing, provided the only means of reaching the grounds.

Those 1887 Mets included in their ranks two former American Associa-tion batting kings, Dave Orr and Thomas J. (Dude) Esterbrook. Both were normally first basemen, but Esterbrook expressed a willingness to play shortstop, and it was anticipated that the Mets would that year be a ferocious bundle of batters. But Orr missed 54 games because of an injured leg and Esterbrook developed a carbuncle on his arm that kept him out of action most of the season.

Those injuries forced the management to engage in a patchwork pattern of play that foretold doom. Paul Radford, an outfielder, was hauled in from right to replace Esterbrook at short, and he became the team's leadoff man and one of only three players to appear in as many as 100 of the team's 138 games, the other two being Frank Hankinson at third and William (Darby) O'Brien in left.

Radford is of more than routine interest because he was one of the first players to refuse to appear on Sunday. He came from a family that was comfortably fixed, and it was reported that his father always sent him five dollars whenever he made a base-hit. This is a policy that would have cost the father of Ty Cobb $20,955, but the elder Radford could have been tapped for no more than $6,525, as his son batted safely 1,305 times in a dozen seasons.

The Mets also had a pitcher named Jack Lynch who, like Yogi Berra today, was the central figure in many an apocryphal story. It has been written that Lynch, while playing for the Nationals of Washington in 1879, went in for moonlighting, taking a side job as gatekeeper at the National Cemetery.

One day a large party of sightseers toured the establishment, and one of the customers, wondering whether Confederate or Union soldiers were buried there, said to Lynch, "What kind of soldiers are buried here?"

And Jack, according to legend, glowered at the tourist and replied, "Dead soldiers."

There was also on that Metropolitan roster a young first baseman who pitched on occasion, Daniel R. Ryan. For everything I know about Ryan I am indebted to Thomas P. Shea of Hingham, Mass., one of the game's great authorities. Ryan was torn between twin loves, baseball and the stage, and for years he toured the nation in vaudeville with his own company. It is probable that old playbills bearing the words "Daniel R. Ryan and Co." exist in historical societies and libraries all over the land. And certainly Ryan is the only major league player of all time to play the role of Richard III.

This is an accomplishment which is probably even beyond the powers of Charles Dillon Stengel.

That last Met team was also handicapped by a bad break in the schedule. Only two of the first 21 games were at home and the first ten of the contests yielded defeat. Bob Ferguson, one of the earnest professionals, started the year as manager, but gave up on June 11 and was replaced by O.P. (for Oliver Perry) Caylor.

Caylor was a baseball writer who dipped his pen in sulphuric acid and who had previously managed Cincinnati.

One of Caylor's experiments was to induce Lipman E. Pike, the first major league player of Jewish ancestry, to attempt a comeback at the age of 42. Pike played just one game, went hitless, and called it a career, devoting the six remaining years of his life to running a haberdashery near the Brooklyn Bridge.

When the season of 1887 was over, Wiman sold out his baseball interests. He dismantled the park and sold the grandstand to the Jersey City club of the International League. The contracts of the players were sold to Kansas City, and that city's Cowboys replaced the Mets as a member of the Association.

Then came a strange turn of events. A year after the Mets moved to Kansas City, there was born on Agnew Avenue in that community the man, Casey Stengel, who was destined to lead the team back to New York not quite three-quarters of a century later.

TEXAS LEAGUERS

MAY 2, 1962. LOU BROCK, OUTFIELDER AND LEADOFF MAN of the Cubs, achieved some sort of distinction when he became the first player ever to go to bat in a major league game played in the state of Texas. This happened, of course, in the first tussle at Colt Stadium, April 10, and the fact that Brock was fanned by Bobby Shantz detracts not a whit from his footnote to baseball history.

Championship National League games have been contested in such unlikely settings as Elmira, N.Y. (the Buffalo club took Providence there for a double-header on October 10, 1885), but the circuit was in existence 86 years before Houston got into the act. Still, Texas has long provided more than its share of big league players and it has enriched the game's language through the phrase "Texas Leaguer."

William B. Ruggles, who in 1932 published the official history of the Texas League, has written more authoritatively about baseball in the Lone Star State than any other person. Ruggles says the first appearance of professional players in Texas took place in 1877 when the Indianapolis team met a local amateur nine at Galveston. Edward (The Only) Nolan pitched that game for Indianapolis, Ruggles states, and struck out 26.

Ruggles does not list the date of this game, but for the record it was played on March 11, 1877, with Indianapolis winning, 50 to 0, a margin of victory that might be termed decisive. However, this was not really the first game played by professionals in Texas, because Indianapolis had stopped at Dallas before visiting Galveston, and defeated an amateur team from that city by an even larger score, 59 to 0, on March 10.

The Indianapolis batting order that season was as follows: Joe Quest, 2b; John (Trick) McSorley, 3b; Denny Mack, ss; Charlie Houtz, 1b; Mike Golden, lf; Frank (Silver) Flint, c; Fred Warner, cf; Adam Rocap, rf; and Nolan, p. Indianapolis was an independent team and did not enter the National League until 1878, but every one of those nine players appeared in the majors at one time or another. Flint was the best of them, a catching mainstay for Cap Anson's White Stockings for 11 years.

But some of the others in that crew that introduced the game in Texas were of more than routine interest. Quest, for example, was the player who first used the term "Charlie horse." Son of a blacksmith from New Castle, Pa., Quest noticed that players hobbling around with a peculiar muscle injury of the legs reminded him of an old white horse, Charlie, employed at his father's shop. Quest's contribution was published in 1882.

Mack was born Dennis McGee, the eldest son of a man by the same name who was the leader of the Carbon County (Pa.) Bucktails in the Civil War. Young McGee studied for the priesthood, but left school after a quarrel with one of his teachers, a circumstance that broke his father's heart.

Rocap was a Philadelphian and a brother of Billy Rocap, for years a famed boxing writer for the Philadelphia Public Ledger. Houtz and McSorley were from St. Louis. Both returned there when their baseball days were done, Houtz to become a night watchman at the South Side Race Track, and McSorley to join the police force.

Nolan was a product of Paterson, N.J., and a wonderful pitcher in 1877, but in league ranks he never equalled expectations. Although Indianapolis played no set schedule, it was technically a member of a minor organization known as the League Alliance, a loose confederation of 13 clubs, some of which never met each other. But during the long season Indianapolis played 121 games, winning 73, losing 40 and tying eight.

The visit of that team to Texas made no lasting impression, and no attempt was made until 1884 to form a professional league in the state. Then local players were employed, with only the batteries imported, and the circuit did not flourish. The real birth of the Texas League occurred in 1888, with the start of the competition launched by Honest John McCloskey, a fabulous character of the game's early days who spent most of his 78 years organizing leagues, managing teams and scouting.

McCloskey entered Texas in the autumn of 1887 with a team from Joplin, Mo., that formed the nucleus of his new league. Honest John used the Joplin players at Austin in 1888, then moved most of them to Houston in 1889 and won that city's first pennant.

As a minor league member, Houston made a record far more impressive that most clubs can boast, largely because of being affiliated with the Cardinal chain gang during that empire's greatest affluence. It is probable that Houston's period of baseball glory lies in the path immediately ahead. But the Texas League has already permitted the fans of the city to watch such performers as the Dean brothers, Jerome and Paul; Gus Mancuso, Bill Hallahan, Fred Frankhouse, Tex Carleton, Jim Bottomley, Carey Selph, Heinie Schuble, George Watkins, Chick Hafey, Heinie Mueller, Ray Blades and Joe Medwick.

The Texas League has also produced two extraordinary records. Justin (Nig) Clarke of Corsicana hit eight home runs in a game against Texarkana, June 15, 1902, his club winning, 51 to 3, and Gene Rye, a half-pint outfielder with Waco, hit three home runs in one inning against Beaumont, August 6, 1930.

CUBA

JUNE 2, 1962.   ALTHOUGH IT HAS BEEN ONLY IN RECENT years that Cuba has become an important source of baseball talent (54 players produced for the major leagues since World War II), the game has been firmly entrenched on the island since 1874, and it appears highly doubtful that the current regime of terror can suppress it. Baseball there survived the Spanish-American War, and at that time it was expressly forbidden by the authorities. Now it is so much a part of the life of the people that it will almost certainly flourish once the boys with the beards retreat to the ignominy they deserve.

Somewhere in Havana there is, or at least there was, a statue devoted to the memory of the man who introduced the game there. This was William Henry (Steve) Bellan, a Cuban who grew up in the United States and became one of the Haymakers of Troy, that legendary team which was a member of the first major league, the National Association of 1871. Bellan, an infielder, attended Fordham University. He returned to Cuba in 1874, popularized the game there, and organized the island's first league. Players from the United States first noticed the statue when they visited Cuba following the season of 1910.

The real start of Cubans in Organized Ball occurred in 1910 when Dan O'Neil of Holyoke, Mass., acquired the New Britain franchise in the Class B Connecticut League. He bought the club for $3,500, and immediately introduced four Cubans: Armando Marsans, an outfielder; Rafael Almeida and Alfredo Cabrera, infielders; and one Padrone, first name unknown, a pitcher. To be entirely accurate, Cabrera, though raised in Cuba, was actually a Guanche, the name for the native inhabitants of the Canary Islands.

They were wonderful players, and New Britain moved up from the second division and finished third, missing the pennant by two games. The contracts of Almeida and Marsans were sold to the Cincinnati Reds, then managed by Clark Griffith, and both appeared in National League games in 1911.

They broke into the Reds' lineup for the first time in a morning game at Chicago on the Fourth of July, although it would have been better for the box office if the club had introduced them at home. Marsans, a first-class outfielder, became a cause to celebrate when he jumped to the St. Louis Federals in 1914, and he was still on the scene with the Yankees in 1918.

Senor Almeida, though a part-time performer, remained with the Reds for three seasons.

Griffith moved to Washington in 1912, and it was probably the memory of Marsans and Almeida and the success he had with them that induced him to begin importing others from the island. His first Cuban recruits for the Senators were Balmadero Acosta and Jacinto Calvo, a pair of outfielders, in 1913.

By this time, other clubs were getting into the act. Mike Gonzalez, a catcher and one of the best known of all Cuban players, joined the Braves in 1912.

Two years after that, the same team introduced Adolfo Luque, best of all the Cuban pitchers. The St. Louis Federal League club introduced Manuel Cueto, a shortstop and later a utilityman for Pat Moran's Cincinnati champions of 1919.

The Yankees also exhibited briefly in 1914 a Cuban outfielder, Angel Aragon. The Giants brought up a pitcher, Emilo Palmero, in 1915, and a first baseman, Jose Rodriguez, in 1916. Eusebio Gonzalez, a shortstop, appeared with the Red Sox in 1918, and that same year Oscar Tuero, a pitcher, showed up with the Cardinals.

Luque was the best of the lot, and was a distinguished pitcher for the Reds from 1918 to 1929. Known particularly for his ability to beat the Giants, he was a hard-luck pitcher in many of his seasons and usually had to struggle for lack of support at the bat. But in 1923 he had a record of 27-8, and for years he was coveted by John McGraw. The Reds, in one of the worst deals ever made by the team, traded him even up for the late Doug McWeeny, a pitcher who did not win a single game for the Cincinnati club.

McGraw finally landed Adolfo in 1932 and he served the Giants through 1935, contributing a victory in relief in 1933 World's Series. Then he became a coach and imported some of his pitching magic to Sal Maglie.

But during the decade of the '20s, there were only three new Cuban players: Pedro Dibut, a pitcher with the Reds in 1924; Ramon Herrera, a second baseman with the Red Sox in 1925; and Oscar Estrada, a pitcher tried by the Browns in 1929. It has often been believed that Luque brought Dibut into camp, but the veteran Cincinnati writer, Tom Swope, recalls that Luque hardly spoke to Pedro and helped him not at all. Dibut cheated on his age by nine years. The records show he was born in Havana on June 24, 1901, but his real place of birth was Cienfuegos, and the correct date was November 18, 1892.

After Estrada, there was not one Cuban rookie in the game until 1937, when Fermin (Mickey) Guerra joined the Senators as a catcher. But then they began appearing in quantity. Baseball today would certainly be poorer without Minnie Minoso, Roman Mejias, Tony Gonzalez, Zoilo Versalles,

Chico Cardenas, Tony Taylor, Camilo Pascual, Pete Ramos, Mike de la Hoz, Chico Fernandez and Mike Fornieles, not to mention such ones of recent memory as Sandy Amoros, Nap Reyes, Willy Miranda, Sandy Consuegra and Ray Noble.

THE RETURN OF THE STEAL

JUNE 30, 1962. THIS WEEK'S SERMON CONCERNS THE STOLEN base, after which the congregation will please rise and sing a hymn to Maury Wills.

It is not really expected here that Maury will exceed Ty Cobb's sacred modern record of 96 thefts in a season, or even Bob Bescher's modern National League mark of 80, but that he should even be given a chance to do so indicates that the steal, once again, has become an important tactic in the game. For it is not just Maury, that pilfering panther whose habitat is a ravine in Los Angeles, but both major leagues that are demonstrating a revived interest in the embezzlement business.

What killed the steal in the first place? Not lack of speed, for the modern athlete can run as fast as, if not faster than, his father. It was a general tightening of the game that first put the bandits in the shade, and then the change in strategy dictated by Babe Ruth and the lively ball put on the crusher. But another corner has now been turned, and we can look for more larceny.

Complete figures for stolen bases are available for the National League starting with 1886, the first year in which steals were recorded. But figures for the American League were not listed in the guides until 1910.

This study, then, will consider the five decades beginning with 1911, a slice of time in which the National and American enjoyed peaceful coexistence and a schedule of the same length. During that time all the runners in both leagues traveled 1,176 miles in stealing 66,270 bases, about the distance from Nashville, Tenn., to Pierre, S.D., regardless of whether you are sent outright or on option. In the following table the notation "S.P.G." refers to "steals per game."

Year	National League			American League			Both Majors		
	G.	S.B.	S.P.G.	G	S.B.	S.P.G.	G	S.B.	S.P.G.
1911-20	6,035	13,108	2,171	6,013	13,626	2,259	12,066	26,734	2.215
1921-30	6,159	6,806	1.105	6,163	6,953	1,128	12,322	13,759	1.116
1931-40	6,159	4,137	.671	6,153	5,372	.873	12,312	9,509	.772
1941-50	6,197	4,141	.668	6,181	4,430	.716	12,378	8,571	.692
1951-60	6,189	4,003	.646	6,183	3,694	.597	12,372	7,697	.622
Total	30,739	32,195	1.047	30,711	34,075	1.109	61,450	66,270	1.078

Careful regard for those figures shows that the introduction of the lively ball in 1921 cut the number of steals almost in half, ending the era in which runners tried stealing almost as often as they reached first base. Then each succeeding decade showed another decline.

It is doubtful if fans would want to return to the game as it was from 1911 to 1920, when each game produced more than two steals. But they probably would want more running than there was in the 1950s, when bases were swiped at a rate of only slightly more than one for every two games played.

The claim has been made that the trend has been reversed, and here is the proof. This year the National League recorded 282 steals in its first 295 games and has a chance to average one per game for the first time since 1929. The American League is slightly behind that pace.

Form seems to count for more in base-stealing than it does in batting. The lists of league leaders in thefts is dotted with second offenders and three and four-time winners. Max Carey, elected to the Hall of Fame and one of the greatest runners of them all, led the National in steals ten different years. His record of 51 in 53 tries in 1922 staggers the imagination.

Luis Aparicio has paced the American for the past six seasons, but now finds himself threatened by Dick Howser and Jake Wood.

Cobb was also at the top of the list in a half-dozen years, as was the fleet George Case. Honus Wagner led the National five different times: Bob Bescher, Willie Mays and Kiki Cuyler, four and Frankie Frisch, Pepper Martin, and Bill Bruton, three. Ben Chapman, George Sisler and Eddie Collins each led the American four times, Minnie Minoso and Bob Dillinger, each three.

In the very early days the best runners were Billy Hamilton, Harry Stovey, John Montgomery Ward, Curt Welch, and the forgotten Thomas T. Brown, who led both the Players' League and the old American Association in thefts.

The last player to steal 100 in one season (and he hit that figure exactly) was Bill Lange of Chicago in 1896. Lange, a superb outfielder and an uncle of George Kelly, first baseman of the Giants, quit the game for personal reasons at the height of his career after the season of 1899. They called him Little Eva and one day in Cincinnati he hit a home run that broke up a poker game in a building beyond the center field fence but that is a story for a column about assault rather than burglary.

There have been other fast ones, and names that come to mind are Jackie Robinson, Sam Jethroe, the unfortunate George Stirnweiss, Clyde Milan, Bill Werber, Pete Reiser, Johnny Mostil, Frank Chance and Jimmy Sheckard.

Bottom was reached in 1950 when the American League saw only 278 steals. The leader, Dom DiMaggio, had 15.

Don't think that Dom's great brother, Joe, couldn't run either. He didn't go very often, but he was not thrown out on a steal attempt in his first 425 games.

So modern baseball has more to offer than home runs. There is no play that offers more excitement than the steal, with its first break, the catcher's bullet peg, and a slide.

You'll be seeing a lot more of these base-stealing artists. For where there's a Wills, there's a way.

BABE RUTH'S FIRST CATCHER

JULY 28, 1962. THE MAN PERHAPS MOST QUALIFIED TO THROW light on the early baseball career of Babe Ruth is Arthur (Ben) Egan, 78, a former catcher and major league coach who now is comfortably retired in the little (pop. 2,922) community of Sherrill, N.Y., west of Utica, famed as the home of Oneida silverware.

Egan was Ruth's catcher on the Baltimore Orioles of 1914, from the day Babe left St. Mary's Industrial Home for Boys to join the team at the training base in Fayetteville, N.C. It is part of baseball legend now that Ruth, entirely lacking in previous experience, advanced to the Red Sox in July, launching his incredible career, first as a pitcher and then as an unparalleled producer of home runs. But Egan takes no bows for Ruth's rapid rise.

"It would be pleasant to say that I developed Ruth as a pitcher," Egan said as we sat in the sunlight of his front porch. "But that would be hogwash. Babe knew how to pitch the first day I saw him. I didn't have to tell him anything. He knew how to hold runners on base, and he knew how to work on the hitters, so I'd say he was a pretty good pitcher — on his own.

"That was a funny camp at Fayetteville," Egan went on. "Jack Dunn, who owned the ball club, wasn't there when we started practice. He had put me in charge of the team, but there was a coach, Sam Steinman, who took it upon himself to issue orders to the players. One day, when it rained, he told them all to work out in an armory, in a room so small they were all endangered by thrown balls. That made me mad, so I sent a wire to Dunn and told him there was dissension. 'You'd better get down here right away,' I wired him and then waited for him to respond to my S.O.S.

"Two days later Dunn was there, and after breakfast we went out for a walk. 'How's the kid from Baltimore look?' he asked me. 'Dunnie,' I said, 'you won't be able to keep him a half-season. He's got wonderful control, just perfect, and he can hit a ball a mile, but he's a wild kid.'

"What do you mean, 'wild'?" Dunn asked.

"Just then Ruth came along on a bicycle, tried to pass a hay wagon and crashed into the back of it. When we got to him, he was lying there in the street. 'Kid,' Dunn told him, 'if you want to go back to that home, just keep riding those bicycles.'

"Ruth wasn't a bad kid, just wild. If he saw a bicycle on the street, he'd get on it and ride off. One morning he found a horse hitched to a post, so he mounted it and rode into a Greek confectionery, scattering the employees and customers all over the place.

"But how he could hit! One day we were playing the Phillies a practice game. Ruth was pitching and Josh Devore was in right field for the Phils. I was a baserunner on second and Sherry Magee, who was playing second, kept motioning to Devore to come in more so he could catch me at the plate should the batter single. Well, Ruth hit the ball so far over Devore's head we never could find out where it hit. The ball landed in a potato patch, but it rained during the night, and when we went out the next morning to see if we could find the ball, we found it was impossible to locate it."

Three months or so later, Ruth was sold to the Red Sox along with Egan and Ernie Shore for $8,500, and the price for Ruth in that package was figured at $2,900.

"I can't take any credit for Babe's development," Egan said, "but I think I was responsible for his going to Boston. We were rained out one day at Jersey City and caught the B. & O. for Baltimore. When the train stopped at Philadelphia, the Red Sox boarded it, and I found myself talking to Joe Lannin, who owned the club, and Bill Carrigan, who managed it. I previously had recommended Ruth to seven or eight big league teams, but none of them showed any interest.

"A couple of days later, Dunnie said to me, 'Ben, would you like to go to the big league?' 'If you can make a deal, okay,' I said. So they made the deal. But I never played a game for Boston. I was traded to Cleveland in a deal for Dean Gregg. When I got to Cleveland, Jack Graney, the outfielder, said to me, 'Where in the hell do you find pitchers like Ruth and Shore? I've looked at both of them now, and I'm never going to get a hit off either one.'"

Egan, who previously had had cups of coffee with the Athletics in 1908 and 1912, remained in the game almost until World War II. He coached for Eddie Collins with the White Sox for two years, and for Bucky Harris at Washington, then had a long career as manager in the minors before he called it a career.

Christened Arthur Augustus Egan, he was born at Augusta, N.Y., a place even smaller than Sherrill, November 20, 1883. As a youngster, he used to hang around with a boy named Ben Stewart. Whenever someone wanted to locate him, they would look for Ben, and soon they began calling Egan "Ben."

He attended elementary school at Sherrill for eight years, then went to work in the silverware industry for five cents an hour. He had ten brothers and two sisters, all of whom lived to adulthood.

"If I have any regret," Egan said, "it is that I did not recommend Ruth to John McGraw. What an attraction he would have been for the Giants, and I think they could have used him. The Reds had a crack at Ruth, though. They had the right to select two players from Baltimore that year, and they passed up Ruth and Shore and picked Claude Derrick, shortstop, and an outfielder named George Twombly."

THE FIRST NIGHT-TIME HITTER

AUGUST 11, 1962. BILLY MYERS WAS A SHORTSTOP OF MORE than ordinary attainments, a much better ball player than some fans thought, during the seven years he spent in the National League, six with the Reds starting in 1935, before a final fling with the Cubs. He ranged well, could move far to his right to make the play in the hole, and had an exceptional arm. He had occasional power, and it was a fly ball from his bat that pushed over the winning run when the Reds defeated the Tigers in the deciding seventh game of the 1940 World's Series.

Now he is a railroader operating out of Harrisburg, Pa., and when he read that his old dugout boss, Bill McKechnie, had been elected to membership in the Hall of Fame, he and Mrs. Myers piled into the family car and zoomed up the northeast extension of the Pennsylvania Turnpike to see the cere-mony. Arriving late at night without tickets or even a hotel reservation, they soon had both. "We just couldn't miss it," Billy said.

Myers has one distinction that few of the game's addicts recall: He was the first player in the major leagues to make a hit at night. The occasion, of course, was the first night game ever played in the National League, a chilly battle in which the Reds defeated the Phillies, 2 to 1, at Crosley Field on Friday, May 24, 1935. Leading off in the first inning, Myers doubled off Joe Bowman, and seconds later crossed the plate with the first big league run made after dark.

Originally the property of the Cardinals, Myers made most of the stops in the chain during seven years of apprenticeship in the minors. Starting in 1928 with Waynesboro of the Blue Ridge, he soon saw the sights at Danville of the Three I, Fort Wayne of the Central, Danville again, then Houston, Springfield, Rochester, Elmira and Columbus.

When he played the whole schedule and batted .313 for Columbus in 1934, the parent Cardinals, secure at shortstop because of the presence of Leo Durocher, peddled him to the Giants.

At this time, Larry MacPhail was engaged in revamping the Reds, inaugurating a youth movement that brought in Lew Riggs and Ival Goodman and would eventually include Frank McCormick, Johnny Vander Meer and others. Needing a shortstop and noting that Myers would be so much excess baggage on the Giants because that team had just obtained Dick Bartell in a big deal with the Phillies, Larry obtained Myers from Bill Terry for Mark Koenig and Allyn Stout.

Chuck Dressen was MacPhail's field manager at Cincinnati in those days, and promised the city a fighting team after four long years in the cellar. Towards that end Dressen appointed Myers captain, and one of his duties was to intervene in any altercations that developed.

The Reds rose to sixth in 1935, climbed to fifth in 1936, but then dropped back to eighth again in 1937. The home fans, more often than not disgruntled by events on the field, took their wrath out on Myers, who, in his role as captain, often jawed with the umpires, providing an easy target for razzberries.

Warren Giles replaced MacPhail as head man of the Reds after the 1936 season, and after another year, McKechnie came on to succeed Dressen. The team, with the judicious addition of Bucky Walters, climbed to fourth in 1938; and with Bill Werber added, won the first of two successive pennants in 1939. Myers that year batted .281 for his best season and contributed a game-winning home run in the final series with the Cardinals that decided the flag.

In his playing days, Billy was not especially known as a sentimentalist. But the game gets into the bloodstream, and in the nostalgic atmosphere of Cooperstown, he was buzzing with the eagerness of a Little Leaguer. When last observed, he and his wife, Evelyn, were proudly obtaining the autograph of Jackie Robinson.

He also reminisced about his days as a Cardinal chattel.

"Did you ever hear of a team losing 30 games in one day?" he asked. Confronted with a blank stare, he offered the explanation:

"During the spring of 1931, Dizzy Dean was telling everyone he would win 30 for the Cardinals. But they sent him back to Houston before the season opened. I was rooming with Jim Lindsey, the veteran relief pitcher, at the training camp, and when Diz was sent back, Lindsey said to me, 'Billy, you're witnessing history. This is the only time in the history of the game that a club lost 30 games in one day.' Of course, Diz later did win 30 in a season to make good his boast."

The first man to make a big league hit at night does not see many games today, but he follows its affairs in the pages of The Sporting News and the daily newspapers. And if his hairline is receding, his enthusiasm for baseball is growing, warming his memories as the years roll on. Occasionally, around Harrisburg, he will run into such old friends as Ray Mueller and Les Bell, men who can share the pleasure of recalling days that have fled.

"This is my first trip to Cooperstown," he said. "I've wanted to come many times, and when Bill McKechnie was elected, I just had to. There is a man!"

THE BARBER WHO BANGED THREE BAGGERS

DECEMBER 1, 1962. HERE IS A HYMN TO THE THREE-BASE HIT or, as it is called in certain segments of society, the triple.

Once a dangerous offensive missile, the triple is becoming as rare as the whooping crane. If you consider this exaggerated, ponder these facts: In 1912, the two major leagues hit 1,353 triples and 433 home runs, but in 1962, over a longer schedule and with four more teams, there were 853 triples and 3,001 homers.

The three-base hit is a thing of beauty, if I may copy a phrase from the late Mr. Keats. It usually resulted in a mad dash by the baserunner, an equally desperate spurt by the outfielder, a long throw, a slide and an attempt by the third baseman to clutch the ball and make the tag. It is a play loaded with suspense. The runner can fall down, or miss a base or overslide third. The fielder can let the ball get through him or make a wild throw. The third baseman can muff the ball or he can tag the runner out. Contrast all that activity with the vacuum of action that follows a home run hit out of the park.

This is not to deprecate the homer, which brings delight to millions and fills the ball parks. But those reactionaries who admire the triple constitute a minority with definite rights.

Quick now, can anyone name the National League leader in three-base hits in the season that has just slipped by? There were actually four of them: Maury Wills and Willie Davis of the Dodgers, Johnny Callison of the Phils and Bill Virdon, the bespectacled Pirate. Each hit ten, and that is the lowest number for a National League leader since 1878, when Rutherford B. Hayes, beard and all, was in the White House and Tom York, leftfielder of the Providence Grays, while playing a 60-game schedule, connected for nine.

The joint accomplishment of Wills, Davis, Callison and Virdon did not, however, constitute a major league low. Bob Allison, with the 1959 Senators, led the American League while hitting only nine. The entire AL that year hit only 267, another record.

Sam Crawford, the hardest-hitting barber who ever came out of Wahoo, Neb., is beyond all doubt the greatest producer of triples the game has ever known. He splashed 312 of them around the outfield lawns of his day, leading his league six different times, once with the Reds and on five occasions when he was a Tiger standout.

It is probable that Crawford's record is safe for all time. Ty Cobb, at 297, is second to him, and the National League leader, Honus Wagner, had 252.

The fact that Crawford obtained his start in life as a barber was as well-publicized, in his day, as similar stories which would, much later, be circulated about Perry Como.

The famed baseball wit, Charlie Dryden, who specialized in hilarious fake interviews, once printed his fictitious exchange with Crawford in the old Philadelphia North American:

"To what do you attribute your superb physique?"

"Whacking at the wind-whipped whiskers of Wahoo," was the mysterious answer.

Sam wasted no time in reaching the majors after starting as a professional with Chatham, Ont., of the Canadian League, in 1899. In his first professional game, he hit a triple off a pitcher named Bradford at Hamilton on May 10.

After little more than a month, Crawford was sold, along with Billy Sullivan, later famous as a White Sox catcher and one of three men ever to catch a ball dropped from the Washington Monument, to Columbus of the Western League.

Soon that franchise was shifted to Grand Rapids. Sam went along, but was soon sold to the Reds. He reported to Cincinnati on Sunday, September 10, just in time to engage in a freak double-header against Cleveland and Louisville. It was in the second game that day that he banged out his first big league triple, off Bert Cunningham of the Colonels.

When peace was made between the National and American Leagues, Wahoo Sam was awarded to Detroit. He had signed contracts with both the Reds and Tigers, and that is how Cincinnati lost the man who might have been the club's greatest star.

Crawford was a lefthanded hitter with exceptional power. It was believed, at the height of his career, that he was robbed of base-hits more than any other player.

Fielder Jones, manager and centerfielder of the White Sox, was his particular nemesis, and year after year he seemed to make one exceptional play after another at Sam's expense. But Jones considered Crawford the hardest hitter in the game, and said so more than once.

"None of them can hit quite as hard as Crawford," Fielder once said. "He stands up at the plate like a brick house. And he hits all the pitchers, without playing favorites.

"When Sam's hitting, they all look alike."

THE RAJAH'S GREATEST SEASON

JANUARY 26, 1963. TODAY'S NEWS IS TOMORROW'S HISTORY, but when a man such as Rogers Hornsby passes, time is suspended for those who are old enough to remember him in his prime.

There is a confusion of tense, and you feel that it was only yesterday that Hornsby stood there, deep in the box, his eyes sparkling as, silent as granite, he awaited the pitch, before lashing it safely into the outfield green. It is the way he would like to be remembered — as a hitter.

Surely his feat of batting .424 in 1924 must be numbered among the greatest seasonal accomplishments of them all. As Lefty Gomez, speaking with his usual ebullience, once observed of the Tiger star, Charlie Gehringer, "He's in a rut. Gehringer goes two for five on Opening Day and stays that way all season."

What is one to say, then, of Hornsby in 1924, who went two-for-five on opening day (off Vic Aldridge of the Cubs) and then improved on the percentage before the year was out?

The Cardinals played 154 games that season, and Hornsby missed 11 of them, three in early May because of a dislocated thumb, eight in late August and early September because of a wrenched back. In the 143 contests in which he appeared, he hit safety in 119 and was blanked in only 24. He hit safely once in 44 games, twice in 46, three times in 25 and four times in four.

Nor did it matter who supplied the opposition. The Cubs had the best luck with Hornsby, holding him to an average of .387, but that would have been good enough to enable him to lead the National League.

Opponent	At-Bats	Hits	Avg.
Braves	75	36	.480
Giants	78	34	.436
Phillies	82	35	.427
Dodgers	92	39	.424
Reds	73	30	.411
Pirates	61	24	.393
Cubs	75	29	.387
Totals	536	227	.424

But some proud pitcher must have enjoyed good fortune against Hornsby that year, and when news of the Rajah's death came to this place of his enshrinement, I looked up the box scores to try to identify him.

The result was interesting, to say the least. It seems unlikely that a single person in the world, including the pitcher himself, knows the identity of the man who, in Hornsby's greatest year, got him out with less difficulty than any other.

The man was Johnny Cooney, now a coach for the White Sox. Hornsby, to repeat, was blanked in 24 games. Cooney, then with the Braves, shut him out in three different battles.

For many reasons, Cooney is a memorable player. He was, like Jimmy Ryan, Hal Chase and Rube Bressler, one of the very few, aside from pitchers, who threw lefthanded and batted right. He also had the rare experience of becoming an outfield star after his arm failed him. Cooney won eight games and lost nine for the Braves in 1924, a team that finished in the cellar, and in each of the games in which he whitewashed Hornsby he went the route and won, 4 to 3, 9 to 2, and 1 to 0.

Another southpaw, Clarence Mitchell of the Phillies, held Hornsby hitless twice. No other pitcher in the league accomplished this feat more than once.

Of the remaining 19 games in which the Rajah did not make at least one safety, two can be disregarded. Both were against the Giants, and each time John McGraw employed many pitchers to stop him (Jack Bentley, Rosie Ryan, Ernie Maun and Walter Huntzinger in one; Mule Watson, Ryan, Claude Jonnard, Maun and Huntzinger in the other).

So that leaves 17 other games in which Hornsby did not hit. In all of them the starting pitcher went most of the way, and to call off their names is to open floodgates of memory: Larry Benton of the Braves; Dazzy Vance and Bill Doak of the Dodgers; Vic Keen, Tony Kaufmann, Floyd Wheeler and Aldridge of the Cubs; Dolf Luque, Rube Benton and Eppa Rixey of the Reds; Bentley, Denny Gearin and Art Nehf of the Giants; Whitey Glazner, Jimmy Ring and Huck Betts of the Phillies and Ray Kremer of the Pirates.

So, there is a salvo to the men who got Hornsby out, at least in that one year.

But on other days and in other years, they, like all pitchers, felt the wrath of his bat, and it is for them that the obituaries of Rogers Hornsby had real meaning.

NAP'S CROWNING GLORY

FEBRUARY 9, 1963. IN THE COURSE OF A HYMN TO ROGERS Hornsby in this space two weeks ago, it was mentioned that the Rajah, in his greatest batting percentage year — 1924, when he hit .424 — was blanked only 24 times.

Despite the greatness of that feat, the thought persisted that there must have been other players in other years who went hitless on even fewer occasions.

One who did was the incomparable Larry Lajoie in 1901. Also a second baseman, Lajoie that season was at the height of his powers and batted .422 for the Athletics. He was shut out in only 17 of his 131 games. It was the first year that the American League enjoyed major status, and Larry got off to what was probably the greatest start ever made by a batter in the big show.

On Opening Day against the Senators Larry made three safeties, repeated with three more the following day, then connected for four against Boston — ten hits in his first three games.

He batted safely in his first 16 engagements until stopped by Doughnut Bill Carrick of Washington on May 17.

Lajoie and Hornsby are both Hall of Famers, of course. They were alike in that they played the same position and both batted righthanded, but they were also quite different. Hornsby was a batting stylist, but the Frenchman had many styles. The Rajah made the pitchers get the ball in the strike zone, but Larry would offer at bad balls.

They both had power, but were basically line-drive hitters, aiming between the outfielders.

That Lajoie was a great hitter goes without saying, but his feat of batting .422 is by no means as impressive as Hornsby's .424. The reason is that in the American League of 1901, fouls did not count as strikes, an obvious advantage to the batter.

The National League adopted the foul-strike rule in 1901, largely at the behest of James A. Hart, president of the Chicago team, but the American did not follow suit until 1903.

Just as Hornsby, in 1924, was blanked three times by Johnny Cooney of the Braves, Lajoie had his own nemesis. Three times he was held hitless by Clark Griffith, then manager and star righthander of the White Sox, who went on to win that first American League pennant. Later, as owner of the Senators, Griffith was known as the Old Fox, a sobriquet derived largely from his canniness in business affairs. But as a pitcher he demonstrated fox-like qualities, too, and as early as August, 1901, the Chicago Inter-Ocean, a paper long since departed, referred to him regularly as the Human Fox.

The White Sox gave Lajoie more trouble in 1901 than any other team, blanking him six times. Roy Patterson, a gifted but largely forgotten righthander, shut him out twice, and Jimmie Callahan, who two years later would succeed Griff as manager, did it once.

Carrick, the first pitcher to stop Lajoie, did it again later in the season, and another pitcher who accomplished the feat twice was little Joe Yeager of the Tigers.

The only other pitchers who held Larry hitless during the entire season were Jerry Nops of Baltimore, George Winter, Frank Morrissey and Parson Ted Lewis of Boston, John McNeal and Pete Dowling of Cleveland and Roscoe Hiller of Detroit.

The inclusion of Morrissey in the select list offers a real surprise, for Frank did not win a game for Boston all year, and the single victory he picked up in 1902 marked the only time he ever recorded a triumph in his brief career.

Unlikely as it seems, Lajoie's batting figure of .422 did not even constitute a personal high. As a rookie in the professional ranks with Fall River of the New England League in 1896, he batted .429, making him the most exciting public figure in that town since Lizzie Borden.

Lajoie's lifetime major league record is indeed a glittering document of diamond skill. He logged the remarkable total of 3,251 hits, and his career batting average in the majors was .339.

Lajoie, unlike Hornsby, was equally celebrated for his work in the field, and he has often been called the most graceful player of all time. His normal style was to glide toward the ball, gather it in nonchalantly, as if picking fruit, and send it sailing to first in time to put the runner out of business. He was an artist.

The late J.G. Taylor Spink once sent me to interview Lajoie at his last home at Holly Hill, Fla. As I approached his cottage in the gathering dusk, I found him in his driveway, polishing his automobile.

He was then over 70, but he moved with the ghostlike grace you had come to expect.

We sat there on his front porch until long after his normal bedtime, and he reviewed his career in a manner that contained just the right mixture of humility and proper pride.

There was a dispute at the time as to whether he had batted .422 or .405 in 1901, a complicated story too long to go into here, but he could not have cared less as to which figure was correct.

The incident of his playing days that seemed more vivid to him than any other was the time he was managing Cleveland and one of his players,

George Stovall, encountered him in a hotel lobby and hit him over the head with a heavy chair, smashing it to bits.

"What did you do to him for that?" It seemed a normal thing to ask.

"Nothing at all," he replied. "George didn't mean anything by it."

IT WASN'T EPPA JEPHTHA

FEBRUARY 23, 1963. THE LONG-DISTANCE TELEPHONE CALL was not used so extensively in 1924 as it is today, but when Eppa Rixey hit two singles, a double and a home run off Jesse Haines in a game at Sportsman's Park on June 28 of that year, he decided to phone his fiancee, Dorothy Meyers, in Cincinnati and tell her the extraordinary news.

"Goodness, Eppa," she said. "You hit a home run? Something dreadful must be about to happen in St. Louis."

On the following day, the Mound City was visited by a rare tornado, bearing out the prophecy, but later in the year Dorothy became Mrs. Eppa Rixey, so the episode had a proud climax.

Rixey was elected to the Hall of Fame for his pitching skill, not his ability to hit balls out of the parks. Until Warren Spahn appeared on the scene, Eppa had won more games than any southpaw in National League annals, 266, pitching exclusively for the Phillies and Reds in a career that stretched from 1912 to 1933.

Towering five inches over six feet in height and weighing in at 210, Eppa liked to toy with the hitters. Seldom did he walk them, but it seemed as if he were always behind them, always 3-and-2, and he appeared to throw an unnecessarily large number of balls in a game. But it was a system that paid off. In 4,494 innings, he walked only 1,082 men, an average of 2.16 per nine-inning game. Still, he could not resist making the hitter go after bad pitches.

His full name is Eppa Rixey, Jr., and not Eppa Jephtha Rixey, which was a facetious designation selected for him by the late William A. Phelon, the Cincinnati writer who delighted in bizarre nomenclature. Rixey has gone to great lengths to disclaim the phony middle name, which still creeps into print on occasion.

Rixey's total of victories would have been swelled if he had had the good fortune to connect with better clubs. In 12 of his 21 seasons in the majors, his team finished in the second division, including outright tailenders. But he went plodding along and almost always had a respectable total of wins. He was a 20-game victor four times, and his best season was 1922, when he was 25-13.

To one who watched him pitch in Cincinnati in the '20s and early '30s, two distinct impressions remain. It seems as if he always worked on Sunday and always against Pittsburgh.

There was a good reason for this. Pennsylvania did not schedule Sunday ball in that era, and the Pirates often hopped over to Cincinnati on the Sabbath. They usually found there a well-rested Rixey, who always enjoyed success against the Bucs.

But it was Rixey's constant use against Pittsburgh that led him to retire from the game. He won six and lost three for the Reds in 1933 at the age of 42, and was still a competent pitcher. But that winter Larry MacPhail took over the Reds and Rixey said to him, "I'm going to hang up my glove if I can't work against other teams."

MacPhail would not guarantee that the new manager, Bob O'Farrell, would change Rixey's schedule, so Eppa quit.

Rixey was discovered at the University of Virginia by the old National League umpire Charley Rigler, who happened to be coaching there, for a promised bonus that was never forthcoming.

At the time, Eppa planned to be a chemist and had no intention of making baseball his life work. But he was thrilled by a big league offer and the opportunity to travel and earn public distinction, so he joined the club, discovered the life was pleasant and remained for more than two decades.

Late in his career, Rixey said, "If I had my life to live over again, I would do exactly as I have done. I would welcome an opportunity to play big league baseball. The old game has bestowed upon me a far wider reputation than I would ever have gained by holding test tubes over Bunsen burners in a chemical laboratory."

When Rixey finally did lay aside his glove, he was too old to proceed with work in chemistry, but by that time he had built an affluent insurance business and was a popular figure in the social life of Cincinnati, where he still resides at suburban Terrace Park. He has also worked hard and selflessly in the promotion of Knothole Baseball.

The home run smashed off Haines that unleashed a tornado and led Eppa to phone his affianced, was one of three that he hit in 21 seasons. He struck his first one as a Phil in 1920.

His last one, off Joe Genewich of the Braves, involves an amusing story. Prior to the season of 1928, the Braves acquired Rogers Hornsby from the Giants. The late Judge Emil Fuchs, who owned the club, installed a jury box of seats in left field, not so much to catch spectators as to catch home runs from the Rajah's bat.

Hornsby hit .387 that year, but few of his blows went into the jury box while opposing players blasted drives into the synthetic seats with regularity.

The climax came when the Reds moved into Boston on June 1. On that day the Cincinnati pitcher, Ray Kolp, connected for a homer off Hal Goldsmith.

On the next day, Pete Donohue, another Red pitcher, belted one off Henry Wertz. Then, in the series finale, Rixey tagged Genewich. That was enough for Judge Fuchs and the jury box was removed for all time.

Rixey pitched many thrilling victories that could warm his dreams, but you know pitchers, and the probability is that he recalls even more vividly those three home runs.

THE CONSISTENT SAM RICE

MARCH 9, 1963. SAM RICE WAS A BRILLIANT, FINISHED PLAYER with no eccentric mannerisms. Possessing a personality closely resembling that of Charley Gehringer, Sam attained success largely because of his durability and high consistency of performance.

He was a lefthanded hitter who stood up straight, even with the plate and very close to it and he took a quick cut at the ball. His stance hardly varied from the time that Washington bought him from Petersburg of the Virginia League in 1915, until he retired after the season of 1934. He seldom argued with umpires, went about his work quietly and was not considered colorful.

In the outfield, he had plenty of range and once held the American League record for total chances, 478 in 1920. On the bases, he was a daring runner, with a seasonal high of 63 steals, but after Goose Goslin became a regular with the Senators in 1922, Rice, for strategic reasons, did not try to steal so frequently.

He was a fast-ball hitter and liked to torment Lefty Grove of the Athletics in particular.

"If I can't nick Grove for a couple of hits," Rice once said, "I think there's something wrong."

Rube Walberg, not so fast as Grove when both were pitching for the A's, gave him much more trouble. But the change-of-pace boys were the best bets to stop Sam, such fellows as Jean Dubuc and Jim (Sarge) Bagby. Clark Griffith ordered Rice to take two strikes against Bagby every time he faced him.

The trail that leads to Hall of Fame membership varies with each successful candidate, and the path Sam followed was a long and strange one.

He got off to a much later start than most players. Born on a farm near Morocco, Ind., he worked in the wheat fields in the Dakotas and Minnesota, served as a railroad section hand and bottled whiskey at the Green River distillery in Louisville. He then drifted to Norfolk, where he enlisted in the

Navy and was assigned to the USS New Hampshire. He made the ship's baseball team and did his first playing at Guantanamo, then saw service in Mexico, helping restore order after the assassination of Madero.

On leave at Petersburg, at the age of 24 in 1914, he tried out with the local team as a pitcher and looked so good that Doc Lee, who owned the club, bought him out of the Navy. When the Virginia League blew up in 1915, Lee, who owed Griffith $800, sent him Rice in lieu of that amount and it was as a pitcher that Sam reported to the Senators.

But his ability to hit was well known. Early in the season of 1916, he made nine pinch-hits in 11 tries, three of them off Elmer Myers of the Athletics, who told him, "You'd better quit pitching."

Eddie Foster, who played second and third for the Senators and was one of the greatest hit-and-run men of all time, advised Griff to use Rice in the outfield. But with Clyde Milan, Howard Shanks and Dan Moeller forming a high-class Washington picket line, there did not seem to be room. Then, as the 1916 season drew to a close, Sam beat out Moeller for the job in right and was up to stay.

From 1919 through 1930, he never appeared in less than 141 games. He seldom struck out and usually took only one swing. He went to bat 600 or more times in eight different seasons and had a lifetime major-league average of .322.

The two facts most frequently recalled about Sam's career are that he made a highly controversial catch during the World's Series of 1925 and that he quit the game with 2,987 hits, passing up the opportunity to join the select ranks of those who batted safely 3,000 times.

It is improbable that Rice, under similar circumstances today, would quit the game. But in 1934, when he was winding up his career with the Indians after 19 seasons in Washington, slight attention was paid to such records.

Rice, in fact, wanted to quit as early as 1929, but Griff talked him out of it. By that time he was fixed for life financially because of his temperate habits, industry and all-round good sense.

Now let's have a look at that catch.

The Senators and Pirates split the first two games of the 1925 classic and then moved to Washington, where a crowd of 36,495, including President and Mrs. Coolidge, jammed the ball park on a cold and windy day. A temporary bleacher handled the overflow.

In the seventh inning, the Senators scored twice to take the lead, 4 to 3. Then Fred Marberry, first of the great relief pitchers, replaced Alex Ferguson. To further strengthen the defense, Joe Harris, who had been playing in right, was benched, with Earl McNeely going to center and Rice moving to right.

Marberry started the inning by striking out Glenn Wright and George Grantham. Earl Smith, the Pirate catcher, then hit a terrific drive to right-center, headed for that temporary stand. Rice turned, raced, reached the ball with his gloved hand and then toppled into the crowd.

Several seconds passed before he crawled into view with the ball in his hand, and then Charley Rigler, the National League umpire who was working at second base, ruled that the catch had been made. There was a furious uproar from the Pirate bench, but it was ineffectual and Washington won the game without further scoring.

The Pirates were so rattled by the decision that they failed to notice that Marberry batted out of turn in the last half of the inning. Too late now, boys!

ELMER THE BAT-MAKER

MARCH 23, 1963. WHEN ELMER FLICK REPORTED TO THE Phillies at their chilly but economical training camp at Cape May, N. J., in 1898, he brought along as a recommendation a batting average of .396 earned the season before with Dayton of the Interstate League.

He also brought along his own bat, which he had turned for himself on a lathe during the winter and which he kept in a canvas bag. But he was given little chance to break into the Philadelphia outfield, a formidable array of pickets that included Ed Delahanty in left, Dick Cooley in center and Big Sam Thompson in right. Thompson, plagued with back trouble, had jumped the club the season before, but now he was apparently all right.

"Flick is going to make the outfielders hustle to hold their positions," wrote Francis Richter, the veteran Philadelphia scribe, before the season began. "He is the fastest and most promising youngster the Phillies have ever had."

It was a shrewd judgment. Although Thompson started the season in right field, his back troubled him again. After the first six games, he was unable to take the field against Boston on April 26, and Flick, making his major league debut that afternoon, singled twice in three trips off Fred Klobedanz. Thompson then took over again, but after playing in eight games, deserted the team once more in the belief that he was finished as a player.

On the day that Thompson left, May 13, Flick was again placed in the lineup and he remained as a standout regular performer in the majors for 13 years.

He was such a hit from the start that by July he had made the fans forget all about Thompson, who had batted .403 in 1894 and .394 in 1895. He showed one of the strongest arms in the league and one afternoon in Pittsburgh he made a catch described by the press as the greatest ever seen in that city. It was a leaping, one-handed stab rewarded by a shower of silver from the bleacher bugs, rare homage to a visitor.

Flick batted .319 in that maiden year, upped the figure to .343 in 1899 and .378 in 1900. But the ways of baseball are strange. When Elmer is recalled today, it is principally because, as a member of the Cleveland team in 1905, he led the American League with an average of .306, lowest ever for a monarch.

Overlooked is the fact that he sported a lifetime average of .315 for his 13 seasons in the big show.

When war erupted between the National and American Leagues in 1901, Flick remained loyal to the Phillies, but a year later he jumped to the Athletics along with Frosty Bill Duggleby, a pitcher, and Monte Cross, the veteran shortstop.

The year before, the Phillies had lost Larry Lajoie, along with pitchers Bill Bernhard and Chick Fraser, to the A's. When the Pennsylvania Supreme Court granted an injunction restraining the trio from playing with the Athletics, Flick, feeling he was in the same category although not named in the injuction, joined Cleveland, to which team Lajoie soon followed him.

During the remainder of the season, Flick and Lajoie were unable to appear in games at Philadelphia, but when peace was restored in 1903, the situation became clarified.

Perhaps one of the greatest tributes to Flick came when Hughie Jennings, manager of the Tigers, offered Ty Cobb for Elmer even up, an extraordinary proposition that Charlie Somers, owner of the Cleveland club, turned down.

The facts concerning this proposed trade have become garbled. The late Whitey Lewis, author of "The Cleveland Indians," thought that Jennings made the offer in 1908, after Ty had won his first batting title. But Whitey was a year off in his reckoning.

In late March, 1907, at Meridian, Miss., Cobb and Charlie Schmidt, the Tiger catcher, engaged in a fist fight before a game.

It was not Ty's first scrap of the year and Jennings decided that he wanted to get rid of him.

He called Somers at Macon, Ga., where Cleveland was training, and suggested the trade.

Somers replied that he would never consider disposing of Flick, but he offered Bunk Congalton, an outfielder who had batted .320 in 1906, for Cobb. Jennings turned that one down.

Clark Griffith, then manager of Highlanders (Yankees), hopefully offered Frank Delahanty for the Georgia Peach, and the Browns weighed in with an offer of Charlie Hemphill for Ty, but Jennings decided to stand pat.

At the time, it was believed that Cobb would not last long. He raced his motor so much and his style of play was so frantic that it was widely believed he was headed for collapse.

But life is ironic, and it was Flick, not Cobb, whose career was shortened by illness. Stomach trouble laid Elmer low in the spring of 1908, and he was out of the game most of that season. He made a comeback of sorts in 1909 but had lost much of his speed. After the season of 1910, he left the big league scene.

But he had done enough in his 13 seasons to leave a record of his greatness. Now he joins Cobb in the pantheon, his achievements secure for the ages.

SENSITIVE JOHN CLARKSON

APRIL 6, 1963. THERE ARE CERTAIN INDIVIDUALS IN LIFE SO sensitive of nature that they become scalded by criticism and withered by blame, but who are so warmed by praise and strengthened by encouragement that in a kind environment they can produce real beauty for an indifferent world.

Such a man was John G. Clarkson.

Adrian Anson, who managed Chicago in Clarkson's best days, was a blunt man not ordinarily given to sentiment, but when he heard of the former pitcher's death in 1909, he said:

"Clarkson was one of the greatest pitchers of all time, certainly the best Chicago ever had. Many regard him as the greatest, but not many know of his peculiar temperament and the amount of encouragement needed to keep him going. Scold him, find fault with him and he could not pitch at all. Praise him and he was unbeatable. In knowing exactly what kind of a ball a batter could not hit and in his ability to serve up just that kind of a ball, I don't think I have ever seen the equal of Clarkson."

It is fortunate for Clarkson that Anson recognized his emotional need. This is the trait that separates the great manager from the ordinary one. This is the trait, so often shown in regard to pitchers, that accounts for the wizardry of such men as Frank Selee, Miller Huggins, Joe McCarthy and Bill McKechnie.

But Clarkson pitched so long ago that he has become enveloped in the shadows of the years.

His election to the Hall of Fame did little except ring a vague bell in the collective unconscious minds of the oldest fans around.

Clarkson! It is just a name, but to the knowing it carries magic, like such names as Galvin, Brouthers, Beckley, Connor, Ewing, Keefe and Ward. For John Clarkson was flesh and blood. He was an extremely handsome man, dark of complexion, quiet of disposition and of average size. Born at Cambridge, Mass., July 1, 1861, three weeks before the First Battle of Bull

Run, he was the son of a well-to-do manufacturing jeweler. Two of his four younger brothers, Arthur and Walter, attended Harvard and also became major league pitchers.

Anson first saw him pitching in Grand Rapids in 1884 and obtained him from Chicago to replace Larry Corcoran, a declining star of the box. Almost singlehandedly, Clarkson pitched Chicago to pennants in 1886 and 1887, and that latter one was the last the team would win until 1906.

Why did Chicago sell him to Boston? At Poughkeepsie, N.Y. on St. Valentine's Day in 1887, Chicago sold the contract of Mike (King) Kelly, catcher and outfielder and the most colorful player of his day, to Boston for $10,000, a figure then considered astronomical. It was a transaction that demonstrated how much real value a player's contract had. So, a year later, Clarkson was sold to the same club for the same price.

Some historians have cited the sale of Clarkson as an example of the avariciousness of the Chicago management. But that is a bad rap. Clarkson preferred to pitch at Boston, which was his home, and in making the deal, Anson and the Chicago president, Al Spalding, merely catered to the pitcher's wish.

By the time he reached Boston, Clarkson no longer had a singing fast ball, but he developed a remarkable drop, the pitch now referred to as the sinker. His work in 1889 almost enabled Boston to snatch a pennant from the Giants, although at the end of the season the team was one game short.

Although plagued by the first sore arm of his career in 1892, Clarkson enjoyed a unique distinction. That year, for the only time in its history, the National League adopted a split season. Boston, with Clarkson a member of the team, won the first half.

Then he was traded to Cleveland and that team captured the second championship, enabling him to be with two pennant winners in the same league in the same year.

After his retirement, Clarkson operated a cigar store in Bay City, Mich., but he became ill and in 1909 returned to his father's home in Cambridge to die of pneumonia. He was only 47.

Francis Richter, a Philadelphia baseball editor, was a conservative in all things and, as a consequence, was not given to overstatement. But when he learned of the death of Clarkson, he wrote:

"On all counts the deceased will always rank in history as one of the few great masters of the art of pitching."

A REMARKABLE FAMILY

"Subtract us into nakedness and night again, and you shall see begin Crete four thousand years ago the love that ended yesterday in Texas."

Thomas Wolfe

APRIL 20, 1963. THIS IS A TALE THAT BEGAN MORE THAN A century ago not in Crete but in Brooklyn and ended early this year not in Texas but in Palm Cemetery, Winter Park, Fla., where a former pitcher named Del Mason was buried.

One of the pioneers of baseball was Jimmy Wood, born in Brooklyn in 1847. At the age of ten, he was already a member of an organized team, the Marions, a junior club, and in 1857 he graduated to the Eckfords. For 13 years he starred for the Eckfords at second base, competing against such famed Brooklyn outfits as the Atlantics and Mutuals.

After the Cincinnati Red Stockings formed a professional team and in 1869 toured the nation without suffering a single defeat, a group of Chicago enthusiasts decided to import the best players available and form a combination that could beat the Red Stockings. The man chosen to captain the team was Wood, who was induced to leave the Eckfords for an annual salary of $2,000.

That first professional team in Chicago played its games on a diamond laid out at a racetrack, Dexter Park, about six miles southwest of the Loop, near 42nd and Halstead Streets. The uniform included a blue cap, white shirt, blue pants, white stockings and white buckskin shoes.

The White Stockings not only dethroned Cincinnati in 1870 but went on to become a charter member of the National Association, the first professional league, in 1871.

Then, in October of that year, the great Chicago fire put an end to baseball in the city for two seasons.

Jimmy captained the Haymakers of Troy in 1872, and when that club folded, rejoined the Eckfords. The year after that he was at Philadelphia. But when Chicago organized another team and entered the ranks again in 1874, Wood once more went to Chicago as captain.

Early in that season, an abscess appeared on Wood's left thigh. Not thinking it serious, he opened it with a pocket knife to drain it. But before he closed the knife, it slipped from his hands and the blade entered his right leg just below the knee. Poison from the abscess entered the flesh, the knee stiffened, and Wood's career as a player was over. On July 10, 1874, doctors amputated the leg just above the knee.

Jimmy remained with the Chicago club as captain in 1875, but when the National League was then organized, he left baseball for good. Record books, which list him as James Burr Wood, show that he died on November 30, 1886, but he did no such thing. The player who did die on that date was Burr Wood, an amateur pitcher from Canastota, N.Y.

Our man, whose full name was James Leon Wood, moved to Florida with his wife and daughter, Carrie Lee, as early as 1881. He invested in citrus groves near Starke and immediately prospered.

The daughter, Carrie Lee, fell in love with an ambitious young man named William Chase Temple who then moved to Pittsburgh, rapidly made a fortune in the steel business and became a baron of industry with interests in coal, plate glass and railroads.

In 1892, he bought a large slice of the Pittsburgh Pirates and became the club's president.

At this time, the National League, operating with 12 teams, had no competition, and consequently there was no World's Series. In order to fill that void, Temple suggested a post-season series between the first and second-place clubs and offered a silver cup two feet high as a trophy.

For four seasons beginning in 1894, the Temple Cup competition decided the championship, but when the second-place team won in three of those years, public interest slackened and the series was abandoned. Eventually, the Temple Cup was acquired by the Hall of Fame and today it is examined annually by thousands, serving as a nostalgic reminder of the nineteenth century game and a primitive symbol of what has grown to be the World's Series.

The Temples had a daughter named Dorothy, and she grew up to marry Del Mason, a former major league pitcher who coached at Rollins in 1909. Mason came originally from Newfane, N. Y., a hamlet in the western part of the state near Niagara Falls.

Patsy Donovan gave Del a trial with the Senators in 1904, and Ned Hanlon obtained him for the Reds in the fall of 1906. Mason started the 1907 season as a regular Red pitcher, but ran into a no-hitter pitched by Big Jeff Pfeffer at Boston early in the year and thereafter seemed jinxed, ending with a 5-12 record. When the season was over, he accepted the coaching job at Rollins, his alma mater.

Mason became a distinguished citizen of Winter Park after his marriage to Dorothy Temple, operated an automobile business for more than 20 years and served two terms as city commissioner.

He died at 79 on the final day of 1962, and his widow lives there now, warmed by her memories of a remarkable baseball family. Her grandfather introduced professional baseball to Chicago, her father was president of the Pirates, her husband was a big league pitcher.

And what became of Jimmy Wood, who started it all? He abandoned the lush life of Florida in the time of World War I, and went back at last to Brooklyn. There he died, probably in 1926 or 1927. The exact date is not known, for the City of New York has so far been unable to locate his death certificate. How many stories are there in the naked city? Seven million? His has been one and some day the facts will all be known.

THE FIRST INDIAN PLAYER?

JUNE 15, 1963. COOPERSTOWN, N.Y. THE SEARCH LIGHT OF truth has piercing rays, and in those beams dissolved some of baseball's most cherished beliefs. The game's past, like a gigantic jig-saw puzzle, is gradually being pieced together under its glow.

It often has been printed that the first American Indian to appear in the majors was Louis Sockalexis, that folk hero out of the Penobscot country of Maine, who joined the Cleveland team of the National League in 1897, dazzled briefly and then faded. Queries about Sockalexis still reach this desk occasionally, because he is supposed to have inspired the Frank Merriwell series of stories, that exercise in heroics created by Gilbert Patten.

But now it develops that Sockalexis was not the first of the natives, that the honor should go to James Madison Toy of Beaver Falls, Pa., a first baseman with Cleveland of the American Association in 1887 and a catcher with Brooklyn of the same circuit in 1890. A nephew of Toy who still lives in Beaver Falls writes that his uncle was a Sioux, although it is not probable that he was fullblooded.

Toy was a righthanded pitcher and thrower and a little fellow, standing five-six and weighing a stocky 160.

A strange accident not only ended his career but blighted his life. While catching for Brooklyn one afternoon, he was struck in the groin by a pitched ball that bounced off the corner of home plate. The resulting injury was so painful that for the rest of his life he had to take morphine under supervision. He went back to Beaver Falls, worked whenever he could as a stove molder, and lived until 1919.

Toy, then, was the first major league Indian yet discovered, the paterfamilias of a breed that has added a colorful page to the game's ethnology. One of them, Chief Bender, the crafty Chippewa, reached the Hall of Fame. In Pittsburgh they still remember Moses Yellowhorse, who was a pitcher and a Pawnee.

Jim Thorpe, who might have become a star had he been able to hit the curve for McGraw, was partly of Sac and Fox origin. Contrary to legend, he

was not fullblooded either, for his father, Hiram Thorpe, a ranchman, had
roots that were Welsh, Dutch and Irish.

Within a half-hour's drive of Cooperstown lived Louis Bruce, 86, a retired
Methodist preacher. Half Iroquois and half Scotch, he was an outfielder who
broke into thirty games for Connie Mack with the Athletics in 1904.

Bill Phelon, that eccentric of the press box who once covered baseball in
Chicago and Cincinnati, was fascinated by Indians in the game and has
preserved with affection his memory of them in the following verse:

The Irish player rages on the field,
    Fights with the umpire, frequently is canned
Is worshipped by the bleachers, and, quite oft,
    Spends all his salary with lavish hand.
The slow, methodic German seldom kicks,
    Counts it "a business," works for those who pay
His salary—works earnestly, and it's a cinch—
    Plants heaps of shekels for a rainy day.
The Indian, sad, morose, receives applause
    Without a smile upon his Sphinx-like face,
And, inwardly, thinks he gets even when
    He draws big wampum from the pale-skinned race!

Some years ago, The New Yorker published a delightful though brief
anecdote concerning an Indian who, after hoisting a few, entered an elevator
at the Waldorf to find himself confronted with a group of paleface people in
evening dress. "Go home, foreigners!" was his salutation: he had a point.

But baseball had earlier known a similar story, though with reverse
English. The Athletics had an Indian pitcher named Ed Pinnance in 1903,
discovered by Harris Davis, the first baseman, while taking the baths at Mt.
Clements, Mich. Pinnance reported, carrying a suitcase made from the skin
of an elk he had shot with bow and arrow.

A reporter asked one of the Athletics' catchers what he thought of
Pinnance.

"I don't know about letting these foreigners into the game," was the reply.

The wampum earned by Indian players in Phelon's day was, of course,
nothing compared with today's rewards. Allie Reynolds, Superchief of the
Yankees, is probably the most prosperous of them all. Now president of a
corporation in Oklahoma City, Reynolds is mostly Scotch-Irish but one-
fourth Creek.

The glorious return to Cleveland of Early Wynn provides that team with
a real Indian, perhaps one who can inspire his mates to go on the warpath
once again. Cleveland's team was first called the Indians, because the roster
included Sockalexis, in the late '90s. Prior to that, they had been the Spiders.

Then, when the American League was formed, they became the Blues or Bluebirds because of their blue uniforms.

Sockalexis, by providing the game with an enduring name for a team, has perpetuated his race. But now it is known that he was not the first of his kind. So until an earlier claimant is unearthed, let the honor rest with James M. Toy.

ADDIE JOSS

JUNE 29, 1963. ADDIE JOSS! WHAT EMOTIONS ARE STIRRED BY that name! It is not necessary to have seen him pitch to know his greatness, for the record is there for all to read, and the years have not dimmed his accomplishments, even though he was cut down cruelly in his prime by meningitis. Pitcher of a no-hit game one year and dead the next — that was the fate of Addie Joss, but he hasn't been forgotten in the City on the Lake.

When you talk about pitchers in Cleveland, there will be three names that come to mind immediately: Cy Young, Bob Feller and Joss.

Addie was extremely tall for his time, three inches over six feet, a righthander with a side-arm motion and a fast ball that smoked. Many pitchers of that time fielded their position in a slovenly manner, but Joss was graceful and alert and it seemed as if he could move to any part of the infield in one gigantic stride.

Out of the Wisconsin woods he had come, from a little town called Juneau to grow up in Toledo. There Cleveland found him, pitching for Toledo of the Western Association when the National and American Leagues were at war in 1901.

Joss pitched a one-hitter in his debut, holding the St. Louis Browns to an infield scratch by Jess Burkett on April 26, 1902, winning, 3 to 0. He was a regular from the start and soon a favorite on a team that included Nap Lajoie, Bill Bradley, Elmer Flick, Deerfoot Harry Bay and George Stovall.

For four straight years he won 20 or more games. He didn't win them all, of course. One afternoon Rube Waddell beat him, 2 to 1, in a 14-inning game that was reeled off in two hours and ten minutes.

But this most celebrated pitching feat took place in the closing days of the 1908 season when Cleveland was fighting for the pennant that eventually went to Detroit by half a game.

At Cleveland on the season's final Friday, Joss hooked up with Ed Walsh of the White Sox in a game that has since been called by many the greatest pitching battle of all time.

Walsh that afternoon was superb. Working his spitball to perfection, he struck out 15 batters in eight innings. But Joss was better. Not one Chicago player reached base and only four balls were hit to the outfield. Cleveland scratched out the victory with one run when Joe Birmingham singled, made a delayed steal and scored on a wild pitch.

It was only the fourth perfect game in major league history. John Lee Richmond and John Montgomery Ward pitched the first two in the National League, within five days of each other in 1880. Cy Young issued the third, for Boston against the Athletics, in 1904. Then came Joss.

Now, here at the Hall of Fame more than a half-century later, stood the pitcher's son, a pleasant man of about 60 with a sandy complexion and a soft-spoken manner that understated the importance of his many diamond memories.

"It's a funny thing," Norman Joss said. "There have been so few perfect games. So very few. And John Lee Richmond, who pitched the first one, ended up as a mathematics teacher at Scott High School in Toledo. I was in his plane geometry class and a nice old man he was. But on the first day of school, he said to me, 'Now look. Your father pitched a perfect game. Well, so did I. And it doesn't mean anything here. The fact that your father did the same thing isn't going to help you with plane geometry.'"

The perfect game was not quite the end of the trail for Addie Joss. He pitched another no-hitter, this time walking two, also against the White Sox in 1910. But later that season, in an afternoon's work at Philadelphia, he hurt his arm.

During spring training in 1911, he fainted one day on the bench, but shrugged it off. Several days afterward he appeared to have pleurisy and doctors sent him home to Toledo. When Cleveland opened the season at St. Louis, he could not join his mates and, two days later, on April 14, he died.

The funeral was one of the largest ever seen in Toledo. The entire Cleveland team was present and Billy Sunday preached the sermon.

"I was only nine when my father died," Norman Joss said. "I can't remember too much about his pitching. But mother lived until about eight years ago.

"Occasionally she'd hear from fans and I remember that when Whitey Lewis wrote his story of the Cleveland Indians he looked her up.

"And, oh yes, there's one other thing. If you're going to write anything about this, you've probably seen him listed in the records books as Adrian C. Joss. But he had no middle name and no middle initial. The sports writers listed him as Adrian C. because Anson whose first name was also Adrian had the middle initial 'C' for Constantine. But it was just plain Adrian Joss."

He might have added that it is a name that will never be forgotten as long as baseball is played. And that promises to be forever.

A GIANT'S STORY

AUGUST 3, 1963. LAUGHING LARRY DOYLE HAS NOT MUCH to laugh about of late.

The former captain of John McGraw's Giants who has fought tuberculosis in the deep Adirondack retreat of Saranac Lake for more than 20 years, now carries the added burdens of emphysema and failing eyesight.

But his spirits remain buoyant and he is cheered by mail from such old friends and mates as John Lobert, Fred Snodgrass, George Cutshaw and Chief Meyers.

His life is comfortable and, in winter, cold. It is nothing for the temperature to sink to 40 degrees below zero. But even winter has its compensations and, last February, Doyle, who is the town's most noted citizen, was acclaimed by the Chamber of Commerce as "King of the Winter Carnival."

"Every king deserves a queen," Larry told the committee, "so you have to get me one."

They followed instructions perfectly and came up with Loretta Ann Rissell, better known as Miss Rheingold, and the royal couple was crowned in coronation ceremonies at a local theater.

Larry was the regular second baseman for the Giants for 14 years starting in 1907. He replaced Billy Gilbert at that position and eventually yielded to Frank Frisch. During those years at the Polo Grounds, the Giants won four pennants and Doyle also won a personal championship, the batting crown of 1915. He accomplished this with an average of .320, the lowest figure that ever earned the NL award.

When you consider all the great players that the Giants have produced over the years, it seems very strange that only five of them have ever won the batting title. During a period of 40 years, Doyle was the only one.

Roger Connor was the first in 1885, then came Jack Glasscock in 1890. Doyle did it in 1915 and there were no others until 1930, when Bill Terry hit .401. The only one since Terry was Willie Mays in 1954. It also seems strange that of those five Giant batting monarchs, four were infielders. Connor, like Terry, was a first baseman and Glasscock was a shortstop.

It was Dan Brouthers, Hall of Famer and slugging first baseman of the '80s, who found Doyle for McGraw. During the early days of the 1907 season, he noticed him playing for Springfield, Ill., in the Three I League. The asking price was $4,500, but Brouthers liked the boy's aggressiveness and his level, lefthanded swing and the deal was made.

Larry reported at the Polo Grounds on July 22 and McGraw threw him into the game that afternoon against the Cubs. Ed Reulbach shut out the Giants, 2-0, on five hits, but Doyle made one of the safeties and was in the lineup to stay.

A product of Irish mining stock, Doyle was born at Caseyville, Ill., across the Mississippi from St. Louis. By a singular coincidence, Art Fletcher, the shortstop with whom he was paired on the Giants for a dozen seasons, was a native of Collinsville, Ill., only a couple of miles away.

The New York that Doyle found himself in is recalled today as an elegant city of fine restaurants such as Delmonico's and Rector's, a city that offered the Floradora Girls and rides through Central Park in hansom cabs.

But that was not the New York that the Giant players knew. There was no such thing as cafe society, and no celebrated sporting mecca such as Shor's today. The Giants were lodged in boarding houses in the Bronx, split up into pairs, and Doyle lived first with Fred Merkle.

"I'll never forget the day Merkle failed to touch second," Larry said. "I was injured at the time and didn't play that day. I think Buck Herzog was at second. Anyway, Merkle and I went back to our boarding house and he never did have dinner that night, but just stayed in the room.

"McGraw always defended what Merkle did. After all, in that situation it was customary for runners to go to the clubhouse. McGraw had a bad temper, of course, and because I was captain, I heard a lot of it. But I never paid any attention to what he was saying because I always knew that ten minutes later he would have forgotten it. He just liked to win."

It was a good life that Larry Doyle knew in those years after joining the Giants. In fact, he has often been quoted as saying, "It's great to be young and a Giant!" What about that? Had he actually said it and, if so, to whom? Or was it just a felicitous but fake quote that he has not bothered to deny because it has a happy ring?

"I said it," Doyle revealed, "to Damon Runyon. And I meant it."

But that was all more than a half century ago, a day that is distant not only because of the passing of time. The Giants have gone now to the other coast, and Larry is no longer young.

But his regal association with Miss Rheingold would seem to give him kinship with the Mets, providing a strain of old blood for the New Breed.

What did he think of the Mets, anyway?

You forget what he replied, but you remember that he smiled and, surely, like all old Giants, he wished them well. It's great to be old and a Met fan.

THE SOUR TROUBADOURS

AUGUST 24, 1963. COOPERSTOWN, N.Y. THE GORGEOUS IN-competence of the Mets in recently losing 22 consecutive games on the road is a feat of considerable magnitude, but it should not be thought that the accomplishment is without parallel. In fact, news dispatches were careful to point out that Casey Stengel's sad band merely duplicated and did not exceed what had been done in 1890 by the Pittsburgh team of the National League.

Not yet called the Pirates, the Pittsburghs of 1890 were known as the Troubadours, and it was a baleful tune that they serenaded National League company. It was, apparently, a much worse team than the modern Mets, and by the season's end had won 23 and lost 114 for a percentage of .168.

Just as today's Cubs have an athletic director in Robert V. Whitlow, the Troubadours were run by a managing director, one J. Palmer O'Neil, an elegantly-dressed sport who traveled with the team.

On the field, meanwhile, the Troubadours were managed by Guy Hecker, a pitcher who had known some great years at Louisville. Sports-writers of the time, seeking an alternate nickname for the team, sometimes referred to the players as Hecker's Kids or Hecker's Colts, or as O'Neil's Innocents, which they certainly were. At least they were innocent of beating anyone.

Bad as they were, the Troubadours included in their band a few players whose names are still recalled today. Billy Sunday, more famous later as a fervid envangelist, was the regular center fielder. Paul Hines, an outfielder and the first player to use sunglasses, was that year stationed at first base.

Fred Dunlap, king of second basemen in the '80s, started the season at that position but, slipping badly, was soon succeeded by Sam Crane, later a baseball writer for the old New York Journal.

Another performer was a combination outfielder-infielder, Ed Lytle, whose name is known today because of a curious anecdote. Earlier in the 1890 season, Lytle had been a member of Chicago, but was cut loose by Cap Anson after playing one game in right field.

In that contest, Lytle exhibited a strange tendency to shoot all his throws to the second baseman, Bobby Glenalvin, regardless of where the play might be. Finally, after Lytle had thrown to second for the umpteenth time while a runner lazily jogged across the plate, Anson cornered him on the bench and said, "Lytle, why do you always throw to second? Can't you throw anywhere else? Why do you always give the ball to Glenalvin?"

"Because, Captain Anson," the rookie replied, "Glenalvin is the only man on the nine to whom I've been introduced."

He was gone the following day appropriately joining O'Neil's Innocents.

Pittsburgh also introduced a brother act that lasted only one day. In a double-header at Philadelphia on June 23, the Troubadours employed John Gilbert at short and his brother, Harry at second. Hardly anything is known about the Gilberts, except that they hailed from Pottstown, Pa.

They could have been the first pair of twins in major league annals, but whatever the facts of their birth, they never appeared again. John Gilbert went back to Pottstown, operated a hotel and died there in 1903.

The Troubadours were as bad as they were because the Brotherhood War of 1890 siphoned off their best players. While the Pittsburgh team, loyal to the National League, reeled off its games at Recreation Park, the Brotherhood team, managed by Ned Hanlon as its manager and, after finishing last in 1891, did not present the city with another tailender until 1917.

Another strange club of 1890 was the Athletic aggregation of Philadelphia, a member of the American Association. Anticipating in reverse the feat of the Miracle Braves of 1914, who climbed out of the cellar to capture the pennant, the Athletics, in first place July 12, finished seventh.

That team also lost 22 straight, the last 22 played, but for some reason you will not find the feat in the record books.

But the Brotherhood War had nothing to do with the decline of the Athletics that year. The owners of the team entrusted its business affairs to a Mr. Whitaker, first name not known. Mr. Whitaker had a strange reluctance to pay the players' salaries, and the paychecks he gave them in June were the last they were to see. The athletes quit in a body on September 16. Mr. Whitaker replaced them with eager amateurs, who finished the schedule.

The astonishing thing about the Athletics was the ease with which they were beaten. In those final 22 games, the club scored 60 runs while their opponents were collecting 278.

The Mets have been impressively awful at times, but let's not get carried away! There were many worse teams in the previous century. What sets the Mets apart is the faith of their followers and the Old Testament acceptance of fate by Casey Stengel, who is making Job look like a sorehead by comparison.

OGDEN THE SCOUT

NOVEMBER 16, 1963. COOPERSTOWN, N.Y. SCOUTS ARE A breed apart.

In the ball parks, you can find them in the grandstand's rear rows, studying the pitcher in stony silence or quietly watching the backwash of a batter's swing.

In the hotels, you can spot them in the lobbies, often alone, wiping their glasses before attacking the six-point type of the box scores.

So many of the great ones are gone now! The Yankees had Paul Krichell, Joe Devine, Vinegar Bill Essick and Gene McCann with the white tie and straw hat. And there was Ira Thomas, Johnny Nee and, bless his memory, Hank DeBerry, Charlie Barrett and Larry Sutton, and, oh, so many more!

But now there is a new crop of elder statesmen among the scouts, men who, without any publicity, have assumed an honored station in the game.

One of these is John Ogden, 47 years in the game, a professional pitcher for 16 seasons. John McGraw originally found him for the Giants at Swarthmore College and used him in five games in 1918.

A decade later, Ogden appeared with the Browns and eventually with the Reds.

I ran into him recently when he was huddled in scout talk with Eddie Sawyer. Both work for the Phillies, of course, a fact which makes you wonder if Bob Carpenter and John Quinn are not cornering the brains market.

Sawyer's photographic memory is well known, but I didn't know if John Ogden goes in for similar mental gymnastics. The discovery that he is a veritable fountain of facts provided a memorable evening.

One of the first times I saw Ogden, he pitched a great game for Cincinnati against the old Boston Braves in 1931 and eventually won it by that favorite score of pitchers, 1-0. His shutout was saved when Tony Cuccinello (we called him Chick then) pulled the hidden-ball trick on Rabbit Maranville, who had wandered off second.

The occasion also included an old-timers' game, and at the banquet that followed, some wag, with the collusion of kitchen help, managed to hide an official league baseball in Maranville's ice cream, thus surprising Rabbit for the second time.

Now it was 32 years later, but Ogden remembered the game in all its detail.

The evening grew late, but Sawyer and Ogden proved tireless and the gabfest went into extra innings.

Some random Ogden observations:

"The best fast curve ball I ever saw belonged to George Earnshaw. The curve of most pitchers cannot compare in speed with a fast ball, but Earnshaw's could.

"Who had the best pickoff motion? That's easy, Sherry Smith. The best by a righthander was that of Death Valley Jim Scott. Today's best, left or right, is Warren Spahn."

"And don't forget Art Mahaffey," Sawyer said.

"Art Mahaffey," Ogden agreed. "And Grover Alexander had the best change-up. Now, who had the worst throwing arm?"

"Goose Goslin, when his arm was hurt," Sawyer suggested. "He played when his arm was very sore and Bobby Reeves had to hustle to the outfield from second base to take his throws."

"Yeah," Ogden said. "I remember that. But there was a fellow around '22, a murderous hitter who couldn't throw 30 feet."

It was inevitable, and it was Sawyer who said it. "Why don't you pick your all-time, all-star team, John? Yours I'd like to hear."

"Well," Ogden said, "Mickey Cochrane is my catcher, and there would be room on this club for Bill Dickey, too. I want six pitchers. It doesn't matter if they're righthanded or lefthanded.

"I'll take Walter Johnson, Alexander, Christy Mathewson, Ed Walsh, Lefty Grove and Earnshaw.

"Billy Terry can play first base. It's hard to see how I can pick anyone over Sisler, but Terry was great in so many ways, at bat, managing, digging the ball out of the dirt.

"Terry also had class. He proved his class by what he accomplished after he left baseball.

"At second base, Larry Lajoie and Eddie Collins were entirely different types. Both great.

"I'd have to pick Collins. He was the best I ever saw in a certain situation — men on first and second and none out, and you couldn't stop him from hitting the ball safely through shortstop.

"Hans Wagner at short. I've never seen his equal. And Pie Traynor at third. Now the outfield may surprise you. None of this Ty Cobb, Babe Ruth and Tris Speaker stuff for me. Cobb and Ruth, sure! But, in my opinion, the best defensive — I said defensive — outfielder of them all is Willie Mays.

"Speaker was a great outfielder and Johnny Mostil made some sensational catches out there, but Mays does everything better than any outfielder I've ever seen."

A few feet away, a fine-looking young Negro was waiting for the elevator. Ogden noticed him and smiled with satisfaction, for he had signed the boy, who is now on the threshold of greatness with the Phillies.

You'd better remember his name, which is Richie Allen. He just may be one of the great ones.

THE MAN WITH THE CLOTH CAP

MARCH 7, 1964. THE ONLY PUBLIC TRANSPORTATION AVAIL-able from Cooperstown to New York City is a bus that curves down through the Catskills, passing such places as Phoenicia and Big Indian to a point near point near Kingston where it joins one of those superhighways that lead with monotonous perfection to the Big Town. One of the places through which it passes is a speck on the map called Fleischmanns, a village that at this time of year is a resort for skiers.

I never ride through Fleischmanns that I do not think of little Miller Huggins, the Mighty Mite who managed the Yankees in the early days of their greatness, leading them to their first six pennants.

The village of Fleischmanns was named for the family that found fame as manufacturers of gin and yeast. Max and Julius Fleischmann (the latter was once mayor of Cincinnati) owned a large chunk of the Reds in the days when Garry Herrmann ran the club. For their own amusement, they also operated a semi-pro club known as the Mountain Tourists at Fleischmanns, N.Y., and it was with that team that Huggins started his career as a second baseman in 1899. You couldn't prove it by the box scores, however, because Miller, in order to protect his eligibility at the University of Cincinnati, was using the name of Proctor. And it was as Proctor that he started his career in O.B. with Mansfield of the Inter-State League.

Huggins the ball player is largely forgotten and he seems destined to be remembered mostly as the man who fined Babe Ruth $5,000. But he was a capable second baseman in his day and, in the six seasons he guarded that position for Cincinnati, starting in 1904, he was regarded as the club's all-time best, except for Bid McPhee. Then he was traded to the Cardinals in an ill-starred deal along with Ennis (Rebel) Oakes, a competent outfielder, and Fiddler Frank Corridon, a spitball pitcher, for Fred Beebe, a pitcher, and Alan Storke, a third baseman. Storke died at Auburn, N.Y., after an appendicitis operation before he could even report to the Reds.

It was the whim of a woman that made Huggins a big league manager. Helen Hathaway Britton inherited the Cardinals from her uncle, Stanley Robison, upon his death in 1911 and she took an active part in league affairs. Although she had Roger Bresnahan, also a Hall of Famer, as a playing manager, she disposed of him after the season of 1912 and gave the job to Huggins.

Miller was then still a regular player. He was a good leadoff man with a great ability to coax bases on balls from the pitchers and although a little fellow (5-6 1/2,135), he could hold his own in the rough and tumble around second base.

Hug had a tailender in 1913, his first year as manager at St. Louis, but then he pushed the club up to third the next year, and that was the highest spot a St. Louis team had occupied in the NL since 1876. Then the team slid to sixth and eighth before rebounding again to finish in the No. 3 spot in 1917.

At this time, Ban Johnson, the dynamic president of the American League, was looking for ways to strengthen the Yankees, who'd had a succession of mediocre teams. He thought that Huggins was just the man to manage New York, and he asked J.G. Taylor Spink, the late publisher of The Sporting News, to sound him out. Huggins wanted the job all right and Spink arranged that he meet with Colonel Jacob Ruppert, who owned the Yankees in collaboration with another colonel, the improbably named Tillinghast L'Hommedieu Huston. Huggins, a frugal and unsophisticated man, showed up for his interview with Ruppert wearing a cloth cap. The urbane colonel winced and almost decided not to offer him the job.

Miller began managing the Yankees in 1918 and remained with them until his death from erysipelas at the end of the season of 1929. Colonel Huston, who had been overseas in World War I at the time of the Mite Manager's appointment, always regretted that he had not been consulted, as he had his own favorite for the post in Uncle Wilbert Robinson, manager of the Dodgers. Huggins' job at New York was not really safe until Huston sold his interest in the club to Ruppert.

The foundation of Miller's greatness as a manager lay in his use of psychology in handling men. Waite Hoyt, Joe Dugan and various other great Yankees of the '20s who are still around can tell you that. He was a small man physically and in ill health most of the time, but he earned the respect of his players and he was the boss.

It was Huggins who introduced Leo Durocher to the major league scene, and it has always appeared likely that he saw in Durocher a replica of himself, a brash infielder composed of nerve and grace, not a good hitter but a good ball player. Huggins championed Durocher on the Yankees, and after his death it was taken for granted that Leo would move on, which he did, going to the Reds on a waiver exchange for the handsome but largely forgotten Clarke Pittenger.

There is plenty of room in the Hall of Fame for Huggins, who in his 12 seasons with the Yankees won six pennants, finished second twice and third twice.

He finished in the second division only once, in 1925, when the club skidded to seventh.

That was the year in which he plastered Ruth with the $5,000 fine. It must have been a case of Mite makes right.

MONTE THE VERSATILE

MARCH 14, 1964. THE ELECTION OF JOHN MONTGOMERY Ward to membership in the Hall of Fame may be a puzzle to the boys whose memories cannot extend beyond the career of Mickey Mantle, but the fact is that Ward is one of the most versatile and romantic figures in the annals of the game. His election is entirely deserved and his contribution to baseball is almost without parallel.

Perhaps the best way to explain Ward and his work is through the use of an analogy.

Suppose, just suppose that Sandy Koufax would pitch a perfect game. Then suppose that he would become a shortstop and play at that position long enough to make 2,000 hits. Now, suppose that Koufax would become manager of both the Giants and the Dodgers, then form a third league that would almost put the other two out of business, become a lawyer and represent the National League in court, and finally buy the Braves. Can Sandy do it? It seems doubtful to me, but Ward, in his time, did all those things.

He pitched his perfect game for Providence against Buffalo on June 17, 1880, and it would be 24 years before Cy Young could duplicate it. But Ward hurt his arm, so he moved to shortstop and remained an active player through 1894, making 2,151 hits. He joined the Giants in 1883 and was one of the key figures as that club won its first two pennants in 1888 and 1889. In the 1889 interleague playoff against Brooklyn, which had won the American Association pennant, his play was so thrilling that he became a national figure, as well known in his day as, say, Willie Mays is now.

During the season of 1885, Ward had organized the Brotherhood, a player group that was originally benevolent and protective in purpose. It was not opposed to the reserve clause, which Ward believed to be the cornerstone of the game.

However, as time passed, grievances developed and, when some of the club owners tried to enforce a salary classification plan, with $2,000 as the maximum pay permitted, Ward simply found backers and formed a league of his own. Almost every player of note in the game joined him, but fortunately peace was restored after the Brotherhood League operated for only one season, 1890.

Ward managed Brooklyn in 1891 and 1892 finishing sixth and then third. But his heart was on Broadway, so he moved across the bridge to manage the Giants in 1893 and 1894. He finished fifth the first year, then second and went on to win the Temple Cup series, the equivalent of today's World Series, from the Baltimore Orioles, who had finished first. Then, at the height of his career, he quit the game to practice law.

As so often happens when a man prospers and grows older, Ward's economic views became more conservative and he became the chief counsel for the National League. He also took up golf, became expert enough to win many prominent tournaments and almost reached championship ranks in that game.

In the sporting pages of newspapers of the '80s and '90s, he was always referred to as John Montgomery Ward, but his family always called him "Monte," and it seems highly improbable that "John" was really his first name.

In fact, I recall reading once that Jim Mutrie, the first business manager of the Giants (John Clapp was the first actual field manager of the team), bestowed the "John" upon him as a nickname. But it stuck with him and is part of the record now.

Grantland Rice once wrote that Ward would die with his boots on and he did just that. He was on a hunting trip at Augusta, Ga., in March, 1925, contracted pneumonia and had to be taken to a hospital, where he died on his sixty-fifth birthday. Only a few weeks before, he had participated in the National League's Golden Jubilee celebration at the old Broadway Central Hotel and the annual New York baseball writers' dinner at the Hotel Roosevelt.

Baseball had always been in his blood. Although he had a distinguished law practice in New York, he succumbed to the old urge and bought the Boston Braves in 1912, but disposed of them before they won that miracle pennant under George Stallings in 1914, rising from last place on July 19 to cop the flag and then knock off the Athletics with four straight victories in the World Series.

He was one of the game's first collegians, a product of Penn State. He obtained his law degree at Columbia while still an active player, pursuing his studies in the winter. Tracing him was quite a job. His funeral was held in Babylon, Long Island, at St. Ann's Chapel, but the Babylon Leader, in its account of the funeral, failed to mention where he was buried. St. Ann's did not have the record either, but since he had been born at Bellefonte, Pa., a letter to a newspaper there turned up a relative in Little Rock, Ark., who in turn supplied the address of Mrs. Ward.

So there he is — perfect-game pitcher, hard-hitting shortstop, manager, organizer and owner. And now, Hall of Famer.

CHANGE-UP AND HEADWORK

APRIL 4, 1964. TIM KEEFE IS ONE OF ONLY 14 PITCHERS WHO have won 300 or more games.

So from a standpoint of statistics, the eligibility of Timothy John Keefe who won 340 games in the majors, becomes apparent for a spot in the Hall of Fame. But baseball is more than statistics. Who was Tim Keefe and where did he come from?

He was the son of Patrick and Mary Leary Keefe, both born in Ireland, and grew up in Cambridge, Mass., where his father was a builder of factories. Two of his uncles, Frank and John, were killed in the Civil War. Tim's father was constructing a plant below the Mason-Dixon line at the time the terrible war began. When he refused to fight against his brothers, he spent three years in a Confederate prison making bullets.

Tim was only nine years old when his father returned to Cambridge, but even at that time he had demonstrated a love for baseball. His father, anxious that the boy learn mathematics and the science of precise measurement, considered baseball a waste of time and administered many a thrashing to Tim for his stolen moments of joy.

Parental disapproval of baseball provides a familiar story, but it is of general interest only when the boy involved rises to greatness, as in the case of Lou Gehrig. Tim, a righthander, first pitched for the Franklin Juniors of Cambridge, an amateur nine, in 1874. Then in a long apprenticeship he was with, in succeeding years, the Tremonts of Cambridge; the Mutuals of Boston; the Androscoggins of Lewiston, Me; the Our-Boys of Boston; and Westboro, New Bedford and Clinton, all in Massachusetts.

His first professional engagement was with Utica of the National Association (a minor league) in 1879, and later that same season he was with New Bedford and Albany. Starting with Albany again in 1880, he joined Troy of the National League and pitched his first game on August 6, beating Cincinnati at Troy, 4 to 2.

Keefe had good speed and a curve and was also one of the first pitchers to employ the change-up, throwing it with the same motion as his fast one.

The mathematical skill that his father hoped he would demonstrate was also apparent; he was one of the first pitchers celebrated for his headwork.

Off the field, Tim was quiet and gentlemanly in demeanor. Well liked, he was serious, and expert at shorthand and a reader.

The Troy franchise was transferred to New York in 1883 and Keefe went along, but he did not at first join the team that was to be called the Giants. He spent two years with the original Mets of the American Association, then joined the Giants in 1885.

His success was immediate. Teaming with Smiling Mickey Welch, he assured the Giants of a well-pitched game almost every day. In 1886, he won 42 games, but his greatest fame came in 1888, when the Giants roared to their first pennant and Tim was credited with 19 consecutive victories, a streak since equalled only by Rube Marquard.

Some authorities have questioned one of the victories in that string, a game from which he retired with a 9 to 0 lead against Chicago after two innings on July 16. But since credit for games won and lost was in those days not included in the box score, it is a case of each authority making his own rules.

Keefe joined the Phillies in 1891 and closed out his career with that team two years later. Then he went back to Cambridge, where he became a realtor. Tim died there of heart trouble in 1933.

Tim and John Montgomery Ward, who will officially enter the Hall of Fame with him in July, married sisters, a coincidence that is singular to say the least. The girls were Helen and Clara Gibson, who came from Cincinnati.

Helen, a beauty of the stage, was known as Helen Dauvray and she became the bride of John Ward in 1887. The marriage did not last and she went back to the stage.

If you happened to see that thriller of the 1920s, "The Cat and the Canary," and remember the old woman who was sewing when the curtain rose and revealed the first act, that was Helen Dauvray.

Keefe and Clara were married at Worcester, Mass., on August 19, 1889, and remained together for life.

When Tim was elected to the Hall of Fame, I was unable to find any trace of his descendants in Cambridge. Thinking that if anyone in Boston could be of help, it would be Harold Kaese of the Globe, I phoned him and was happy to hear him say: "You're in luck. About a half-hour ago, I got a call from a Miss Paula Brodbine, who is Tim Keefe's niece. She has a scrapbook concerning her uncle's career."

Now the pertinent facts of Tim's career are in his file here and, before long, he will join in immortality such old teammates as Ward, Buck Ewing and Orator Jim O'Rourke.

MUSCLEMAN FROM MUSCLE SHOALS

MAY 2, 1964. HEINIE MANUSH IS A FUN-LOVING MAN OF 62, with a face as ruddy as a smoked ham, a murderous, lefthanded hitter in his day, a former pipe-fitter and the seventh son of his father.

The six other Manush (accent on the second syllable) boys — Frank, William, Charles, Ernest, Harry and George — were all ball players, five of them joining the professional ranks. Frank, the eldest, had a whirl at third base for the Athletics in 1908 and, at the age of 80, is living in pleasant retirement at Laguna Beach, Calif.

But Henry Emmett, the youngest, was the most proficient of the ball-playing brothers. He was born at Tuscumbia, a little town in northern Alabama not far from Muscle Shoals, and any Tennessee Valley Authority could have told you that on the local kid teams, Heinie was the best hitter in the whole dam area.

A couple of years at Massey Military Academy at Pulaski, Tenn. whetted his yearning to travel and he set out for Salt Lake City, apprenticed to a pipefitter at a refinery. He also played first base for the company team and the ringing line drives from his bat began to earn professional offers.

The Tigers landed Manush and sent him to Edmonton of the Western Canadian League for his debut. He was moved to the outfield because Edmonton had another first baseman who could hit, Babe Herman. But Heinie batted .321 and moved up the O.B. ladder, accompanying Herman to Omaha of the Western League in 1922. There he batted .376. The Tigers decided he was ready and he was.

The Detroit team that Manush joined in 1923 was managed by Ty Cobb and it seems unlikely that any machine ever assembled had outfielders who could hit more devastatingly. In the year of Heinie's debut, he batted .334, but Harry Heilmann led the American League with .403 and Cobb, aging but still a master, hit .340. Now that entire regular picket line from Detroit is in the Hall of Fame. Even the reserve outfielders could sock: Bobby Veach, a relic of the Cobb-Veach-Crawford era, connected for .321, and Bob Fothergill, then a sophomore, swatted .315.

Inferior pitching kept the Tigers from ever winning a pennant under Cobb, but Manush thinks that Tyrus was extremely helpful to him at the plate, aiding him in fashioning the style that made him so greatly feared. Unlike most sluggers, Heinie choked up on the bat and never tried for home runs. He hit stinging line drives and, in his early years, pulled almost everything to right. Later, he learned to go to the opposite field.

Walter Johnson was still around when Manush broke in and Lefty Grove soon came along to blaze his torrid path to fame, but neither of them bothered Heinie particularly. If he had a nemesis, it was the indestructible spitballer with junk stuff, Jack Quinn.

Manush kept improving. In 1926, he led the American League at .378 while Heilmann and Fothergill each batted .367 and Cobb, in his last Detroit year, .339.

But Heinie slumped to .298 in 1927 and George Moriarty, who succeeded Cobb as manager, traded him to the Browns, along with first baseman Lu Blue, for Elam Vangilder, a pitcher; Harry Rice, then an outfielder of enormous promise, and Chick Galloway, a reserve infielder who was nearing the end of the line.

From a Detroit standpoint, it was an unfortunate deal. Frank Navin, the Tiger owner, always regretted it. Manush hit .378 with the Browns in 1928 and .355 in 1929. Then, after holding out in 1930, he was shipped to Washington, with pitcher Alvin Crowder, for Goose Goslin.

Clark Griffith always was sorry he sent Goslin to the Browns, but eventually he got him back. Meanwhile, Manush provided the Senators with a powerful bat and his contribution to the 1933 pennant was an average of .336. He raised this to .349 in 1934, but then he slumped to .273 and Griff let the Red Sox have him for a pair of outfielders, Roy Johnson and Carl Reynolds. Boston employed him mostly as a pinch-hitter and gave him his unconditional release after a year in which he batted .291.

Burleigh Grimes then grabbed him for the Dodgers and Heinie, unawed by the National League, hit .333. Through an odd coincidence, Grimes and Manush will now enter the Hall of Fame together on July 27.

Larry MacPhail took over the Brooklyn operation in 1938 and, in May, let Manush go to the Pirates via the waiver route. Heinie did his last big league playing at Pittsburgh in 1939, then managed in the minors before rejoining the Senators as a coach in 1953.

OLD <u>DURABLE</u>

JULY 25, 1964. THE WHITE SOX, LOCKED IN SEVENTH PLACE, were going nowhere in the fading days of 1930, and Donie Bush decided to call in youngsters from the minors: Clarence Hoffman from Indianapolis, Irvine Jeffries and Bob Weiland from Toledo, George Blackerby from Dallas, Chick Autry from Louisville, and a kid shortstop, Luke Appling, from Atlanta.

Appling reported on the morning of September 10, slapped a single off Danny MacFayden of the Red Sox in four tries and remained in the American League for two decades. The White Sox used him in a half-dozen games before he broke a finger on his right hand and he hit safely in every one, bashing the best offerings of such established pitchers as Hod Lisenbee, Fred Marberry, Bump Hadley, Alvin Crowder and the original Sad Sam Jones.

Since his election to membership in the Hall of Fame, Appling has been referred to in wire-service stories as Old Aches And Pains, and celebrated for his ability to foul off pitches.

Such allusions are irrelevant to his skill and project a false image of him as a player. If Luke were injured frequently, how did he find time to take part in 2,218 games at shortstop, more than any other player in the history of baseball, and break into 204 additional box scores as a third baseman or pinch-hitter?

If he hit so many foul balls, what about the 2,749 safe hits he made? There is no doubt that he could foul them off, a science that has worn out many a pitcher, but in Appling's case, emphasis should be on the hits he got. Shortstops who can hit are a rare commodity in baseball.

You think of Honus Wagner, of course, (.329 lifetime), Arky Vaughan (.318) and Joe Cronin (.302). But Appling could wield the sapling, too, as his mark of .310 attests. When he batted .388 in 1936 he became the first shortstop in history to pace the American League in hitting, and seven years later he repeated with a .328 figure.

To find a shortstop who topped Appling's seasonal high of .388, you have to go back all the way to Hughie Jennings of the Baltimore Orioles, who mauled National League hurlers with a .397 in the year 1896.

Appling is another in the long list of players native to North Carolina. Born at High Point in that state on April 2, 1907 (his correct age did not become a matter of public record until he registered for Selective Service and eventual Army duty in World War II), he first splashed his name on sports pages as a dashing halfback for little Oglethorpe University in Atlanta. Luke was a halfback as a sophomore when Oglethorpe rose to the heights and knocked off mighty Georgia, 13-7.

But he could play baseball, too, and the scouts began to hound him. Nap Rucker, the old Brooklyn pitcher, thought he might land him for the Dodgers and the Cubs were also hot on his trail. But Luke signed with Atlanta of the Southern Association in a deal that earned him a slice of the purchase price when the White Sox grabbed him.

At first, there was some question about his fielding. Most young shortstops are erratic and Luke contributed his share of bobbles.

One afternoon against Cleveland, the Chicago fans rode him unmercifully, but Tris Speaker, the Hall of Fame outfielder who then occupied a broadcast booth for the Indians, urged an end to that nonsense.

"I may be wrong," Speaker told his audience, "but those fans who are booing this kid at shortstop are going to see him in this league for many years and they'll wind up cheering him."

After the game, Appling said in the clubhouse, "The fans may be surprised to know that during my freshman year at Oglethorpe, I waited on table and never made an error, never dropped a tray nor broke a dish."

He took those early errors in stride, coming up smiling, and seemed to be without nerves. On the field, he appeared to amble rather than strut and pressure seemed not to bother him at all.

When Jimmie Dykes became manager of the Pale Hose in 1934, he expressed confidence in Luke, and the young shortstop settled down into the high-level groove that would lead eventually to Cooperstown recognition.

But even before Dykes, Lew Fonseca installed Appling at short, preferring him to the smooth-fielding Hal Rhyne.

A righthanded hitter, Luke liked to swing late and punch the ball to right field. Right fielders played him as if he were a lefthanded pull hitter.

It was this style that made him foul off so many pitches and one alert observer figured out that his foul balls averaged 2.5 for every time at bat or about 1,500 for the season.

Late in his career, Appling told John Hoffman, the Chicago scribe, that he thought his greatest game was a wild contest against the St. Louis Browns on August 5, 1933. He made five hits in six trips, including three doubles, and reached base the sixth time when Lin Storti booted a slow roller.

The White Sox eventually lost the contest, 10-9, when Earl Webb, an outfielder stationed that afternoon at first, booted an easy bounder making a losing pitcher out of Red Faber.

Now Appling and Faber enter the Hall of Fame together.

A MAN CALLED JUMBO

AUGUST 29, 1964. THERE IN THE DOOR OF THE HALL OF FAME library stood the heaviest man who ever played baseball in the major leagues.

"Remember me?" he asked.

And who could forget Walter Brown?

When he was with the Yankees, they used to call him "The man who swallowed a taxicab."

Joe McCarthy used him as a spot starter and reliever and often called upon him in Philadelphia, with the whimsical explanation, "It's the only way I know to fill Shibe Park."

The true playing weight of Walter (Jumbo) Brown always eluded the keepers of the records. The Red and Green books listed him at a conservative 265, and even that figure made him the heaviest performer of them all.

Now the moment of truth arrived, and Brown recalled, "When I was pitching with the Giants from 1937 to 1941 I weighed 295, in shape. After quitting, I ballooned up to 355, the most poundage I ever registered."

He does not weigh that today. Ill with hypertension for most of the last ten years, he checks in at 220. Accompanied by Mrs. Brown, he stopped at the Hall of Fame on his way to a fishing camp in Canada. And he still devotes his life to recreation, as supervisor of games at Jones Beach State Park.

The annals of baseball are jammed with strange stories, and the bittersweet life of Walter Brown, whose capabilities were never fully recorded by the averages, provided one of the strangest.

Born at Greene, R.I., just outside of Providence, as everything in that state must be, Jumbo was of normal weight as a youth. The family moved to Massachusetts and he did his first pitching on the sandlots while attending Brockton High School, an institution that would later produce another heavyweight worth considering, Rocky Marciano.

A scout for the Cubs spotted him just after his graduation in 1925. Rabbit Maranville was having a brief fling as manager of Chicago that season.

So it was that the heaviest citizen in baseball history reported to one of the smallest men in the game.

Brown at that time weighed 197. He appeared in two National League games, then served his apprenticeship in the minors with stops at Sarasota (Florida State), New Orleans (Southern) and Gulfport (Cotton States). Cleveland brought him up for another trial during the final days of the 1927 season.

After that season, he became ill. His tonsils were removed and in the days of idleness that followed he gained 68 pounds. He worked out daily for five hours in the gymnasium after his recovery, but the excess suet simply would not leave his frame.

After that he remained the game's fabulous fatty, but his bulk did not appear to be a disadvantage. He was a glutton for work, but never seemed to get enough of it. He could also hit, swinging a bat made out of orange wood, the hardest timber there is.

Fans in Newark still remember the great year he had there as a Yankee farmhand in 1934. Major league scouts were generally agreed he was the outstanding pitcher in the minors. He led the International League in everything but strikeouts.

He won 20 games and lost six, pitched the most complete games, the most innings, the most shutouts (seven) and turned in the lowest ERA (2.56).

But in his trials with the Yankees he seemed to be pursued by a jinx. Every time he appeared to be working his way into the starting rotation, he was felled by illness or some injury. He would damage an ankle sliding to third, or twist a knee shagging flies in the outfield, or be konked on the wrist with a line drive during batting practice. Then, rusting on the bench, he would put on more weight.

Warren Giles grabbed him for the Reds in 1937. Decked out in a suit of flaming red silk that the club used for night games, he sat in the bull pen with another portly reliever, the late Don Brennan, awaiting the shrill whistle of Charlie Dressen.

Waived to the Giants in September, he pitched for Bill Terry for four more years; he was used sparingly, as always, but often effectively. You wondered what he could accomplish if fortune ever permitted him to take his regular turn.

There was a blonde nurse stationed at the first aid room at the Polo Grounds in those years, a girl named Mildred Garrigan. The players used to notice her admiringly, and during the season of 1940 they used to kid Brown about her.

"You ought to ask her for a date, Brownie!" would be the daily advice of one or another of his teammates.

"I never noticed her," Brown would reply, "Never paid her any attention."

What the players did not know was that during the previous winter Walter and Mildred had slipped down to Elkton, Md., and were married.

So here they were, still together 24 years later. In the wilds of Canada they would fish the streams and escape the weighty problems of a weary world.

BURLEIGH THE BULLDOG

OCTOBER 10, 1964. BURLEIGH GRIMES, BEARER OF 270 PITCH-ing victories, is a quiet man of 71 with an air of calm about him and a high pitched voice not unlike that of Jack Dempsey. It is an appearance that is deceptive.

As a pitcher, he was as mean and persistent as a bulldog with a good grip on the seat of an adversary's trousers. Stocky and muscular, he did not have the blinding speed of a Lefty Grove or the spot control of a Grover Alexander, but he never gave up. He was a horse for work and his idea of an intentional pass was four brushbacks. Appropriately named, he looked burly.

Bill Terry, who batted .401 in 1930, was the last National League player to reach that figure. The first time Grimes faced the Giants in 1931 and Terry came to bat, Burleigh called time, walked toward Terry and said, "What did you hit last year?"

"Four-oh-one," Terry told him, possibly with a trace of annoyance.

"Well, you won't be hitting .400 this year," Grimes said.

His first pitch turned Bill's cap around, and the vendetta resumed.

For Burleigh Grimes, life was a continuous struggle. Born on a farm halfway between the communities of Emerald and Clear Lake, Wis., he was a small boy when his father died. His mother held the family together and Burleigh grew accustomed to hard work and wholesome food.

There was a time when he toiled in a lumber camp from dawn until after dusk for a wage of one dollar a day. Once, driving four horses hitched to a sled, he was buried under seven tiers of 16-foot logs when one of the horses tripped over a stump in the snow. Lumberjacks, astonished that he was not killed, dug him out.

He was the last of the legal spitballers, spinning the moist delivery for 15 years after it was banned to newcomers after 1920.

But he did not rely entirely on the spitter, using it only about a dozen times in each game. He had a good fast ball, the usual assortment of curves and a screwball. He threw overhanded or sidearm, according to circumstances.

His spitball did not break as dazzlingly as that of Ed Walsh, but on his good days it would slide about eight inches and on his bad days about four or five. Unlike Stanley Coveleski, who gripped his spitball loosely, Grimes habitually held it tight and on one occasion he broke his thumbnail when he released the pitch.

He started pitching professionally in 1912 for Eau Claire of the Minnesota-Wisconsin League, a little circuit that included only four teams (Winona, Rochester and LaCrosse were the others) and expired on July 1. But Grimes started in again with Ottumwa of the Central Association in 1913 and reached the majors with the Pirates late in 1916.

Burleigh was traded to the Dodgers in January, 1918, one of five players in a big deal that saw Casey Stengel move from Brooklyn to Pittsburgh. Grimes became a big winner immediately. During his nine seasons in Brooklyn, he won 20 or more in a season four times. Then the trail led to the Giants, Pirates, Braves, Cardinals, Cubs, back to the Cardinals, back to the Pirates and finally to the Yankees, where he closed out his career, except for a final fling with the Bloomington team he managed in the Three I League in 1935.

John McGraw traded him to the Pirates for Vic Aldridge before the '28 season, probably the worst deal McGraw ever made. Burleigh won 25 for the Bucs while Aldridge was 4-7 for McGraw.

In World Series competition, Burleigh started slowly, losing two out of three to Cleveland for Brooklyn in 1920 and dropping a pair to the Athletics for the Cardinals in 1930. But he gained revenge in 1931, winning two without defeat as those same teams clashed, including the crusher in the seventh game, a 4-2 verdict over George Earnshaw.

Now a scout for Baltimore, Burleigh has led a useful baseball life for more than a half-century, including two years as Dodger pilot.

In reading about Grimes recently, I encountered a story that proves once again that it is possible to get almost anything in print. According to this yarn, Grimes reported to the Pirates for his first major league trial in 1916 at Cincinnati and found his hotel room occupied by a man who said, "I'm Larry Doyle of the Giants. We're just leaving town."

Grimes is supposed to have been so overcome by Doyle's friendliness that, when he pitched against him the first time, he purposely grooved the ball and Doyle connected for a home run.

Anyone who knows Grimes knows that he would not groove the ball for anyone. But even if he would, the story can be readily spotted as a phony. Grimes reported to the Pirates and pitched his first game against the Cubs at Chicago on September 10, 1916. The day before, Larry Doyle had broken a leg and was out for the season.

The first time Grimes faced Doyle was in 1917, but there was no home run then, either. For Laughing Larry hit six of them that year — off Lou North of the Cardinals, Leon Cadore of the Dodgers, Hod Eller of the Reds, Dick Rudolph of the Braves, Joe Oeschger of the Phillies and Lee Meadows of the Cardinals.

WHO REALLY MOVED THE BABE?

JANUARY 16, 1965. ED BARROW WAS A TITAN IN HIS TIME, A sort of Cecil Rhodes of baseball, with the emerald empire of the Yankees as his Rhodesia.

He was the president of the International League in 1914, when Babe Ruth began his professional career with the Baltimore club of that circuit. Ed followed the Babe to Boston as his manager in 1918 and trailed him again to New York, where there finally arose the big stadium on the Harlem that Ruth made possible.

It was Barrow, the history books tell us, who converted Ruth from a pitcher to an outfielder in 1918, while with the Red Sox. Although I am well aware of Barrow's contributions to the game and respect him greatly for the work he did in creating the Yankee juggernaut, I have always viewed with jaundiced suspicion the claim that he was the first to toy with the idea of sending Ruth to the outfield.

In a technical sense, this was true because it was in 1918 that Ruth went to the garden to stay and Barrow was then the manager. But Ruth's hitting skill had been recognized from the time he stepped into an Oriole suit four years before and surely, in those seasons, someone must have thought of moving him, superlative pitcher though he was.

Bill Carrigan, who managed the Red Sox when the Babe reported to that team, is now a retired banker living in Lewiston, Me. Though now 81, he was kind enough to write when the matter was put up to him: "Harry Hooper is the man who made an outfielder out of Ruth."

So the trail led to the gifted Hooper, field captain of the Red Sox under Barrow and now a resident of Santa Cruz, Calif. He was kind enough to clear the matter up for all time.

"I ran the club on the field," Hooper wrote. "Heinie Wagner was coach and he and I and Everett Scott, the shortstop, composed a strategy board. We figured that Babe would help us much more with his bat than pitching, so we asked Ed to put him in the outfield. At first, he absolutely refused. He said, 'I would be the laughing stock of the league if I took the best lefthanded pitcher in the league and put him in the outfield.' However, Babe kept asking, and I kept arguing with Ed....People were coming to the games to see Ruth hit....Why not have him in there every day?

"Barrow finally consented. 'Okay,' he said. 'We'll put him in the outfield. But mark my word! The first time he gets into a slump, he'll be down on his knees.' Well, Babe had his slump, and he did pitch a few games after that, but always at the request of the management."

This gem of Ruthiana is only one of various bits of lore currently being unearthed. The Babe, had he lived, would have been seventy years old this February 6, a horrible reminder of the flow of time. Despite the fact that he has been gone for over 16 years, interest in him is constantly maintained.

I should say that it was The Sporting News that printed Ruth's name for the first time in a national publication. This was a note in the issue of March 19, 1914, written from Fayetteville, N.C., where the Orioles were training.

In view of the fact that the name of Ruth became so famous, it is humorous to note, that the Baltimore correspondent, E.L. Schanberger, got it wrong and referred to him as Frank Ruth. "Dunn's team has now been south more than a week," Schanberger informed The Sporting News. "Reports from this camp indicate that he has some good prospects among his rookies. For one there is a youngster named Frank Ruth, a Baltimore boy, who has been the pitching mainstay of a local industrial school team for years. He has shown Dunn so much that the manager makes the bold statement that he will stick with the team this season, both on account of his hitting and his portside flinging."

When Baltimore opened the International League season at home against Buffalo, Ruth did not pitch but watched Dave Danforth shut out the Bisons, 7-0. The Babe did pitch the second day, and he repeated the whitewash, 6-0, and made two singles.

The day after his debut as a pitcher, Ruth was called upon as a pinch-hitter for the first time. Swinging for another pitcher, Frank Jarman, he slapped a long triple, evidence that he could hit as well as pitch.

The birth of Ruth as a national celebrity took place during the season of 1919 when he established a record for home runs in a season with 29. Wherever the Red Sox appeared, the crowds were enormous because of him and his every time at bat was an exciting experience for the fans.

It was that same year that Ruth started showing up at hospitals to cheer stricken children, a habit he retained throughout his lifetime. His love for children was genuine, and for every visit of this type that received publicity, there were ten that went unnoticed.

It is probable that his first appearance for a charitable cause was on August 19, 1919, when he showed up at Bridgeport, Conn., to lend his services to a benefit game for tuberculosis sufferers. He pitched three innings for both teams that day, hit several home runs and, quite typically, had been stopped en route for speeding by a highway patrolman. But when he explained his mission to the officer, he was waved on, as he would be so often in the golden years to come.

PUD THE DESERVING

FEBRUARY 20, 1965. IT IS DIFFICULT TO RECALL WHEN A PLAY-er elected to membership in the Hall of Fame brought with him more robust qualifications than James Francis Galvin.

Consider the following points:

1. He won 361 major league games, more than any pitcher in history except Cy Young, Walter Johnson, Christy Mathewson and Grover Alexander.

2. He pitched more innings — 5,959 — than any hurler in history except Young.

3. He pitched two no-hit games, both for Buffalo, against Worcester and Detroit, and his outing against the Wolverines followed a one-hit triumph over the same club.

4. He got the first two victories earned by Pittsburgh in the National League, beating John Clarkson of Chicago, 6-2, and Lady Baldwin of Detroit, 8-3, in 1887.

5. After an apparently unbeatable Providence team had won 20 straight in 1884, Galvin shut out the Grays, 2-0, beating Old Hoss Radbourn.

The Kerry Patch district of St. Louis, a section so Gaelic that the inhabitants referred to their corned beef and cabbage as "Irish turkey," produced a swarm of capable ball players over the years, but the first of that caravan was probably the greatest, and that was Jim Galvin, born there on Christmas in 1856.

Professional baseball was unknown in St. Louis until 1873. Before that, there had been only such strong amateur organizations as the Empires and the Reds. When the Reds turned professional in 1873, they were joined by another play-for-pay organization, the Browns. Galvin, at the time, was the best amateur in the city, and the Reds grabbed him before the Browns could sign him.

Soon they were calling him Pud (perhaps because he made pudding of the batters), Gentle Jeems and the Little Steam Engine. A short, stocky man with a handlebar mustache, he was a tireless worker. Although he grew up after Candy Cummings had popularized the curve ball, Galvin never thought much of the pitch and relied on speed and control. A group of New York Giants was discussing him on the bench at old Recreation Park in Pittsburgh one afternoon and Buck Ewing, the greatest catcher of his age, said, "If I had Galvin to catch, no one would ever steal a base on me. That fellow keeps them glued to the bag. And he also has the best control of any pitcher in this league."

Galvin first attracted national attention in 1876 when he pitched two no-hit games for the St. Louis Reds, one against the Cass Club of Detroit, named for that perennial wheelhorse of Michigan politics, Lewis Cass. The next season he joined the Alleghenies, a member of the International Association, the first minor league. Then he moved on to Buffalo and did his best work for the Bisons in the National League from 1879 to 1885. He won 46 games in 1883 and the same number in 1884. In the first of those two seasons he worked the staggering total of 656 innings.

He went back to Pittsburgh (Allegheny) in 1885, first pitching in the American Association and then in the National League (1887), and for the remainder of his life he made that city his home.

Bidding for the pennant in 1891, the Pirates acquired two veteran pitchers, Mark Baldwin and Silver King, shunting Galvin aside. Deeply hurt and with his salary slashed in half, Gentle Jeems said nothing, but just continued to pitch when asked and he made a better record than either of the newcomers. But, in 1892, he went into decline and closed his major league career with St. Louis. In 1894, he came back with Buffalo, but for only two games, both of which he lost.

A devoted family man, Galvin fathered nine children, two of whom survive. They are thrilled by the election that for so many years they had hoped would come.

When his playing days were over, Galvin spent one year as a National League umpire, then went back to Pittsburgh and opened one of the largest cafes in that city, an emporium that employed nine bartenders. It is interesting to observe that while Galvin went broke running the establishment, each of the nine bartenders opened a place of his own, a fact which perhaps reveals more about human nature than Galvin's business ability.

With his fortunes declining, he moved into a rooming house on Lacock street, in the district called Little Canada on the lower north side of Pittsburgh. There he died at forty-six on March 7, 1902, victim of what his death certificate describes as "catarrh of the stomach." Not far from the house in which he suffered his final illness, the swirling waters of the Ohio were at flood stage, leaving thousands homeless and creating so much excitement that the death of the great pitcher went almost unnoticed.

A righthander, Galvin was inclined to put on weight. In his best form, he checked in at 190, but there were times when he weighed much more.

Galvin had another distinction: He was a warm personal friend of Grover Cleveland. This came to public notice when a band of Chicago players, led by Al Spalding and Cap Anson, called on President Cleveland at the White House.

The President shook hands and greeted them all warmly and then, turning to Anson, said, "How's my old friend, Jimmy Galvin? You know he and I were good friends when I was a sheriff and mayor of Buffalo."

What Anson said in reply has been lost to history, but he probably reported that Galvin was a little hard to hit, but otherwise all right.

TRICKS OF MEMORY

MAY 8, 1965. COOPERSTOWN, N.Y. MEMORY IS A TRICKY PRO-cess that can be a snare, a fact which explains why juries often pay scant attention to the testimony of witnesses.

We think we know something and often we do not. For example, for a period of years I carried around the impression that Lloyd Waner, junior partner in the well-known Pittsburgh firm, threw lefthanded. He did not, but my recollection that he did was so vivid that it became difficult to be persuaded by the facts.

There are even cases in which major league players insist they did not play for teams that employed them. A particularly piquant example is provided by the late August (Gus) Weyhing, a workhorse of the '90s who pitched chiefly for the Phillies and who wound up with 265 victories. Gus took the hill for the last time for the Reds of Bid McPhee in 1901, losing his last effort before he was handed his unconditional release.

One day, shortly before his death in 1955, I caught up with Gus on the telephone in his home city in Louisville and asked him about that farewell appearance for the Reds. Although he recalled other facts about his long career with clarity, he absolutely denied ever working for Cincinnati. I dropped the matter then and there, not wanting to contradict a pleasant old gentleman. But he certainly did pitch for the Reds. The game was played on August 21, 1901, at Cincinnati, and Gus got clobbered by the Cubs, 9-1, with Rube Waddell working for Chicago.

The Sporting News, as well as all the dailies in the land, identified Weyhing as the pitcher and recorded his work, but later he had no recollection of it at all.

There is another story concerning Weyhing that is not without humor. Once his baseball days were done, he opened a refreshment palace in

Louisville that fell on evil times. The property went under the auctioneer's hammer with the sheriff running the show.

Gus was informed that his place would be sold on July 1 in a certain year, and he put a big sign in his window that read, "The first of July will be the last of August."

Ty Cobb was another who totally forgot one aspect of his career in the sunset of life. Cobb had a famous fist fight with Buck Herzog of the Giants in the Oriental Hotel in Dallas in the spring of 1917. He won the scrap, but refused to play in any more exhibitions against the Giants. With the blessing of his manager, Hughie Jennings, he went to Shreveport and finished his conditioning with the Reds.

But Tyrus completely forgot this in his later life, and when asked about it, Cobb said he had come north that year with some other team, he was not sure which one.

So it goes. And here is one for the book. Do you recall when the Philadelphia Athletics had that famous club that included Mickey Cochrane, Lefty Grove, Jimmie Foxx, Al Simmons and Babe Ruth? Yes, Babe Ruth.

If you want to make a bundle, place a friendly wager with your Uncle Herbert that Babe was in Connie Mack's troupe.

The year was 1925, and it is a matter of history now that Ruth was to suffer a humiliating season, not playing at all until June because of influenza, and then being plastered with a $5,000 fine by Miller Huggins, a turning point in his life.

The Babe would come back stronger than ever, but in 1925 he batted .290 in 98 games and it was a season he always regretted and wanted to forget.

Ruth's fate that season was actually predicted by Joe Vila, the veteran writer of the New York Sun. "If Ruth doesn't begin the championship season in perfect physical condition, he'll begin to hit the long slide down which so many other great players have gone down before him. Don't forget that the Bambino is growing old like the rest of us and cannot hit home runs forever."

Babe was at Hot Springs at the time and he weighed 245. He developed a pain in his back and stopped working out. Then shortly after reporting to the Yankees at St. Petersburg, he fractured the third finger of his left hand. This cost him another week of training.

For some reason or another, Huggins then allowed Ruth to join the Athletics at Ft. Myers and appear with them there in an exhibition against Milwaukee, then in the American Association.

The A's beat the Brewers, 5-4, with the following lineup: Max Bishop, 2b; Bing Miller, rf; Ruth, lf; Joe Hauser, 1b; Al Simmons, cf; Mickey Cochrane, c; Jimmie Dykes, 3b; Chick Galloway, ss; Ed Rommel and Lefty Grove, pitchers.

It is possible that Dykes would recall that game. Ruth added nothing to his team's attack, going hitless in three trips against Dinty Gearin, a pocket-size southpaw who had been with the Giants and Braves. The Milwaukee lineup that afternoon included such familiar names as Lance Richbourg, Oscar Melillo, Bunny Brief, Fred Schulte and Fred Skiff.

Connie Mack always felt that Jack Dunn should have sold him Ruth in 1914, and it probably was not much of a consolation to have had him for that one afternoon, March 24, 1925. You can look it up.

You can wonder also, in view of the cases of Weyhing and Cobb, whether Babe ever remembered he had once been a White Elephant.

CALLED ON ACCOUNT OF SUN

DECEMBER 11, 1965. GAMES OF BASEBALL HAVE BEEN CALLED off for a variety of odd reasons over the years. Rain is the most common cause, with darkness second and cold weather third. And there have been contests terminated by wind, snow and fire.

But in the early days of the Astrodome, there was a joke that some day, perhaps, a game would be called because of the sun. Painting the glaring dome ended that joke.

There are few things in baseball that have not happened before and a National League brawl WAS once called because of the sun. It was at Cincinnati between the Reds and Boston on Friday, May 6, 1892. It was a scoreless battle that stretched through 14 innings before Jack Sheridan, the only umpire, decided that the sun was too strong in the eyes of the batters. He then called everything off and it was a decision that strangely offended neither team. "Mr. Sheridan has distinguished himself," reported the Cincinnati Enquirer the next day. "His decision, while it may appear ridiculous on the face of it, was...a just and sensible one."

There were five members of the Hall of Fame in that game: John Clarkson, King Kelly, Hugh Duffy and Tommy McCarthy for the Beaneaters, and Charlie Comiskey for the Reds.

Clarkson allowed Cincinnati four hits and walked five. The Cincinnati pitcher, Elton Chamberlain, called Iceberg or Icebox because of his placid disposition in the face of ominous situations, gave Boston only three safeties and walked one.

Because of that game, it was decided to place home plate in the corner of the Cincinnati lot that it still occupies. The change was made when a new grandstand was constructed in 1894. Since then, it has been the right fielder and not the batter who has received the most direct rays of the sun.

Because most ball parks are now so arranged, with the right fielder in the glare of the East and the batter in the shadow of the West, the pitcher stands with his left arm to the South. This explains why lefthanded pitchers are referred to as southpaws. There are few questions asked here as frequently as that one.

The sun, however, has not provided the most peculiar reason for calling off a game. The most weird cancellation in the game's annals was the result of a murder. On the morning of June 7, 1921, the body of a slain girl was discovered in the ball park at Kingsport, Tenn., a member of the Appalachian League. Bloodhounds were summoned to sniff the trail of the murderer. To prevent that trail from becoming lost, no one was allowed in the park that day and the game with Knoxville had to be postponed by order of the police.

TEDDY BALLGAME

JULY 15, 1967. WHEN TED WILLIAMS BEGINS TO TALK ABOUT baseball, he bends his knees, flexes his muscles, and his whole body begins to transmit a current of enthusiastic excitement that is electric and infectious. To watch him and listen is like watching Ray Bolger or Fred Astaire dance.

There was such a moment a year ago, on the morning of the day Ted was to be officially admitted as a member of the Hall of Fame. He arrived here at seven that morning in the company of Bobby Doerr, the second base star of the Red Sox who now coaches for his old team; Joe Buzas, a shortstop who now operates the Oneonta (New York-Pennsylvania) club for the Yankees, and Matt Sczesny (pronounced says-knee), who managed Oneonta last year but who is now at Greenville in the Western Carolinas League. Ted dominated the group like a mother hen, studying each exhibit with extreme care and commenting on everything he saw with the rare shrewdness that he directs to everything pertaining to baseball.

He was especially fascinated by a statistical tabulation of the game's lifetime batting leaders that occupies an entire wall, and you could see the emotion swell throughout his frame as he read the names that rank so high — Cobb, Speaker, Hornsby, Wagner, Ruth, Musial, Gehrig and, of course, Williams.

Suddenly he wheeled and cried to Doerr, "Do you know who was one of the greatest batters of all time? Ernie Lombardi! You don't see his name here because catchers don't bat often enough to compile the records that men who hit high in the order can make, but what a hitter!

"I remember," he continued, "when we used to come north with the Reds in the spring, playing at places like Durham and Winston-Salem and Lynchburg. The hitting background in some of those parks was terrible, just terrible. I could hardly see the pitches. As if that wasn't bad enough, the Red Sox had a flock of hard-throwing kids like Bill Butland and Woody Rich and Bill Sayles. They were often wild and batting against them against such a background was no picnic. But it didn't bother Lombardi. He just took his cuts in the game each day and from the way he crashed liners over the infield you might have thought he was batting in the Little League. I don't know how he did it.

"What was Lombardi's lifetime?" Williams asked. "Three-oh-six? Well, if he had had normal speed, he would have made batting marks that would still be on the books."

Ted knows all the arguments that help explain why batting averages today are generally so low. He knows about night ball, which probably has cut 20 points from the combined average of every player in the majors. He knows about the slider, which reduces the batter's chance of guessing what is coming from one in three to one in four. He knows that swinging for home runs, and that is where the money is of course, has added total bases at the expense of batting percentage. And he knows about the fresh pitcher, especially the fresh pitcher.

"You can't mention this fresh pitcher business enough, " he said. "It used to be that a pitcher finished his games because he was expected to finish. In the late innings he was tired, and you could figure on getting to him. But now when he gets tired, you don't see him. I have batted four times in games against four different pitchers. How are you going to get a chance to figure them out? I don't want to take anything away from the old-timers, but you take a player years ago who made more than 3,000 hits. How many do you suppose were made against tired pitchers?"

Williams is thought of mostly because of his tremendous hitting ability, but he could do more. No fan who saw him fracture his left elbow while crashing into the wall at Chicago in the 1950 All-Star Game will ever forget it. That unfortunate play occurred in the first inning, but Ted insisted on staying in the lineup until the ninth. He even singled for an RBI in the eighth inning. The injury kept him out of all but 19 games in the second half of the season.

But if the conditions of his time were not revealed in the cold figures, what about Doerr, whose principal forte was fielding, although fielding cannot be measured to the same fine degree that batting is. Fielding percentage is almost meaningless, and lifetime fielding is almost never ever published. When Joe Gordon was flashing at second for the Yankees and Doerr was simultaneously shining for the Red Sox, their fans were constantly wrangling about which was the better player.

There is one way in which fielding ability can be demonstrated to some extent, and that is to rate players by the chances they accept per game. Obviously, a man cannot accept more chances than a rival without covering more ground. But in counting chances, you have to include errors because a great player will get errors on chances that an ordinary fielder will not reach.

ART SHIRES, SELF-PUBLICIST

JULY 29, 1967. THE LAST TIME I SAW ART SHIRES WAS IN 1954, when he was running the most exclusive restaurant in Dallas. He discouraged potential customers, kept the door locked, and if you wanted one of his strip sirloins at $7.50, you had to beg him to let you in. I went there one evening with the intention of eating a steak and staying for a couple of hours. I stayed three days. There were no other customers.

We sat in the back room with a chef. Art was unshaved, wore a faded blue bathrobe, and kept putting nitroglycerin tablets under his tongue to relieve the intermittent pain of a chronic heart condition. He was a sensitive and appealing man. During the course of the visit, he brought out all his scrapbooks, which he said he hadn't looked at in years, and as he lived again the turbulent events of his strange career, tears kept streaming down his cheeks.

The steaks were the best that Kansas City could pack, and when I complimented the chef on his handling of them, he replied, "You know, it's a funny thing. Do you know who taught me to cook? Art did. He is one of the greatest chefs in the United States."

They buried Shires a few days back, put him to rest in Italy, deep in the cotton country between Waco and Waxahachie. It was inevitable that the obituaries would refer to the fact that as a member of the White Sox he had socked Lena Blackburne, his manager, in the eye, in a clubhouse brawl.

Blackburne, now approaching his 81st birthday at his home in Palmyra, N.J., has a different recollection of that trivial incident.

"I never bothered to correct the record," Lena said. "Art was always horsing around, and on this day he borrowed a red cap from an usher and wore it during batting practice. Big Ed Walsh, who was coaching for me, told me about it, and I made him take the cap off. He made some remarks on the bench, and I ordered him to the clubhouse.

"After the game, I went to the clubhouse and found Shires fighting with Lou Barbour, our traveling secretary. I tried to separate them, but the poke I got in the eye happened when Barbour's head hit me. We all forgot about the thing immediately. Art was a fine hitter, a great personality, and he had tremendous courage."

To understand the complex man that Shires was requires a review of his entire life, which began at Milford, Mass., in 1907. His father came from Cork, his mother from Kilarney, and when Art was eight, the family moved to Texas. James Shires, his father, was a lawyer and cotton broker.

Art ran away from home at 11 and went to Beaumont, where his brother, Jack, was playing ball, and got a job as an office boy at the Magnolia Petroleum Company.

When he was 17 and a pitcher, he spurned an offer of $15 a game and asked for $25. To get it he purchased an old flivver, decorated it with banners saying, "The Great Shires Will Pitch Today," hired a schoolboy friend, dressed him in livery and soon was earning $40 a game, giving the driver $15.

Before Art started in O.B. with Waco in 1927, he began to play first base in a copper league in Arizona near the Mexican border, learning the details of the position from that skulking phantom of the game's most tragic era, Hal Chase. It was a league of ghosts like Chick Gandil, Buck Weaver and Jimmy O'Connell.

His campaign to glorify himself was not a result of conceit, but a shrewd bid for attention and money. When he reported to the White Sox in 1928 and made a triple and three singles off Red Ruffing in his first game, he had a wardrobe that consisted of 50 suits, 100 hats, 40 pairs of spats, 300 neckties and 20 canes, along with a morning suit, silk hat, a half-dozen tuxedos, golf, riding, motoring and yachting attire and two dirty baseball uniforms.

He was hobbled by injuries and was passed along to Washington in 1930. The Braves gave him a trial in 1932, but his knee would not hold up and he was through.

While with the White Sox, Shires moonlighted as a prizefighter and had six bouts before Judge Landis, in what surely today would be considered a violation of his civil rights, made him choose between baseball and pugilism. In the ring he was a tremendous draw, appearing in a crimson robe that had ART THE GREAT in bold white letters on the back. He was trained to fight by Jack Blackburn, who later would teach Joe Louis a thing or two. One of his opponents was George Trafton of the Chicago Bears.

He became a wrestler then had a brief fling as a Houston florist, and then opened his restaurant. By the time I caught up with him at Dallas in 1954, the spats and walking sticks were long gone, but he carried a wad of bills that would choke Buckpasser today.

But mostly I think of that blue bathrobe. And his once-fiery mop of hair that was graying. Like Hal Chase before him, but for entirely different reasons, he had become a ghost.

A BASEBALL METHUSELAH

SEPTEMBER 9, 1967. JACK QUINN, A VETERAN OF EIGHT DIFFER-ent major league teams and more minor and semi-pro outfits than he could count, was still paid to pitch for the Reds at the age of 49 in 1933, drawing his release only because economic conditions dictated a major amputation of the payroll. Pitching for the Dodgers at 48 in 1932, Quinn had finished 31 of 42 relief jobs.

Everything about Quinn was mysterious, including his name, age and sequence of clubs. The record books invariably listed him as John Quinn (real name Picus), born at Hazleton, Pa., July 5, 1885, but the suspicion was that he had been born earlier.

When the late S.C. Thompson was gathering material for the first edition of his Official Encyclopedia of Baseball, he asked me to track down Quinn's correct data, and I was able to obtain a baptismal certificate from his church showing that he was born at Jeansville, Pa., July 5, 1884, so Jack was cheating by only one year.

Jeansville was anthracite country then with most of the miners Polish or Welsh. Picus is a truncated form of a Polish name Paykos. It is certainly not Welsh, and Quinn is obviously Jack's nom de baseball. I also understand that Quinn once pitched under the name of Johnson.

As a youth he slaved at the humiliation labor of the mines, engaged in the degrading task of picking slate from coal in a breaker near Pottsville. The mine operators, of course, would say this was a fine way to build character, but Jack had other ideas. Rather than spend the rest of his life in the bowels of the earth, he jumped a freight with an older companion and went as far west as Montana. On the return trip east, he unexpectedly began his career as a ballplayer in Dunbar, Pa.

He arrived in that town dirty and without proper clothing on the morning of the Fourth of July. The big event in Dunbar was the ball game between semi-pro teams from that place and Connellsville. Attracted by the crowd, Quinn attended the pre-game practice. When a ball rolled toward him and a voice instructed him to stop it and throw it back, he threw it so hard that John Malloy, manager of the Dunbar club, ran out to him and offered him a job as a pitcher, promising to pay $5 for a victory and $2.50 for a defeat. Jack earned the five spot and launched his career.

Where he pitched after that before he reached Macon in 1907 would not be known if he had not had a dispute with his manager at Macon, Perry Lipe. He wrote a letter about that hassle to John E. Bruce, secretary of the National Commission, then the game's governing body, and it now is in his file at the Hall of Fame, one of the thousands of documents from the office of Garry Herrman. In the letter, Quinn wrote, "I have pitched for seven years for Dunbar, Connellsville, Mt. Pleasant, Ursina, Barlin, Washington and Pottsville, all in Pennsylvania."

Quinn started 1908 with Toledo, pitching for Billy Armour, who was Ty Cobb's first manager at Detroit. You won't find Quinn's Toledo record in any record book, and it came to light only because in 1928 the pitcher told Bill Dooly of the old Philadelphia Record that he had won four games without defeat at Toledo, then joined Richmond and won 14 without losing. The truth is that Quinn pitched three times without a decision for the Mud Hens, then drew his release because Armour didn't like the way he exposed his thumb when throwing a curve. But the Richmond bit is true, and when he won 14, including a no-hitter without losing, the Yankees drafted him, kept him until 1912, then let him out as "too old."

As a consequence, he lasted in the majors for only 20 years or so thereafter, pitching in turn for the Braves, Baltimore Feds, White Sox, Yankees again, Red Sox, Athletics, Dodgers and Reds.

He was a righthander and spitballer who faked the moist delivery on every pitch. He managed to be on pennant winners with the Yankees in 1921 and the Athletics in 1929-30.

I remember seeing him on the day the Reds handed him his last big league release, looking very dapper in street clothes as he stood at a concessions stand and munched on a hot dog lavishly smeared with mustard.

Even then he wouldn't hang up his uniform. In his 50th year, he started pitching for Hollywood of the PCL in 1934 and split a pair of decisions before drawing his release. In 1935, he got into a few games for Johnstown of the Mid-Atlantic League, close to Dunbar, where he had started but 34 years before.

Jack Quinn thought highly of baseball as a way of life. It beats silicosis!

THE FUTURE OF BASEBALL

SEPTEMBER 23, 1967. A GENTLEMAN IN NEW ORLEANS, DAVID F. Dixon, who is one of a group interested in a domed stadium for that city, says that pro football can be supported, but that baseball is a dying sport. This charge is now 97 years old.

It is not pleasant to take issue with anyone from New Orleans, certainly one of the most civilized cities in the United States. Any town capable of producing shrimp remoulade, Louis Armstrong and the Ramos Gin Fizz has nothing to apologize for, and any person who has ever seen the dawn come up over Canal Street and then visited Gluck's on Royal Street (now unhappily burned out) for bacon and hot biscuits knows something of the charm of life.

But, nevertheless, to put the matter as elegantly as possible, Mr. Dixon is all wet. There is no way of knowing if he could obtain a major league franchise if he wanted one; but the obtaining of one might assure that his domed stadium does not turn out to be a doomed stadium.

The first charge I know of that baseball had no future was made in the pages of the Cincinnati Gazette following the season of 1870. The Cincinnati Red Stockings, organized as the first professional team in 1869, had traveled from Boston to San Francisco without losing a game, but they had dropped six of 80 played in 1870 with the result that interest declined, the management sold the grandstand to a lumber yard to meet its outstanding bills and the Gazette issued this lugubrious prophecy: "The baseball mania has run its course. It has no future as a professional endeavor."

But it was the Gazette and not baseball that had no future. The paper was swallowed up by a rival, the Commercial, on January 4, 1883, and the combined paper was absorbed by still another rival, the Tribune, in 1897. As the Commercial Tribune, it survived until 1930, when the Enquirer bought it. Baseball, meanwhile, grew to become a national addiction that has now survived the Spanish-American War, World War I, World War II, the Korean War, the Great Depression and any number of civil disturbances in its own ranks such as the Union Association, the Brotherhood War and the Federal League. I should like to suggest that it will certainly survive Mr. Dixon and me. We are mortal, but baseball is not, and when Bill Klem said the game with him was a religion, he was guilty of an understatement.

Anyone who is interested enough to join the thousands who annually visit the Hall of Fame and see eight-year-old boys stand in genuine awe before the plaque of Babe Ruth, can learn for himself that baseball is nowhere near ready for the coroner's table that awaits us all.

Another early charge that baseball was slipping came from Al Spalding, of all people. Although Spalding was destined to become a member of the Hall of Fame and a millionaire through the sale of baseball equipment and the regalia of other sports, he told O.P. Caylor, sports editor of the Cincinnati Enquirer, in January, 1881, "Professional baseball is on the wane. Salaries must come down or the interest of the public must be increased in some way. If one or the other does not happen, bankruptcy stares every team in the face."

During the 1890's, George Wright, also to become a Hall of Fame member, millionaire and manufacturer of sporting goods, attended a game in Boston, but went away sneering, "Imagine, players wearing gloves! We didn't need them in our day."

No, they did not, but a different game was evolving, to the eternal satisfaction of George Wright, who sold baseball gloves and lived comfortably on the proceeds until he was 90.

Since that day, there have been many wails that baseball was on the wane. But the game has been every bit as fabulous an invalid as the theater.

One of the soundest statements ever made about baseball was delivered by Rev. Thomas E. Green at the Eighth Presbyterian Church in Chicago, October 4, 1885, when he said, "As an amusement, baseball is in every way superior to nine-tenths of what we call amusements. It is not so dignified as some of the learned professions, but I had rather be a good baseball player and win the pennant for my club than be a poor, dishonest merchant, constantly failing and swindling my creditors, or a briefless lawyer hunting up divorce scandals for a livelihood. There are plenty of things worse than professional ball playing that are higher esteemed."

It has always seemed curious that most of the prophecies of the early demise of baseball come from people interested in other sports. Yet, I have never heard a baseball official knock football, basketball, or even parchesi or mumbly-peg. Many of them attend rival games and enjoy them immensely. There is room in this country for all the games we have.

Perhaps it is the fact that baseball has been known as the national game for almost a century that its rivals, in their envy, feel it necessary to predict its doom. For as Jack Dempsey once said, "If they knock you, you know you're on top."

'GOOFY' WAS SIX AND O

OCTOBER 7, 1967. AT THE HEIGHT OF THE AMERICAN LEAGUE pennant race, with all thoughts on the forthcoming World Series, who should suddenly appear in the Hall of Fame library but the only pitcher in the history of the classic to win six games without defeat, Vernon (Lefty) Gomez.

Jack Coombs and Herb Pennock each won five World Series battles without losing, but only El Senor made it six. You are apt to run into him anywhere in the United States, and this time he was here to make one of his innumerable banquet addresses, a chore which he invariably fulfills with suavity and his unique blend of Castilian and Irish wit.

"Welcome, Senor," was the greeting to him. "Come in and inspect some of your records."

"I never broke any records," he confessed. "But, now, wait a minute! Yes I did. My son had a record I broke once — I think it was Rudolph the Red-Nosed Reindeer. But I wasn't much of a record-breaker. In fact, I was the only ball player ever sent back to the minors by the Bulova Watch Company."

"How's that again?"

"Well, you know, Bulova used to give watches to major league players who made home runs. That was in 1930 when I broke in with the Yankees. And they hit so many off me that I found myself back in St. Paul."

It was more than a slight exaggeration, but the Gomez style of humor, like that of Jack Benny, is based on self-deprecation, and it adds to his charm.

"I wish I had time to get over to Buffalo and see my old manager, Joe McCarthy," he said. "Now there was a fellow who never missed anything that happpened, on the field or off. I'll never forget one year. I think it was in 1937. I won 21 that year and a couple of more against the Giants in the World Series.

"Anyway, we had an off day that summer and my wife, June, was opening in 'You Said It,' a musical in which she was the leading lady to Lou Holtz. It opened in Buffalo, and I managed to find a way to get there and see it. The next day I pitched in Boston and got beat, 2-1, when a little dribbler rolled right up my arm.

"I didn't know McCarthy even knew I had been in Buffalo, but the next spring in St. Pete, he said to me on the bench, 'Lefty, how many did you win last year?' 'Twenty One,' I told him. 'Well,' he said, 'it should have been 22. Remember that game in Boston when the ball rolled up your sleeve? You hadn't had much sleep the night before. You were trying to get to Boston from Buffalo after seeing that play."

"I used to drive McCarthy crazy by chinning myself on the dugout rail right in front of where he was sitting. He couldn't see to give the signs, and he used to make me sit down next to him. Joe used to chew gum when he got nervous and stick the gum next to him under the bench. So I'd sit down next to him and one time I reached under the bench and there was a mound of chewing gum as big as an eggplant. 'What causes you to chew all that gum?' I asked him. 'Those bases on balls of yours are responsible for half of it,' he said.

"I like this part of the country," he went on. "You know, I managed for a couple of years at Binghamton. Terrible clubs. Finished in the cellar both seasons. Bill McCorry was the general manager — good old Bill, living in retirement now at Augusta. Well, we'd lost about 13 in a row one time, and I had an engagement that evening and was late getting back to the hotel.

"McCorry was worried about me and phoned the desk. 'What floor you got Gomez on?' he asked the operator. 'The second,' she told him. 'Oh, well, then I won't worry about him,' McCorry said. 'He can't hurt himself jumping out of a second-floor window.'"

A thin southpaw who never weighed more than 178, although he is six feet two, Gomez started with Salt Lake in 1928 and reached the Yankees in 1930. His father was a dairy rancher at Rodeo, Calif., and in 1932, three weeks after winning his first World Series game against the Cubs, Lefty found himself back on the ranch milking cows.

"I thought I was pretty hot stuff until then," he said. "But when I'd be sitting there and a cow's tail would hit me in the face, I'd think, 'Boy, I'm glad my teammates can't see the Great Gomez now.'"

He added two World Series wins against the Giants in 1936, another pair against the same team in 1937, and one against the Cubs in 1938. He tried for a seventh straight against the Reds in the third game in 1939, but his arm was sore that day and the late Bump Hadley had to relieve him in the second.

He wound up his career with Washington in 1943, but since managing at Binghamton in 1946 and 1947, has worked in the sporting goods business and toured the banquet circuit. For years, he has made his home at Durham, Conn., but now plans to move back to California.

"I've been back to the Coast quite a bit," he said, "I fact, I was there a couple of weeks ago, and I was talking to this sports writer who said to me, 'Why aren't the ball players as colorful as they used to be?' 'I don't know,' I told him. 'Now let me ask you one. Why aren't the sports writers as colorful as they used to be?'"

He just might have something.

THE 'I' ALL-STARS

DECEMBER 9, 1967. BOCA RATON, FLA. WHEN ROBERTO Enrique (Hank) Izquierdo came up from Denver early last August and made his major league debut by catching for the Twins and batting .269 in 16 games, he automatically won a job on my all-time, all-star team of players whose names begin with "I."

Maybe you think that isn't an honor!

In all of big league history, there have been 10,253 players and only 20, or one out of 513, had a surname that started with "I." Six of them were pitchers, so there is little room to maneuver at the other positions. Picking a team of stars from the material available is a chore, so Izquierdo's arrival is a boon. He strengthens what had been the weakest position on the team.

There have actually been only two other catchers in the majors whose names started with the all-important letter. One was Ed Irvin, one of the Detroit strikebreakers at Philadelphia in 1912, but he got into only that single game. The other was Charlie Ingraham, who also appeared in only one contest, for Baltimore of the American Association in 1883.

When Ford Frick, the game's third commissioner, visited Cooperstown last summer to witness the Hall of Fame game and ceremonies, he remarked that the first big league player he ever met in his native Indiana was Bert Inks, a pitcher from the town of Ligonier, who saw service in the '90s with six of the National League's 12 clubs.

It so happens that Inks is the starting pitcher for the all-star "I" aggregation. With 28 victories in five seasons, he could hardly be kept off the squad.

But there is a sentimental, rather than statistical reason for the inclusion of Inks. For in his minor league days, he had a catcher with the beautiful name of Nicholas Ivory. Baseball writers of the day, ever alert to play on words and delighted with the spectrum before them, always referred to the pair as "Inks & Ivory, the Piano Battery."

Inks was sharp, but unfortunately Ivory was flat and never reached the top of his profession. If he had, Izquierdo might have difficulty making the club today. If Ivory were to appear today, television announcers would almost surely call him "Soapy." In personality, he would be flaky and go on the disabled list with either bone or soap chips.

Izquierdo is the first "I" player at any position to reach the majors since Monte Irvin joined Leo Durocher's Giants in 1949. Irvin, with a .293 lifetime in 764 games, is the greatest player on the mythical team and is stationed in center, flanked by Fred (Happy) Iott of the 1903 Cleveland club in left, and William (Scotty) Ingerton of the 1911 Boston Nationals in right. Iott, who came from Bangor, Me., and whose death is so far unrecorded, is, sorrowfully, the worst player on the team now that the catching has been so strengthened by Izquierdo. Iott begs for replacement. He appeared in only three games for Cleveland, batting .200. Ingerton was a regular and for him no apology need be made.

The infield, however, is the source of the club's strength. At first base is Frank Isbell, his normal station being there, although the Hitless Wonder White Sox employed him at second in 1906. At second with the "I" boys, however, is Harold (Grump)Irelan of the 1914 Phillies.

It is the left side of the infield that is stronger, with Arthur Irwin at short and the unrelated Charlie at third. Arthur lasted in the National League from 1880 to 1894 and managed teams in the minors for many years after that, hanging around long enough, at least, to employ Waite Hoyt as a pitcher. Charlie was a defensive whiz with the Cubs and Reds in the '90s.

It is a great pity that there is no room on this team for Robert Ingersoll, who pitched briefly for the Reds in 1914. He was a member of two distinct minority groups. Not only did his name began with "I," but he was born in South Dakota, a state that has produced only a handful of players. And as if that were not distinction enough, he bore the same name as Robert Ingersoll, the celebrated agnostic, whose nomination of James G. Blaine, the Plumed Knight, at the Republican convention of 1876 at Cincinnati constituted one of the most eloquent moments in the party's history.

But Ingersoll is one of the "I" players who will have to ride the bench. There he joins Herman (Ham) Iburg and Harry (Doc) Imlay, pitchers for the Phillies early in the century; Mel Ingram, an infielder who pinch-hit three times for the 1929 Pirates; Clarence (Hooks) Iott, a southpaw with the Browns and Giants before and after World War II; John Irwin, a brother and contemporary of Arthur and three more Irwins; Tom, a shortstop with the 1938 Indians; Walter, a pinch-hitter for the 1921 Cardinals; and Bill, who pitched for the Reds in 1886.

Arthur Irwin can manage the club from his position at short, and any of the reserve players can coach.

It will probably be necessary also to have a team physician, and the choice is the late Dr. Ilarion Gopadze, who served the Philadelphia Athletics in that capacity for many years. Although it is true that Dr. Gopadze's last name does not start with "I," his first one does, and, after all, you can't have everything!

THE SWEET SWEETLAND

"My country 'tis a thee, Sweetland and Willoughby, of thee I sing."

DECEMBER 30, 1967. PALM BAY, FLA. LONG BEFORE PLAYING the National Anthem became standard procedure in ball parks, George E. Phair, A New York baseball writer and a man of astringent wit, customarily intoned the above lines every time he entered the press coop at rickety old Baker Bowl in Philadelphia. He had invented the chant because it seemed to him that every game there began with either Lester (Sugar) Sweetland or Claude Willoughby pitching for the Phillies.

In the late twenties, those Phils were notable for their slugging, with Chuck Klein, Lefty O'Doul, Don Hurst and Pinky Whitney on hand. The pitching was — to be discreet — disappointing. But Sweetland and Willoughby were the best Burt Shotton had.

Willoughby, a righthander, was shorter in stature than southpaw Sweetland, but had a slightly better record. He lives today in McPherson, Kan. Sweetland I just located here, thanks to the good assistance of Joe Simenic of the Cleveland Plain Dealer, who risked conjunctivitis or astigmatism or whatever it is you risk when you glower at too many phone books.

Palm Bay is not on the Gold Coast, but in fisherman's Florida, and Sugar, despite a very bad leg, is able to slip away to Sebastian Inlet and tease the red snapper, pompano and blue. Also, only a countdown to the north is Cape Kennedy, and he can stand in his front yard to see the fire and hear the thunder of Apollo.

"You know," Sugar told me, "I was born as far north as you can get in the United States, at St. Ignace, Mich., where my father worked on boats on the Saginaw straits. Then he became a millwright and we moved to Seattle, then Texas, New Orleans and finally Melbourne, a few miles north of here, where I grew up. Dad was putting in a cypress mill there.

"I began pitching semi-pro ball, then started with Jacksonville and Orlando of the Florida State League. Then it was Charlotte and Spartanburg, where I pitched for Mike Kelly, and that's where the Phillies found me in midseason of 1927.

"Stuffy McInnis managed the Phils for that one year, and I wasn't scared when I reported, because I figured I'd never pitch. But two days later, he gave me the ball, I started against the Braves and managed to beat them. My trouble was wildness. I had a good sinker, but hardly any curve ball at all, and when I got wild, I had a hard time getting back on the track.

"I guessed the best game I ever pitched was on opening day in 1930 at Ebbets Field. I beat another southpaw, Watson Clark, 1-0, allowing three hits and retiring the last 21 men. I also scored the winning run by hitting a double in the eighth before Klein singled. But I never had any more days like that one.

"My biggest disappointment was in not pitching against Babe Ruth. I always hoped to meet him in an exhibition game in Florida. But we were just the downtrodden Phillies, and they were the Yankees, so they would never schedule us."

Sweetland remained with the Phils through 1930, just as Willoughby did. His best year was in 1929 when he won 13 and dropped 11. William A. Wrigley paid the Phils $25,000 for his contract, and he won eight and lost seven for the Cubs in 1931, including five triumphs in a row, but he did not get along too well with Rogers Hornsby, his manager at Chicago, and was dropped.

Then he went back to the minors — Los Angeles, Jersey City and Montreal. Finally, he hit Little Rock.

By 1936, his knee hurt him constantly and he was unable to pitch. The great depression still shrouded the land and, in order to get a job, he went to Detroit, figuring he could connect in the automobile factories. But employment agencies told him that the plants were not hiring but laying off. Then he had a happy inspiration.

"I knew Mickey Cochrane pretty well," he said. "We had played against each other often in the Philadelphia city series each spring. Cochrane had won the pennant for Detroit in 1934 and the pennant and World's Series in 1935. I figured he could get anything he wanted in Detroit, so I went to him and I said, 'Mickey, things are tough, and I just have to get a job.' Cochrane then wrote a letter to Walter Briggs, who owned the Tigers, and I went to work at Chrysler the day after he received the letter. I stayed there for more than 25 years, working as a production man, stamping metal. Then I was pensioned and moved back here."

He seldom sees baseball people now and sticks pretty much to the house. He does watch the World Series on television and he reads regularly about the game, for which he retains all his old affection. He and his wife live here with their little dog, a curbstone setter who is mostly terrier. But the mutt is smart enough to go out into the yard each morning and pick up the paper so Sugar can learn what the Phillies did.

THE SMOOTH TALKER

FEBRUARY 10, 1968. EDITH HANKE GREETED ME CORDIALLY, pointed to a comfortable chair in her living room and said, "Whenever my father had occasion to find fault with me or had to correct me, he did it in words of five syllables."

We both smiled because her father, dead now for almost 50 years, was celebrated for his verbosity.

His name was James Henry (Orator Jim) O'Rourke, and he was celebrated for a great deal more. A member of the Hall of Fame, he was a major league catcher, third baseman and outfielder for 23 seasons. He visited England with baseball's first missionary band in 1874, made the first hit ever recorded in a National League game in 1876, graduated from the Yale Law School and became a practicing attorney, caught a full game for John McGraw's New York Giants at the age of 52 in 1904, served as president of the old Connecticut League and played on that circuit's Bridgeport team in the company of his son, James Stephen O'Rourke.

But mostly he was known for the luxuriousness of his vocabulary. A letter that he once wrote to a widow named Gilligan who had grabbed a pitchfork and routed a lion she found in her barn (the creature had escaped from Ringling's headquarters) is a baseball classic and can be found today in the anthologies.

On another occasion, O'Rourke was managing Buffalo when one of his players, John Peters, asked for a raise.

"I'm sorry," O'Rourke said, "but the exigencies of the occasion and the condition of our exchequer will not permit anything of the sort at this period of our existence. Subsequent developments in the field of finance may remove the present gloom and we may emerge into a condition where we may see fit to reply in the affirmative to your exceedingly modest request."

Peters, understandably, did not try again.

Much later in his career, the Orator handled a ticklish conflict-of-interest situation with amazing aplomb. He was catching for Bridgeport at a time when he was president of the league, lost his temper and swore at the umpire.

Recovering his poise almost immediately, he removed his cap and shouted, "As president of the Connecticut League, I hereby fine player James O'Rourke ten dollars for swearing at an umpire." Then the cap went back on and play proceeded.

In addition to his son, O'Rourke had seven daughters, and Edith Hanke is the youngest. The others were Irene, Lillian, Ida, Sadie, Anna and Agnes. Most of them, with their children, have visited the Hall of Fame at one time or another, but so modest are they that they have never made known their identity, and I was able to trace Edith only after a search of many years.

The Orator was a poor farm boy left fatherless at an early age. He and his brother John helped their mother on the farm, but played baseball at every opportunity. When Ben Douglas of Hartford was organizing the Mansfields of Middletown, Conn., in 1872, he visited the farm and signed Jim, but only after placating the mother by securing a farm worker to help John. Seven years later, John left the farm and joined Boston as an outfielder.

The Mansfields folded, and Harry Wright brought the Orator to Boston in 1873. Brahmins controlled the city, signs bearing the legend "No Irish Need Apply" were posted on factory walls and Wright asked young O'Rourke if he would mind appearing in box scores as "Rourke," a rather clumsy attempt to hide his Celtic origin.

"Mr. Wright," the Orator said, "I would rather die than give up any part of my father's name. A million would not tempt me."

So he remained in Boston as O'Rourke and became a public favorite. He played for Providence, Buffalo and then New York, being a member of the first Giant team to win a pennant in 1888. His last year as a regular was with Washington in 1893, then he umpired in the National League for two seasons before returning to Bridgeport to buy the local ball club and practice law.

"My father died of pneumonia in January, 1919," Mrs. Hanke said. "He was the kind of lawyer who was too kind-hearted to charge a fee to anyone in modest circumstances.

"I remember it was New Year's Day and very cold, and father had promised to meet a client in Bridgeport. We urged him to take a trolley because of the cold. He waited for one, but when it didn't come, he decided to walk. He caught a cold, it turned into pneumonia, and seven days later he died."

If you have ever driven from St. Petersburg Beach, where the Mets stay each spring, to Clearwater, where the Phillies train, you have perhaps gone through Madeira Beach without knowing it had any baseball significance. Most of the motels in the area have words like breeze and coral and dolphin in their names. But there's one you'll notice called the Southern Gentleman, and it's owned by Raymond Hanke, a Naval officer in World War II and a grandson of Jim O'Rourke. He has also visited the Hall of Fame without revealing who he was, but the secret is out now.

MICHIGAN WATERFALLS

MARCH 2, 1968. EXTREME CARE HAS TO BE EXERCISED WITH this one, otherwise I could be found at the bottom of Lake Michigan wearing a concrete overcoat, the sort of haberdashery that students of crime assure me adorns the body of Judge Crater in the East River.

It all started 30 years ago this week. I was attending the School of Journalism at Columbia when I received a telegram from Gabe Paul, then road secretary and press agent (the euphemism is "public relations director") of the Reds, asking me to report to the team at Tampa as his assistant.

The chance to get into baseball excited me so much I left Columbia without informing anyone or even removing my books from the desk. So far as I know, I may still be enrolled there.

At any rate, I arrived in Tampa early one morning and Gabe said to me, "You're addressing two service clubs today, Rotary at the Floridan at twelve, Kiwanis at the Tampa Terrace at one. Good luck!"

There was time at the Kiwanis session for a question-and-answer period, and the first question was, "How long have you been with the Reds?"

A veteran of several hours of service to the team, I replied, "All my life. I've been interested in the Reds all my life." I doubt if the late Branch Rickey could have conceived of a more apparently truthful but essentially evasive answer.

The first article I ever wrote for the club was a ghost job for Frank McCormick, "How It Feels to Be a Big Leaguer," which appeared in Joe Aston's column in the old Cincinnati Post. When I asked Frank what he wanted to say, he replied, "I haven't made the team yet." But he made it all right! More than six hundred hits his first three years, that's all he did; and if he hadn't hurt his back jumping off a diving board in Puerto Rico in 1940 — well, he might have become a righthanded Lou Gehrig, that's all. As it is, he left a lifetime .299 for 13 seasons.

The Reds were looking at a lot of kids in those years, and the Floridan was crowded, so Gabe roomed me with a pitcher whose identity will have to be disguised. This guy was right out of Ring Lardner, and you'll know I mean it when I tell you he let the water run in the bathtub all night because it reminded him of the waterfall near his home in Michigan. He wore all my neckties at will, and when I saw him using my toothbrush, I bought another, in the belief that Emily Post would recommend such a course.

One day Gabe told me to play mother hen to the B Squad, taking the team to Plant City for an exhibition game. Our hero, my roommate, was the starting pitcher, and the manager was Bobby Wallace, Hall of Famer, great shortstop and the squarest man (in the best sense) who ever scooped up a grounder. My roommate, who was big and tough and looked as if he could throw the ball through the side of a battleship, easily retired the first two men. Elated, he threw his glove high in the air and marched off the mound. But Wallace met him at the foul line and said, "You fool! You have to get three men out to retire the side!"

"Oh!" replied our hero, and he retrieved his glove and began to pitch again. He never did get the third man, as hits began to rattle all over the field.

They sent him — let's say they sent him to Waterloo, but that was not the place. And the agreement was that if he were kept after a certain date, he would get a bonus of $1,500. As the date approached, it was discovered that he was older than listed and definitely not a prospect, so they cut him loose.

Late that season, the Reds visited Chicago and as Gabe entered the pass gate one afternoon at Wrigley Field, our hero was waiting for him.

"I want to talk to you, Gabe," he said, grabbing him by the arm about as gently as Frank Howard grips a bat.

"Why did you fellows release me at Waterloo?" was the first question. "I was doing all right."

"I'll tell you, Pete," Gabe said, for Pete was not really his name.

"Do you remember Lee Allen who you roomed with in Tampa?"

"Yeah, what about him?"

"Well, he got you released."

"He did?"

"Yes, sir. He told Bill McKechnie that you wore his neckties. That's why we had to let you go."

"Well, I'll be damned," the pitcher said. "So that's how it was. And the damned things weren't any good anyway."

It was an uncharitable way to refer to my $2.50 ties, but I must say that to this day I am somewhat ill at ease at Wrigley Field. And it's not the wind blowing in off the lake that bothers me. Instead, I seem to hear the running of water in a bathtub, and I clutch my throat to see if my tie is there. I know that this is true, that Gabe remembers, too; but it was all of 30 years ago in a different world, a time and place in which problems seemed to have solutions. Pete, I hope that time has been kind to you, and wherever you are, I hope you get that third man out.

THE ROUND MEN

MARCH 16, 1968.   IT ALWAYS HAS SEEMED TO ME THAT heavy players, those who packed a lot of weight, almost always had crowd appeal. Old Giant fans will never forget catcher Shanty Hogan, who had a signal system with hotel waiters so that he could order a pie a la mode and have it appear on his dinner check as asparagus. One day the announcer at the Polo Grounds informed the crowd that Andy Cohen was running for Hogan, and a man in the bleachers leaped to his feet, cupped his hands and yelled, "Murphy now leaving the ball park!"

In Detroit, lovers of the game retain fond memories of Bob Fothergill, a round outfielder who was a murderous hitter. His name was Robert Roy Fothergill, and he had the initials R.R.F. on his leather suitcase, and when people asked him what they stood for, he would proudly say, "Runs Responsible For."

It seems likely even that had Smoky Burgess been built along the lines of Frank Sinatra, his resounding pinch hits would have carried less authority. Poundage is popular!

In the mail the other day was a letter from Elly Luderus, nephew of Fred Luderus, who played a lot of first base for the Phillies from 1910 through 1920, informing me that some anonymous sponsor had paid my dues and made me a full-fledged member of the Old-Time Ball Players' Association of Wisconsin. Maybe you think this has nothing to do with the subject of this column, but it has. I knew immediately that my benefactor must have been Garland Buckeye, one of the heaviest players who ever was in the majors.

Buckeye, a big bird from Heron Lake, Minn., was a hefty southpaw. He was 13-8 for Tris Speaker at Cleveland in 1925, pitching for a club that finished sixth, a better record by far than such other pitchers on the club as George Uhle, Walter Miller, Benny Karr, Sherry Smith, Joe Shaute and Byron Speece were able to compile.

I always listed Buckeye as weighing 238, and tried to reach him recently to verify the figure. I knew he had operated a Ford agency for years in Toledo, but found he has given it up and now has two homes, one in Gary, Ind., and a summer place at Stone Lake, Wis.

"I weighed over 250 all the time I was in the big leagues," Buckeye wrote me, "and in 1928, when Billy Evans was general manager of the Indians and Roger Peckinpaugh manager, Evans had me come to Cleveland to sign my 1928 contract. I got on a scale in the Cleveland ball club office and weighed 269. I played pro football for years at the time I played baseball, and one winter I had to play handball continually to keep under 275. Ask Casey Stengel how much I weighed. I was playing for his Toledo Mud Hens when I got married on August 9, 1928."

Garland, or Gob, as his friends call him, also informed me that he was pitching against Rip Collins of Detroit the day Johnny Neun made the unassisted triple play, the last ever made in the majors, on May 31, 1927. Buckeye lost, 1-0, and the play came in the ninth when Homer Summa lined the ball to Neun at first. Charlie Jamieson and Glenn Myatt were the other outs.

About a year ago, I was driving through the backwoods of Georgia, looking for a town called Barwick, where I thought I could find an old Tiger pitcher, Ken Holloway, raising pecans. Barwick is really off the beaten track, and I stopped for lunch and to ask directions at a place called Quitman, joining a cafeteria line and settling for meatloaf, cornbread and baked beans. I had never heard of Quitman before and never expected to again, but now Buckeye informs me that he has just returned from there, having watched the running of the Continental Quail Championships at Mrs. Livingston's Dixie Plantation.

But it became my unfortunate duty to inform Gob that he was not the heaviest player of them all. The honor goes to the late Walter (Jumbo) Brown. Shortly before his death, Brownie came to the Hall of Fame to see Ken Smith and me, and he told us that he actually weighed 295 when he closed out his career with the Giants in 1941. Poor Jumbo! His widow, Midge, told me that he just couldn't give up smoking, and during his last bout with heart trouble, he used to sneak out of the oxygen tent, duck down the corridor and light a cigarette.

Buckeye did not say what he weighs now, but the amount must be considerable, yet, he moves around the country and does as he pleases, a privilege he has earned. He's all fixed, and I'm sure he's the one who paid my dues to the Old-Timers in Wisconsin. I guess I'll have to pick up his tab at Mrs. Livingston's Dixie Plantation in Quitman.

And, by the way, Ken Holloway has given up raising pecans at Barwick. He's moved to Thomasville.

EDDIE'S LAST SPRING

MARCH 30, 1968. THE FIRST TIME YOU WATCH EDDIE Mathews this year, go to the park early and see him take his cuts in batting practice. He presents as youthful an appearance as ever, and you can follow him as he slices a few and then lays one down and legs it to first.

It would be foolish to say that he is as fast as ever, for Eddie is starting his 17th season in the majors. But, as a Tiger, he will enjoy at Detroit a friendlier park than was his lot a year ago at the Hofheinz Taj Mahal at Houston.

However, he finds himself locked in a battle for the first base job with Norm Cash, an established star, and Don Pepper, a rookie worth his salt.

While taking his practice swings here the other day, Eddie was closely watched by coach Wally Moses, who leaned on the batting cage, rested his right elbow on his right leg, and stroked his chin with his fingers as he peered at Mathews through spectacles.

"Are you trying to teach Eddie to hit?" someone asked.

"He's a pretty good hitter right now," Moses replied.

At breakfast the next day, Eddie explained why Wally was watching him so closely.

"If you'll look carefully at my career record," Mathews said, "you'll notice that I hit 30 or more home runs for nine straight years, and then fell just one short with 29 in 1962. There was a good reason for that. One day against Turk Farrell of Houston I took a tremendous swing, missed the ball completely and tore all the tendons and ligaments in my shoulder. The injury was slow to heal, and even after it did, I became a defensive hitter and developed some bad batting habits. I didn't hit over 30 homers again until 1965. Moses is a good batting coach, and he watches me to make certain I'm in the right groove."

"It's a funny thing," Mathews said. "Last year at this time, Mantle had only three more home runs lifetime than I did. But he played more than I did and hit more. But what makes it funny is that Mantle and I have never discussed home runs or our records. Maybe this season we'll get a chance to sit down and talk about them."

Hank Aguirre and Bill Freehan strolled in and sat down with us just as the waitress took the order.

"You fellows discussing anything personal?" Aguirre asked.

"Nothing any more personal than home runs." Mathews said as he ordered ham and scrambled eggs.

"When you're a kid," Eddie said, "what fun the game is! You grab a bat and glove and ball, and that's it. I know what Ted Williams and Stan Musial meant when they said it got tougher to get in shape every year."

He said it wistfully, and you were reminded of the scene in a novel by Thomas Wolfe in which the hero encountered on a train a player the author called Nebraska Crane, one of the few characters in all of Wolfe's work who had no counterpart in real life, but who merely represented Wolfe's childhood ambition to become a player. Crane explained what hard work professional baseball was, especially to a veteran, mentioning the tensions and the August heat of the baked diamonds.

"But I feel good this spring," Eddie said, "and if I have a better year than I had last year, I may go on for another one after that.

"I've been playing on organized teams since I was in the sixth grade," Eddie said. "Not uniformed teams at first, but organized. They have them that way in California. My father was a Western Union wire chief, and one of his duties was to tap out the accounts of ball games in the Pacific Coast League. He died in 1954, and I've always been glad that he lived to see me make it in the majors.

"I've had a funny career," he said. "I played in Atlanta in the minors in 1950 and 1951 and, and when I came back to Atlanta in the majors in 1966, I renewed acquaintances with many of the same fans. I also played with Milwaukee in the minors in 1951 and in the majors two years later. And, of course, I played with the Braves in three different cities, Boston, Milwaukee and Atlanta. I don't know if it's true or not, but someone told me I've hit home runs in more major league parks than any player in history."

"Even Jersey City?"

"Even Jersey City."

He was right. Although appearing in only two games against the Dodgers in Jersey City, he connected for a homer in each, on July 31, 1956, off Carl Erskine, and on June 10, 1957, off Don Newcombe.

Eddie has known just about everything the game can offer. When he came up as a third baseman, he was a very ordinary fielder, but by hard work he made himself a master of the position.

Now it is twilight, and as you watch him in his familiar stance, notice that his cap fits as neatly as ever, and his swing is level, and he looks youthful. He isn't but, Eddie, hit a few more for us!

THREE A.M.

APRIL 6, 1968. AT THREE IN THE MORNING, I AWOKE WITH A nauseating feeling of discomfort in my stomach, as if Yogi Berra had been jumping on it all night with his spikes on, or that I had swallowed one of Jim Lonborg's skis.

It was terrible. As I sat up, immobile in the darkness, a name crept into my half-awakened consciousness, and it was spelled D-E-N-I-E-N-S. It puzzled me at first, but then I knew it was a name in the encyclopedias of baseball that stood for a catcher in one game for the Chicago Federal League team of 1914. The longer I sat there, the more it seemed that there could be no such person as Deniens, that it must have been a typographical error in some box score from which the first of these encyclopedias was compiled. Ernie Lanigan, my predecessor at Cooperstown, used to refer to such players as "phantoms." That was it. Deniens was a phantom. Deniens indeed! There could be no such player, for the message came from my unconscious.

That awful feeling in my stomach had occurred before and the best therapy always had been not a powder or a pill but hard work. I dressed quietly, slipped into my workshop, turned on the microfilm reader and began to construct a chart of the positions played daily by the Chicago Federal League players of 1914. That club, managed by Joe Tinker, in another year would be known as the Whales, but then they were the Chifeds (horrible word), the Northsiders or the Tinks.

But you know how it is. You start looking for one thing and find several others, and before the arrival of dawn I learned a number of things about baseball that I had never known before, such as the identity of the inventor of the rubber home plate, an early claim to the invention of the chest protector and the earliest example yet found of the squeeze play.

But the first thing that caught my eye was a rule adopted by the International League in 1914. Before the season began, the league instructed its umpires that should a game require two hours or more to play, they must file a report explaining the reason for such dawdling.

Then appeared the business of the rubber home plate. In earlier times, the home base had been constructed of iron, stone, marble or wood. The refinement of employing rubber, which now seems so natural, had evolved quietly. I had never heard whose idea it was. But the man was Ed Keating, a pitcher with Baltimore of the American Association, then a major league, in 1887. He patented the idea.

Some enterprising reporter of 1914 looked him up in Pittsburgh and asked him about it. Keating answered the inquiry about his invention in unbelievable language. "Not only did I invent the rubber home plate," he said, "but I have invented various cycloidal, isperimetrical and spiral catenaries."

My dictionary does not contain the word "isperimetrical," although it defines "cycloidal" as resembling a circle, and a catenary is the curve assumed by a chain hanging from two points not in the same vertical line. Interesting!

But Keating was in only one game and he lost it. His trouble was wildness. Either his cycloidal, isperimetrical and spiral catenaries were too wide for home plate or the plate was too small. Whatever it was, he was more of a success as an inventor than a pitcher.

An item about the first chest protector gave credit for the equipment to Charlie Bennett, one of the greatest catchers of the 1880s saying that he appeared on the field so clad as a member of the Detroit team for which he played from 1881 through 1888. But the exact year was not given, so it is impossible to say that Bennett's contribution was a "first," a very dangerous word to employ in writing baseball history. For it is unknown that in 1884 Jack Clements, the greatest of all the lefthanded catchers, appeared on the field that year in a protector, and jeering sports writers referred to it as a "sheepskin."

So Bennett may or may not have been the inventor, but in any event he was a memorable player. The first field occupied by the Tigers in the American League was named for him and he was the victim of one of the game's first real tragedies.

Following the season of 1893, Bennett was riding on a train in Kansas. He got off at Wellesville to speak to a friend, saw the train begin to move and, in his anxiety to get back on, slipped under the wheels, losing both legs. For years after that, until his death in 1927, he operated a newsstand in Detroit.

The squeeze play, which I always had thought to be the brainchild of Clark Griffith when he managed the Highlanders in 1904, the team destined to be called the Yankees, was attributed to Cap Anson and King Kelly with Chicago in the 1880s, but without any documentation.

By now the chart of the Chicago Feds was complete, and there was no Deniens. He was a phantom all right, a misprint for Clement L. Clemens, who appeared in 13 games instead of 12 as the records show. It was apparent that a telegrapher, in tapping out the box score, had misread the "Cl" for a "D' and the "m" for "ni." Now the work was accomplished, the truth was out and the stomach ache gone.

WHEN WERE THEY TIGERS?

APRIL 20, 1968. BOCA RATON, FLA. HAL MIDDLESWORTH, director of public relations for the Tigers, is trying to determine when his team first wore that nickname. The earliest reference he has found is the Detroit Free Press of April 16, 1895. Does anyone in the house know if they were called Tigers earlier than that?...The first permanent resident of Naples, Fla., now a plush resort, was W.H. Haldeman, owner of the Louisville team of the N.L. in its pioneer season of 1876...John L. Sullivan, the heavyweight champ, pitched for the Mets (against a picked nine at the old Polo Grounds, in May, 1883)....When Milwaukee was expelled from the National League for failing to pay its bill on December 3, 1878, William P. Rogers, who owned the club, stomped out of the meeting and went to attend

an opera....Early International League teams considered Syracuse an un-
lucky city because so many games were postponed by rain.... The cover of a
baseball in its present form was invented by C. H. Jackson in Massachusetts
in the 1860s when he was ten years old. An old shoemaker gave him two
small pieces, which he stiched together in the exact shape that came to be
in use and was patented by Harwood, a baseball manufacturer in Natick,
Mass..... Players always have been touchy about their ages. When a reader
asked the Chicago Tribune the average age of National League players in
1878, the published reply was "a little above the average."..... Was William
Shakespeare referring to baseball when one of the characters in The Merry
Wives of Windsor proposed, "Now let's have a catch?".... The custom of
having a player select his own model bat started with Providence in 1878....
When Dode Criss, a fine pinch-hitter for the St. Louis Browns in 1908, asked
permission to leave the family farm in Mississippi for a career in baseball, his
father advised him not to sign for less than $1 a day.

Long before the Alous, Albany in 1881 had an outfield of Tom, Mike and
John Mansell... Joe Overfield, poet laureate of the game in Buffalo, has
located a strange reason for calling a game. He found a scorebook at the
Buffalo Historical Society that has written across the scoresheet of a game,
"Called after five innings, Tom Shiels being completely filled with gas and
unable to continue." .... Harry S. New, postmaster general under Warren G.
Harding, covered baseball for the Indianapolis Journal in 1883.... Cushions
were first rented by grandstand customers at the park in Cincinnati on June
25, 1879.... In early times, most players ate a hearty meal before leaving for
the park. Apparently it was Guy Hecker, Louisville pitcher, who first
considered this bad practice and settled for crackers and milk.... Bill Veeck
may not believe it, but the St. Louis Browns of Chris Von Der Ahe exploded
fireworks at games in 1882.... The first tape-measure job was a fungo hit by
C. R. Partridge of Dartmouth College in 1880, and the distance was found
to be 354 feet, ten inches.... The hot dog was invented in 1852 by the
butchers' guild in Germany. Because the union headquarters was at
Frankfurt, the new sausage was called a frankfurter.... The Phillies held a
"bootblack's day" during spring training in 1883, admitting free all boot-
blacks, newsboys and urchins.... Peter Browning was a great hitter, but a poor
outfielder, for Louisville in the 1880s. When he complained of finding a fly
in his soup at the old Laclede Hotel in St. Louis, Ben Armstrong, the
steward, said "Don't worry, Pete. There's no danger of your catching it."...
John J. McGraw, third baseman of Baltimore, announced in March, 1896,
that he had had all the baseball he cared about and that it would be his last
season in the game.... George McManus, business manager of the St. Louis
Browns of 1877, was the father of the George McManus who drew "Bringing
Up Father," the comic strip usually called "Jiggs."

As late as 1910, players were afraid to be sent to the Southern League because of the danger of malaria. ... The rule allowing players to be given first base when struck by a pitched ball first appeared on the books in the American Association in 1884 because John Schappert, who had pitched for St. Louis in 1882, threw at so many hitters.... Following the season of 1895, Gus Schmelz, who had managed the Washington team of the N. L. for $3,000, earned $30,000 as business manager of a touring play, "A Texas Steer." ... Every member of the Boston N. L. team of 1880 voted for Winfield Scott Hancock in the presidential election that year, and all lost when James A. Garfield was the winner.... Phil Reccius, a Louisville player, was one of the game's greatest hunters and killed 341 pheasants in 1885.... Joe Roche may have been the first professional player to break a leg, when he did it sliding into second for the Binghamton Crickets in a contest against Boston, September 1, 1876.... Sam Wise, shortstop for Boston in 1883, always carried a small potato in his vest to guard against rheumatism.... When Tom Zachary reported to the Yankee camp one spring, a New York writer said to him, "I did a nice feature on you during the winter. Did you see it?" "Nope," replied Tom. "What?" asked the writer. "Don't you get our papers in Guilford, N.C.?" "No," Zachary said. "Do you get ours?"... George H. England was a one-armed pitcher with Wheeling in 1889.... Frank Oberlin, pitcher with the Red Sox and Senators early in the century, liked to stay in his hotel room and knit. His house was full of embroidered and crocheted articles he had made. ... Ten Million was the full and correct name of the center fielder of the Victoria, B. C., team of the Northwestern League in 1911. He came from Mt. Vernon, Wash., where his father was a judge.... Jack Benny was a scout for the Cubs in 1912.... John Donaldson, a great Negro pitcher from Kansas City, pitched 30 consecutive innings without allowing a hit in 1915.

KNOXVILLE, ED BAILEY AND FRANK CALLOWAY

MAY 11, 1968. I DROVE TO KNOXVILLE FROM BOCA RATON, Fla., in a single day, a distance of 812 miles, and if my body was tired, my spirits were lifted by a sense of gratitude toward Clarence F. Kohler of York, Pa., and Jack Peterson of Sacramento, Calif.

In a recent column, there was a parenthetic question as to the whereabouts of Rex Barney, former pitcher of the Dodgers, and Gene Bearden, former ditto of the Indians. I had been unable to locate them.

As usual, readers came through like champions. Mr. Kohler informed me that Rex is now tending bar at the Pimlico Hotel in Baltimore and Mr. Peterson said that Gene is a police officer in Sacramento. It occurred to me that in their current capacities Barney might require the services of Bearden rather than vice versa.

Buoyed by the solution to the puzzle, I entered this city at dusk and, noticing a parkway named for Bob Neylan, considered it obvious that this was football country.

A phone call to Marvin West, sports writer for the Knoxville Journal, confirmed that fact, and he said that the local baseball park, Bill Meyer Stadium, named for the late manager of the Pirates, was this year unoccupied by a professional team.

Louise Smith, whose husband, Sam, is president of the Southern League, expressed sorrow over the situation and added that several other fine cities such as Chattanooga, Mobile and Columbus, Ga., have lovely ball parks, but no teams. The Southern is operating with clubs at Asheville and Charlotte, N.C.; Birmingham and Montgomery, Ala; Savannah, Ga., and Evansville, Ind., a town whose citizens are not particularly celebrated for singing "Dixie." All have major league working agreements; the days of independent ownership are as dead as Fulton Street fish.

Ed Bailey, who caught a lot of baseball for the Reds, Giants, Braves, Cubs and Angels from 1953 to 1966, lives here. He explained that Bill Meyer Stadium is still busy with baseball, but at a different level. College ball, high school ball, recreation ball, and Babe Ruth League teams draw good crowds throughout the season. "But this town will not support a professional team unless it is a winner," he said. "They've had such successful football teams that they expect the best."

"What are you doing now?" was the obvious question to Bailey.

"I'm a field representative for Congressman John Duncan."

"What does a Congressman's field representative do?"

"Just takes care of the district — eight counties — when the Congressman is in Washington, that's all."

"Don't you miss talking to the hitters? Earl Lawson always said you enjoyed talking to the hitters."

"I'm talking to constituents," he replied.

It must be pleasant work. Presumably constituents don't have to be knocked down.

Bailey is by no means the only former big leaguer living here. One of the residents is John B. (Bonnie) Hollingsworth, who pitched for the Pirates in 1922, the Senators in 1923, the Dodgers in 1924 and the Braves in 1928.

He provided a portion of one of the game's first big package deals when

Uncle Wilbert Robinson shipped him, along with five other players, from Brooklyn to Minneapolis for Johnny Butler, a third baseman, after the season of 1925.

Hollingsworth could not be located, but another oldtimer, Frank Calloway, who played short and second for the Athletics in 1921-22, was at home.

He is one of the city's most prosperous and best-known men, operating a wholesale and retail sporting goods house, a boat dock and a marine store, the biggest institution of its kind in the South, with a business of several millions annually.

"I was born and raised here," Calloway said. "I pitched high school ball there and went to the University of Tennessee. Chief Bender and Harry Davis discovered me for the A's, and it was a wonderful experience playing for Mr. Mack. He was always very gentle and never corrected the players harshly.

"I might have played a lot longer, but Ty Cobb put me out of business. You see, I normally played short or third, but in 1922 our second baseman, Pep Young, that was Ralph Young, got hurt and I filled in for him. I was awkward there at second, and one day against Detroit I blocked Lu Blue as he was trying to slide in. Cobb raced out and immediately wanted to start a fight. There was no fight, but after that every Tiger heading for second tried to cripple me. Finally, Bob Fothergill knocked my knee out of place and that was the end of me in the majors. I don't blame Fothergill; he was just a nice fellow following orders.

"You want to hear a good one? I think I'm the only man ever paid to quit playing. It happened this way. They traded me to Milwaukee for Wid Matthews and I wouldn't report, so Mr. Mack owed Milwaukee some money in lieu of my services. He offered me five thousand dollars to report, but meanwhile Tom Shibe, the president of the A's, made some other arrangement. Then I decided to report, but Mr. Mack sent Mike Drennan — he's the fellow who discovered Jimmie Dykes, you know — to Knoxville. He offered me $1,800 to quit the game, and I took it."

Darkness had now settled over the city, and it seemed to be too late to drive over to Greeneville to look up Dale Alexander.

PIE-EATING CHAMP

MAY 18, 1968. FOR THE PAST MONTH, THE STATE OF INDIANA has been swarming with politicians seeking the highest office in the land, but the primary reason I came here was to try to find out more about a champion pie-eater of 1877 and establish the fact that, 18 years later, he was not hanged.

North Vernon is a pleasant place of about 5,000, and the house joke is that John Dillinger never bothered to rob the local bank because 120 trains a day went through the town and he saw no reasonable opportunity to escape.

Dillinger is no longer with us, having made the mistake of attending a movie at the Biograph in Chicago in the company of a woman who moonlighted for the FBI, and the trains no longer pass through here at such a rapid rate. But the village thrives on the manufacture of automotive parts. If you look hard, you can find traces of baseball history.

Forest More, a pitcher for the Cardinals and Braves in 1909, was born at Hayden, seven miles to the west. Mike Simon, who caught for the Pirates from 1909 to 1913, started life here, and so did the Daringer brothers, Howard, Rolla and Cliff. Howard never made the majors, but managed in the minors for years. Cliff, an infielder with Kansas City of the Federal league, now lives in Sacramento, Calif. Rolla, a shortstop with the Cardinals in 1914-15, lives in Hayden, but I knocked at his door without avail until a neighbor told me he probably had gone fishing.

But space is short and we must return to the subject of this piece, the champion pie-eater. His name was Harry W. Smith, and he was a catcher for the Cubs (then called White Stockings) and Reds in 1877. One evening while employed by the latter team, he ate $3 worth of the pastry at the railroad station restaurant in Pittsburgh. When you consider that pie was probably then ten cents a portion, his feat was considerable, although not yet listed in "One for the Book" (Most pie eaten by third-string catcher in one evening, season —$3 worth —Harry W. Smith, Cincinnati, 1877).

Baseball anecdotes of the early days are so scarce that it seems impossible that another one involving pie should have originated in that same railroad station in Pittsburgh. But The Sporting News reports on page five of its issue of January 15, 1887, that Harry Wright, manager of the Cincinnati Red Stockings in 1869, had been in the Pittsburgh railway station one evening that summer; that his pie was cold, and that he said to the waiter, "Here! Take this over to the fire and heat it."

Wright, a native of Sheffield, England, spoke with a British accent. The waiter took the pie, looked at it with a puzzled expression, walked over to the stove and ate it.

Toward the end of September in 1895, there was hanged in Decatur, Ill., an old minor league catcher named Charles N. (Pacer) Smith. By the strangest of all coincidences, there was another old ball player in Illinois at the time, Frank W. Harris, who had played first base and the outfield for Altoona of the Union Association in 1884, sentenced to hang on the same day. Smith and Harris had never met on the diamond, but they began a maudlin correspondence from their respective deathhouses that newspapers of the day published in full.

The governor of Illinois, John P. Altgeld (his political enemies called him John Pardon Altgeld because he granted amnesty to the Haymarket rioters) then issued Harris a reprieve, but ignored the case of Smith, who then went to his death on the gallows as scheduled.

Smith's crime was a rather ordinary example of domestic horror. He had married in 1888 at Effingham, Ill., a girl named Maggie Buchert against the wishes of her parents. Two years later, a daughter, Louise, was born. Pacer neglected them and they returned to Aggie's family home at Decatur, where the old catcher often paid them visits. On one such occasion, he showed up with a gun, announced his intention of killing his estranged wife, but missed. He killed her sister by mistake.

Now, the point is that all the newspapers in the land described Smith as a former catcher for Chicago and Cincinnati, but I do not believe it for a minute.

Pacer was not born here in North Vernon, as Harry W. Smith was, but at Pendleton, in an entirely different part of Indiana. He was never a big leaguer, but appeared for such Indiana teams as Nobleview, Greencastle, Elkhart and Muncie, and such Illinois clubs as Decatur, Bloomington, Monmouth, Ottawa and Plano.

It was simply a case of the papers mixing the playing records of the two men. Throughout his days with Cincinnati and Chicago, the pie-eater always was identified as Harry, never as Charles N. Smith. If I could only find a record of him here and could prove that he died at some other time, the case would be cinched.

But I failed. Harry W. Smith is not buried here. He did not die here. My hunch is that he lived out his days in Louisville, where he is known to have caught in 1889.

I had breakfast with Howard Daringer, the oldest of the three playing brothers and a remarkably spry man who is writing a history of baseball in North Vernon.

"I have heard of Harry W. Smith," he told me, "but he was before my time, and my time goes back a long way. But if he had come back here in the 1890s, I would have known it."

We looked at each other hopelessly over the remnants of poached eggs, then said good-bye. I thought some of driving to Louisville, but the mere idea of trying to trace a man named Smith in a city so large was too much. Some other day perhaps.

WOMEN IN BASEBALL

MAY 25, 1968. I HAVE NOTHING TO OFFER BUT BOUQUETS of good wishes to Mrs. Bernice Gera, the Long Island housewife who wants to be an umpire, and my fondest hope is that she will obtain not only a job but a chest protector that fits.

However, in the interest of historical accuracy, it is only fair to advise Mrs. Gera that she is not the first of her kind. More than 60 years ago, Amanda Clement of Hudson, S. D., was well known as an umpire throughout the Dakotas, Iowa and Minnesota. At the age of 17, in 1905 Amanda served as captain of the basketball team at Yankton College and was the foremost tennis player in South Dakota.

But her heart was in umpiring. She tucked her hair neatly under her cap, dressed nattily in a blue suit and announced her decisions with crisp authority. For years she was a popular figure in semipro ranks, and hoped to receive an offer from Organized Baseball, but it never came.

The role of women in baseball history is of minor importance, but not without interest, and the ladies who have contributed to the pastime's annals have added a piquant flavor to the stew of history.

Eleanor Engle of Harrisburg, Pa., the last girl who attempted to enter the playing ranks as a shapely shortstop for Harrisburg of the Inter-State League, surpassed Mrs. Gera, although the latter was unheard of as an umpire when La Engle signed with Harrisburg in June, 1952. A stenographer and wife of a carpenter, she was signed by Dr. Jay Smith, president of the team, though without the knowledge of the disgusted manager, Buck Etchison, formerly a first baseman with the Braves.

I say that Eleanor Engle got farther than Mrs. Gera because she actually took infield practice before a game with Lancaster. Then the late George Trautman, president of the National Association, ruled that women could not be signed to contracts in Organized Baseball, a decision to which Eleanor reacted with shock.

Then there was the classic instance of Virne Beatrice (Jackie) Mitchell striking out Babe Ruth and Lou Gehrig successively at Chattanooga on the afternoon of April 2, 1931. It is noteworthy that the Lookouts of the time were run by Joe Engel (no kin to Eleanor, of course, with the surname spelled differently). A precursor to Bill Veeck, Engel had his eye on the gate when he signed Jackie, and that she struck out Ruth and Gehrig in order is a tribute, not to her pitching, but to their gallantry. Engel, who earlier had traded the contract of a shortstop, Johnny Jones, for a 25-pound turkey, signed Jackie as a sure way of filling the park for his exhibition with the Yankees.

But the Depression was on in earnest and the combination of Ruth and Jackie drew an attendance of only 3,500. Clyde Barfoot, once a Cardinal and Tiger, started that game for the Lookouts, but after yielding a double to Earle Combs and a single to Lyn Lary, he departed and was relieved by Miss Mitchell, who promptly produced her two whiffs, then walked Tony Lazzeri and left the game, disappearing from baseball history.

Where is Jackie Mitchell now and where is Eleanor Engle? The former would be 54 and the latter 40. For that matter, whatever became of Amanda Clement, who, if alive, would be 80 and presumably retired as an umpire.

Women have served the game in almost every known capacity. Joan W. Payson, president of the Mets, had an early counterpart in Helene Hathaway Robison Britton, who inherited the Cardinals from her uncle, M. Stanley Robison, just before the season of 1911 and ran them for eight seasons. It was she who made Miller Huggins a major league manager, giving him the job that had belonged to Roger Bresnahan in 1913. She also made all deals for the team and put up with the cigar smoke of league meetings.

Ed Barrow, in his excellent "autobiography" which actually was penned by Jim Kahn, recalled a girl pitcher, Lizzie Arlington (nee Lizzie Stride at Mahanoy City, Pa.), whom he hired in his minor league days to fill various parks in the old Atlantic Association. That Barrow should have resorted to such a promotion seems curious, since he was later chiefly responsible for the Yankee image of austerity, but perhaps he can be excused for such intelligence on the ground of having been callow and not unreceptive to something new.

Women even have scouted. Bessie Largent was the best of the lot, accompanying her husband, Roy, on the road in behalf of the White Sox for years. Among the players they discovered and signed were Zeke Bonura, Smead Jolley, Art Shires and Luke Appling. The last named of course, became a Hall of Fame shortstop and the others reeked color. Baseball surely could use a Jolley or a Shires today!

But when I survey the field of women in baseball history, my favorite of them all is Florence Knebelkamp, traveling secretary of the Louisville Colonels for many years. She was a sister of William F. Knebelkamp, owner of the club, and took on every duty that her office required. She signed her telegrams to hotels "F. Knebelkamp, Secretary," and on at least one occasion this got her into trouble.

The Colonels were visiting a certain hotel for the first time, and when Miss Knebelkamp approached the reservation desk, the clerk asked, "Who are you?"

"Why, I'm Florence Knebelkamp, the traveling secretary," she replied.

"Oh, yes," he said, looking at a wheel of index cards. "Let's see, I've put you in with Johnny Marcum, one of your pitchers. I'd better give you a room to yourself."

GOD LOVE THE BROWNS

JUNE 1, 1968. IN ONE OF HER MEMORABLE AND BITTERSWEET sonnets, Edna St. Vincent Millay referred to the procession of her years as being "like one hack following another hack."

This moving line always has reminded me of the life experiences of the old St. Louis Browns, the team which expired at the age of 52 in 1953, only to be resurrected in Baltimore as the Orioles the following year.

For the Browns, the years also passed like weary hacks, with one pennant to show for those 52 seasons, a wartime job in 1944 when the thoughts of most fans were occupied with the Normandy beachhead, and two second-place finishes. The Browns, dead last ten times, were a second-division outfit in 40 campaigns.

I found myself working the other week with the Browns of 1912, a chore begun in order to determine whether the C. Miller listed in one game at shortstop was the same man known as Edwin Miller, who played a dozen games at short and first. He was not. C. Miller, whoever he was, appeared as the starting shortstop on June 29, demonstrated that he had a weak throwing arm and could not pivot on a double play, was removed before the game was over and shipped the next day to Chattanooga.

Ed Miller came up in September, a collegian who had been playing at Lowell of the New England League.

It was a typical year for the Browns, with the team finishing seventh, two games ahead of the Yankees. That was the first cellar finish for the Yanks, and they would not suffer that ignominy again until 1966.

Bobby Wallace, the Hall of Fame shortstop, started 1912 as manager of the Browns, but after his team won 12 and dropped 27, he was replaced by George Stovall. It was not a cheap team. In those days, most clubs were content with one coach and one scout, but Colonel Robert Lee Hedges, who owned the Browns, had Lou Criger, Cy Young's old batterymate, as a pitching coach, and a competent scouting corps that included Monte Cross, Charlie Barrett and Bob Gilks.

Even before the season began, there were ominous notes. Training was scheduled for West Baden, Ind., and Bunny Brief, a prize rookie outfielder after a big year at Traverse City, Mich., became homesick in Chicago on his way to report, turned back and did not reach the Browns until late in the year.

It was so cold and rainy at West Baden that workouts were impossible, and the players huddled against radiators for a week before Hedges moved the squad to Montgomery, Ala.

But there were reasons for hope. George Baumgardner, a pitching recruit, was described as "faster than Walter Johnson and with excellent control." Del Pratt, a second baseman up from Montgomery, looked good at his job. Stovall provided solid protection at first, Jimmy Austin played third competently, and on days when Wallace, aging now, did not feel up to playing short, Eddie Hallinan subbed for him.

Burt Shotton was the center fielder and leadoff man, and was flanked by Bill Hogan in left and Frank LaPorte, normally a second baseman, in right.

Jack Powell, though 38, was still a strong pitcher, and the staff also included spitballer Joe Lake, Elmer Brown, Barney Pelty and Earl Hamilton, a stylish southpaw.

The greatest weakness was in the catching department. All of the available men for the position were small. Jim Stephens and Paul Krichell did most of the work, and the latter, who would become one of the greatest scouts in the game's annals and the discoverer of Lou Gehrig, was a weak hitter and frequently was banged up by runners at the plate.

"If this keeps up," he said early in the year, "I'm going to wear spikes on my calves."

Baumgardner more than met expectations. In his first major league start, he beat Ed Walsh of the White Sox, 4-1. In his next outing, also against the Sox, he hooked up against Death Valley Jim Scott and the pair went 15 innings to a scoreless tie.

After Baumgardner's victory over the great Walsh, reporters clustered around him in the clubhouse, and he seemed baffled by the attention.

"Who's Walsh?" he asked. When told that Ed had merely won 40 games for Chicago in 1908, Baumgardner replied, "Well, if he's that good, why doesn't some National League club draft him?" Around Barboursville, W. Va., where he had been raised, the only teams he heard about were Cincinnati and Pittsburgh.

The Browns knew one shining moment that summer. "Ty Cobb Day" had been scheduled for August 30 to celebrate the seventh anniversary of that great player's big league debut, with the Browns as visitors. And, as so often happens on such occasions, another player stole the show. Hamilton that afternoon became the second southpaw in American League history to pitch a no-hitter, beating Jean Dubuc, 5-1, with Cobb scoring the only run for his team on an infield out. Jess Tannehill had been the only previous lefthander to pitch a hitless game in Ban Johnson's young circuit.

But if the years of the Browns proceeded "like one hack following another hack," there were still moments of humor. One day Powell, who had pitched in the majors since 1897, was warming up prior to a game when a fan leaned over the rail from his field box and shouted:

"Who threw out the first ball the year you broke in?"

"Adam," the pitcher shouted back.

IN SEARCH OF HISTORY

JUNE 8, 1968. THE LATE RING LARDNER WAS ADDICTED TO outrageous play on words, and in one of his hilarious spoofs, three characters were in search of a fourth for a game of bridge when one of them said, "Let's invite rigor mortis to set in."

I was reminded of this during the recent home-run splurge of Frank Howard, because every time the imminent death of baseball is predicted by some partisan of another sport, along comes a Mickey Mantle or a Willie Mays, a Sandy Koufax or a Frank Howard to provide some sensational burst of the spectacular to capture public imagination and restore the old game to its position of glory. In other words, rigor mortis has not set in yet, or if it has, the symptoms are not visible in this sylvan village which is the game's home.

On the morning following Howard's tenth home run in six games, a feat which sent to limbo all previous attempts along that line, three young men were observed at a table in The Hitching Post, a local restaurant, excitedly talking about Howard's accomplishment, and one of them, his pancakes finished, was furiously addressing postcards to the big slugger of the Senators. Spread out before them was the Binghamton Press, a newspaper which not only publishes major league box scores in full but, in this day of sloppy proofreading, actually edits them, and on the first sports page was a one-column box that showed in agate exactly what Howard had accomplished on his spree that was destined to be ended that afternoon.

A few minutes later, I opened the door of the Hall of Fame library and almost immediately the three Howard watchers trooped in.

"Hey," one of them said, "you're the fellow who was at the restaurant. How about that? Well, here's what we want. There were four players with the Washington Senators who hit home runs their first time up in the majors. They didn't all hit them for Washington, understand, but they all played with Washington at one time or another, see? I know three of them — Brant Alyea, Buster Narum and John Kennedy. But who was the fourth?"

It beat me, and I confessed my ignorance. But Leonard Gettelson's "One for the Book," published by The Sporting News, was handy, and here, on page 77, was the list of players who spanked home runs on the occasion of their first appearance. It was an easy matter then to pick out the fourth, Don

Leppert, who broke in with a homer for the Pirates in 1961, but then played for the Senators.

The answer seemed to please them. "Leppert," they said jointly, rolling the name over their tongues again and again with the same sense of satisfaction that a man is said to get from a good cigar.

Then we found a fifth, Clyde Vollmer, who slugged one for the Reds his first time up in 1942 and later played for the Senators. It was apparent now that the trio consisted of not just Howard fans but Washington fans. This is all to the good. There is no satisfaction in the game equal to living and dying with a particular team. But Howard's feat superimposes this and provides a thrill for all who love the game itself.

By this time, the phone was ringing, and on the other end was a small, thin voice that certainly belonged to a boy about eight years old.

"Tell me some facts about Babe Ruth," he demanded.

"Where are you calling from?" I asked.

"Boston," the small voice said.

"Well, sonny, there have been many, many books written about Babe Ruth and you will find some of them in the Boston Public Library. I couldn't possibly tell you the facts about Babe Ruth in a telephone conversation, and if I tried to, your daddy would have a hard time paying for the call."

"Do you know how many trophies Ruth won?" the boy persisted.

"No, I'm sorry. But he won many trophies."

"Do you have them all?"

"We have many of them."

"Who has the rest?"

"Mrs. Ruth."

"What's her phone number?"

"I'm not allowed to give you that," I said, "but if you write her in care of the Hall of Fame, the letter will be forwarded."

He hung up then, but ten minutes later the girl at our ticket counter buzzed me to say that the boy had called back and demanded Claire Ruth's number from her. Somewhere in Boston, I suspect, a man next month will receive a telephone bill that includes at least two mysterious long-distance calls, and if the father knows his son, the two to Cooperstown will be a dead giveaway.

Baseball dead? Not yet, thanks. Not when three young men rush from breakfast to search for the name of a fourth man who hit a home run his first time up. Not when an eight-year-old boy phones long distance to inquire about a player who has not played for 33 years and who has been dead for almost 20.

This is not to suggest that baseball does not have imperfections. Of course it has. The present dominance of the pitcher threatens the structure of the game, and something will have to be done about it. But an answer will be found, as it always has been in the past.

And I suspect that other sports have imperfections also. At least I've never heard of Henry Aaron losing a home run because he marked a triple on his scorecard by mistake. And I doubt that the Yankees ever will have to forfeit because Mickey Mantle went to his post with traces of Butazolidin in an ailing ankle.

AN AUTHORITY ON NO-HITTERS

JUNE 15, 1968. OUTSIDE THE RAIN IS COMING DOWN AS STEADily as it did for Sadie Thompson and the Rev. Davidson on Pago Pago, but inside the Hall of Fame library, work proceeds as usual and the day is sunny because of the presence of Colonel Jack Rudolph, who stopped in for three days to conduct research on no-hit games.

I always thought that Allen Lewis, the Philadelphia correspondent of The Sporting News, knew more about no-hit games than anyone I had ever met; and Phil Pepe, the New York writer, has just turned out a delightful book on the same subject. But Colonel Rudolph, who has been studying these things since 1944 and hopes to publish his findings eventually, probably has more raw data on no-hitters than anyone has ever compiled. From Joe Borden in 1875 to Catfish Hunter in 1968, there have been 171 no-hitters, and the colonel, a jovial, stocky man of 60, is pursuing every possible detail of the lives of the men who pitched them.

Colonel Rudolph makes his home at Green Bay, Wis., and his father was the first team physician for that city's Packers. But the son, who retired from the Army in 1953, now comports himself with great versatility as a feature writer for the Green Bay Press-Gazette, performing as a music critic as well as an observer of no-hitters, thus running the risk of confusing Breitenstein and Bach or Haydn and Haddix.

The day in the library is warm for another reason. From another Wisconsin source, Bill Parizek of LaCrosse, comes a letter in the morning mail containing an anecdote of the game that I never had heard of and doubt if many other fans have.

It seems that LaCrosse fielded an entry in Northwestern League in 1887, and the pennant was won by Oshkosh, a notable team which had Frank Selee as its manager and William (Dummy) Hoy in its outfield. Selee went on to win five pennants for Boston in the '90s, then built at Chicago the great machine that Frank Chance took over and shared dominance of the National League with the Giants and Pirates in the first decade of this century. Hoy just missed becoming the game's first centenarian, dying December 15, 1961, about five months before he would have reached birthday No. 100.

The Oshkosh franchise, Parizek informs me, was owned by one Philetus Sawyer, United States Senator and millionaire lumberman, and he knew as much about baseball — to steal a phrase from Rube Waddell — as a hog knows about ice skating.

At one of the games he attended, a line drive zoomed between the left and center fielders, and Sawyer raced in an indignant rush to his team's bench.

"Listen," he told Selee. "We have to stop this. I demand that you hire a man at once to play between left and center. And if that isn't enough, I will engage more players."

Parizek also corrected me on an error I made in a recent column on women in baseball. After saying that Jackie Mitchell, the girl who struck out Ruth and Gehrig in succession in an exhibition at Chattanooga, did her stint as a promotion for Joe Engel, owner of the Lookouts, I added the misinformation that she "disappeared from baseball history."

Not quite. Parizek saw her at LaCrosse on the afternoon of September 22, 1933, pitching against a local team for the House of David. She worked the first inning and allowed two runs.

A year after that, Parizek saw the talented Babe Didrickson Zaharias pitch an inning at LaCrosse for the House of David, and that year the squad, in addition to Babe Didrickson, included Grover Alexander; Earl Smith, former catcher of the Pirates and a tipper of bats beyond parallel; and Poncho Traynor, the younger brother of Pie.

There's another strange aspect of that column concerning women in baseball. I had occasion to mention Amanda Clement, a famed girl umpire from Yankton College who worked semipro games throughout the Midwest for years. I said that if she were still alive, she would be 80. I lacked the sense to write to Yankton and find out if she's living or not. So Kenneth E. Crouch, a fan in Bedford, Va., did so, and the college reported that Miss Clement is living in Sioux Falls, S. D., a fact confirmed by Floyd Torkelson of Hudson, S. D., another reader.

I have learned painfully that it is dangerous to accept at face value statements about the whereabouts of former players. A few columns ago, I reported that Jack Peterson of Sacramento, Calif., informed me that Gene Bearden was a member of that city's police force. In fact, he went on to say that numerous former major leaguers were on the Sacramento force. Buoyed by the news and encouraged by C.C. Johnson Spink, I wrote to the police chief and asked how many players he had around, but never received the courtesy of a reply.

Then Ray Gallaway of West Helena, Ark., who apparently doesn't read

very carefully, ignored the fact that my placing Bearden in Sacramento was
an idea initiated by Peterson. Gallaway wrote me how shocked the people
of Helena, Ark., were because Bearden was running a restaurant there.

I wrote and thanked Gallaway for the information and asked for Bearden's
address. He has not answered, but he did write to Voice of the Fan, repeating
how shocked the people of Helena were. Well, apparently Bearden is in
Helena and his place is called Gene Bearden's Italian Village and is situated
at 12432 Perry St. I obtained that information from Joe Simenic of the
Cleveland Plain Dealer, who is shocked by nothing, and who also can answer
mail.

SIXTY-FEET-SIX

JUNE 22, 1968. HERE IS HOW THE PITCHING DISTANCE HAP-
pened to be set at 60 feet, six inches.

The season of 1892 had been the dreariest experienced by the National
League up to that time. Pitchers dominated the game, and scores were low.
Only 12 players out of 184 who appeared in 15 or more games batted .300 or
above.

A bat with one side flattened was permitted for bunting, and one "hitter"
after another trooped to the plate to lay the ball down. The fans hated the
bunt, which they called the "baby hit," but apologists said the game never
had been so scientifically conducted.

The National League that year had expanded from eight to 12 clubs, and,
despite the novelty of a split season, interest slackened all around the top-
heavy league.

Batting seemed to be on the verge of disappearing, and only a few
reactionaries like Adrian Anson and Ned Hanlon liked the game the way it
was. Something just had to be done.

All sorts of radical schemes began brewing. A man named Cliff B.
Spencer, of Rolla, Mo., suggested a game that used five bases instead of four.
Other revolutionaries suggested reforms almost as drastic. Then W.R.
Lester, sports editor of the Philadelphia Record, thought up a scheme that
had wide appeal.

The pitcher at that time did not work off a slab. Since 1880, the rules had
called for him to work from a box, five and one-half feet long by four feet
wide, 50 feet distant from the center of home plate. Each corner of this space
was marked by a flat, round rubber plate six inches in diameter, fixed in the
ground even with the surface. The extreme rear of this box was thus 55 feet,
six inches from home plate.

The Lester Plan, as it came to be known, contained three planks, as follows:

1. Make the base lines 93 feet in length, instead of 90.

2. Put the pitcher's point in the geometrical center of the diamond and abolish the pitcher's box.

3. Abolish the foul ball and the flat bat and make every foul ball a strike.

No idle dreamer, Lester constructed a diamond to his specifications at Wynnewood, Pa., a suburban Philadelphia community on the famed Main Line. Amateur teams then engaged in games played there under the new code, and the results were pleasing.

Even the owners of the National League clubs, some of them at least, became interested. But Anson, still operating as he had in the 1880s, though his Chicago team had been pennantless since 1886, sniffed, "There is enough batting now and the public is tired of the continuous tampering with the rules." (Anson had hit .274, the lowest mark in his 27 professional seasons, as it turned out.)

"The Lester Plan won't change anything," added Ned Hanlon, new manager of the Baltimore Orioles.

But there was a strong demand for action.

"Why was it that baseball was popular even before the days of curved pitching?" asked J.M. Carroll, a baseball writer in San Francisco. "Simply because there was plenty of action in the play and spectators got their money's worth of pleasure. There was that pleasing uncertainty which kept the onlookers guessing and made the spectators look for a safe hit from even the weakest batter. Baseball has been too long in one rut."

The National League club owners were exactly split over the Lester Plan when they sat down at the old Fifth Avenue Hotel in New York City on March 7, 1893. Boston, Cleveland, Pittsburgh, Chicago, St. Louis and Louisville wanted the game left the way it was. Brooklyn, Philadelphia, New York, Cincinnati, Baltimore (despite Hanlon) and Washington were the dangerous radicals who wanted to try something new that would increase scoring.

Frank DeHaas Robison, the extreme right-winger who owned the Cleveland club, almost broke up the meeting, which lasted until 11 p.m., with his frequent outbursts on behalf of the status quo, and the chairman, Arthur H. Soden, the Boston magnate, kept ruling him out of order.

The Lester Plan, calling as it did for bases 93 feet apart, meant that the pitcher would stand 65 feet, nine inches from home plate. The distance from home plate to second would be exactly twice that, 131 feet, six inches.

What seemed to be a hopeless deadlock was dissolved when the liberals agreed to compromise. And here is how they worked out an agreement:

The distance of 90 feet between bases was maintained, but the pitcher was moved back, after much haggling, five feet. The old pitcher's box (the term, an anachronism, is still employed) was abolished. Lester's suggestion of a pitching rubber was adopted, and it was placed five feet behind the rear of the old box, or 60 feet, six inches from home plate. The flat bat was also ruled out.

But the foul strike rule was not to be adopted by the National League until 1901 and by the American in 1903.

"Now there'll be more bunting than ever," predicted Anson.

But he was wrong. Except for such skilled players as Arlie Latham and John Montgomery Ward, bunting with a round bat was an art that required constant practice to learn.

Sixty-five players batted over .300 in the National League of 1893, and the fans loved it. Anson, by the way, managed to raise his average to .322.

IDAHO

JUNE 29, 1968. UNTIL HARMON KILLEBREW CAME ALONG, Idaho was principally known for its incomparable potatoes, Sun Valley and uncountable herds of elk.

There is something lopsided about the state, which sags west from the Continental Divide, struggling through forests and wilderness to reach the borders of Oregon and Washington.

Major league players born in Idaho have been as scarce as parakeet in Patagonia. I can find only 14 of which Killebrew, born at Payette, is by far the most noted. Yet there are three National League pitchers currently operating who were born there: Larry Jackson of the Phillies, a native of Nampa; Pat House of the Astros, who first saw the sun's golden rays in Boise; and the latest exhibit, Frank Reberger, of Durocher's fierce Cubs, born at Caldwell.

The only pitcher from Idaho that Killebrew ever faced in American League play was John James, who toiled for the Yankees in 1958 and 1960, and for the Yanks and Angels in 1961.

James was born at Bonners Ferry in the panhandle of Boundary County, the northernmost county in the state, a lonely stretch of land bordering on Canada.

There are 44 counties in Idaho, and only ten have produced and exported players for the major leagues. Statehood was not achieved until 1890, but even before that time, one National League performer, George Borchers, a pitcher with Chicago in 1888, made his home in the territory, running a small grocery in a community I cannot recall at the moment. The death of Borchers is unrecorded so far, and it may have occurred in Idaho, but perhaps he went back to his place of birth in California.

The first big leaguer to come out of Idaho was Walter Doane, a pitcher with the Indians in 1909 and 1910. Hailing from Bellevue, a smaller place than Bonners Ferry, he appeared in only ten games in his two seasons, losing his only decision, then remained in the East, dying at Coatesville, Pa., in 1935, a fact neglected by both the Spalding and Reach Guides.

Aside from the players already mentioned, other Idaho players include Clarence Roberts, a catcher with the 1913 Cardinals; Claire Goodwin, an infielder who reached the Kansas City Federals; Ralph Erickson, a pitcher briefly with the Pirates in 1929; Hugh Luby, who joined the Athletics as a second baseman in 1936 and made it back with the Giants in 1944; Bill Salkeld, a catcher with the Pirates, Braves and White Sox, starting in 1945; Vern Law, an outstanding pitcher for the Pirates for 16 seasons before becoming a coach only this year; Bob Martyn, an outfielder with the Athletics for three years beginning in 1957; and Kent Hadley, first baseman for the same club and also with the Yankees from 1958-60.

Few of them went back to Idaho. Roberts worked for an oil refinery in Long Beach, Calif., before his death in 1963; Erickson is now a safety director in a copper mine at Magma, Utah; Luby is in Eugene, Ore., busy as president of the Northwest League; and Salkeld was a representative of a steel company when he died at Sun Valley, Calif., a year ago. Of Goodwin, there is not a trace, although for some reason I associated him with Los Angeles.

But if few players were born in Idaho, even fewer died there. At least, I know of only five. The first was Bob Addy, an outfielder whose career began in the 1860s and who is supposed to have been the first player ever to steal a base by sliding. The records show that he was born at Rochester, N.Y., but Harry Simmons of the commissioner's staff tells me that he thinks Addy originally came from Canada, and respecting Harry's great knowledge of that era (we used to talk about these things 20 years ago over pastrami sandwiches across from the old International League office at 535 Fifth Avenue in New York City) I would hesitate to press the Rochester claim.

At any rate, Addy wandered west when his playing days came to an end in the late '70s, and when he died in 1910, he had been working as a tinsmith in Pocatello. If you ever want to read a wonderful book about that town and that time, beg your second-hand book dealer to locate a copy of "You Can't Win," by Jack Black, the confessions of a competent burglar who ended up as librarian of the San Francisco Call.

The four others who died in Idaho were Thomas Seymour, a pitcher in one game for Pittsburgh in 1882, found dead of exposure at Boise in 1916; Chick Fraser, a good pitcher for many teams from 1896 to 1909, who passed away at Wendell in 1940; Johnny Kane, an outfielder for the Reds and Cubs from 1907-10, fatally struck by an automobile at St. Anthony in 1934; and Jim Keesey, a first baseman with the Athletics in 1925 and again in 1930, who had a heart attack at Boise that claimed his life in 1951.

A player I never will forget and who is living in Idaho now is Freddy Leach, an outfielder with the Phillies, Giants and Braves from 1923 to 1932 and who left a lifetime average of .307. The thing I most remember about Leach is the peculiar stance he affected in the outfield, placing his feet in such a manner that he faced the centerfielder, and had to peer over his right shoulder to see the batter. Leach is a farmer now in the little town of Bliss, and if Paul Kerr would give me the time off, I would gladly drive out there to see him without stopping except to sleep. How good was Leach? Well, after the season of 1928, the Giants gave the Phillies Lefty O'Doul for him and threw in a little money to sweeten the pot.

AN UNUSUAL MAN

JULY 6, 1968. SAM CRAWFORD HAS LEFT US NOW, EMBARKING on the mysterious voyage that awaits us all. At 88, he had earned the reward.

None of the wire service obituaries I saw caught the flavor of his personality, but belabored the obvious facts about his career, his 312 triples, his birth at Wahoo on the Nebraska prairie, and his role as a cleanup hitter for the Tigers.

But you can learn about Sam in Larry Ritter's wonderful book, "The Glory of Their Times." Sam was an individualist, a man who hated telephones, but who could write long and earnest letters, a man whose formal education had been confined to seven years of elementary school, but who came to know the beauty of reading Balzac, Dickens, Ingersoll and Santayana, a free thinker and a free man and, in late years, a desert drifter who exuded love in a world that seemed to produce an increase in petty and irrational hatred.

For the past nine years, I had corresponded with him at intervals, and had come to look forward to his bold script in the green ink he always employed.

The lost art of penmanship was one of his accomplishments, and he liked to ask questions about men and events around Cincinnati at the turn of the century.

"Tell me," he would write, "what was the name of that cigar store on Fountain Square where they used to hang out a big white baseball on the days the Reds were at home?"

I'd tell him that the name of the store was Hawley's and that the building had been razed before my birth, but that it was all there in the newspapers of the '90s.

Poor Sam! How he wanted his 3,000 hits! His lifetime total was 2,964, but he always claimed with the same tenacity that he had battled pitchers that the 87 hits he made for Grand Rapids in the Western League in 1899 should be counted. He asserted that the National Commission, baseball's ruling body before Judge Landis became the first single commissioner, had awarded them to him. But this was just a pleasant delusion.

The Western League was not a major in 1899 and it was not a major when it changed its name to the American League in 1900. And the National Commission, of which Garry Herrmann was chairman, and which included Ban Johnson and whoever happened to be the president of the National League, did not concern itself with playing records at all, but concentrated on the endless contractual disputes between players and their clubs.

It is possible that Garry, in a private conversation with Crawford, gave him his 87 hits. For Garry, who fronted for one of the most notorious gangs that ever ran a city, gave away throughout his life everything that passed through his hands, which explains why he left an estate of only $800 when he died in 1931.

When Sam started playing baseball professionally with Chatham, Ont., in 1899, it took him only a few months to reach the majors. After stopping at Grand Rapids, he joined the Reds on September 10 and engaged in a freak double-header. In the first game, Cincinnati played Cleveland, and Sam, batting fourth and stationed in left, made two singles in four trips against a pitcher named Harry Colliflower. In the second game, the Reds met Louisville, and he added two more singles and the first of his famous triples off Bert Cunningham.

One of the most unfortunate events in Cincinnati baseball history was losing Crawford to Detroit. During the war that raged between the National and American Leagues, Sam signed contracts with both the Reds and Tigers for 1903. But the winter before that season, the leagues made peace. There were a dozen or so players whose contracts were disputed. Sam was one of them and Christy Mathewson was another. As part of the peace deal, Crawford was awarded to Detroit and Mathewson to the Giants.

Sam then put in 15 seasons with the Tigers, glorious years in which he usually followed Ty Cobb in the batting order, a slashing lefthanded hitter who could bat the ball a mile.

Needless to say, with a .309 lifetime average for 19 seasons and following Cobb most of the time, he batted in plenty of runs as did another nearly forgotten Detroit hero, Sam Thompson.

VIC 'THE RICH' RASCHI

JULY 20, 1968. IT IS EXTREMELY UNLIKELY THAT JOHN KENNETH Galbraith had Vic and Sally Raschi in mind when he titled his book "The Affluent Society."

But he well might have. For the once-noted righthander of the Yankees and his wife are ensconced here in Conesus, N.Y., in split-level splendor in a ranch type retreat built on an abandoned golf course that commands a breathtaking view of Lake Conesus, a modest body of water not so well known as its sisters of the east, which are identified as the Finger Lakes.

This is farming and dairy country eight miles east of Geneseo, where they raise trotting horses, and where Vic operates a profitable package store and serves as a physical education instructor at the New York University College of Education. The Raschis have two daughters and a son. Victoria, the elder daughter, teaches Latin at Carthage, N. Y., in the state's desolate northern section. But William, who just graduated from high school, and Maria, 8, are at home. Another member of the household is Bullet, half collie and half golden retriever, who was conceivably named after his master's fast ball.

"But I never had a curve," Raschi said. "Never a curve at all. It was learning a slider from Johnny Schulte that made me a winning pitcher."

His claim to having been a winning pitcher is irrefutable. When the Yankee empire was at its zenith, he was the anchor of the starting rotation that included Allie Reynolds, Ed Lopat and Tommy Byrne. In eight years with the Bombers, he won 120 and lost 50 for a percentage of .706, and in each of three straight seasons, starting in 1949, he won 21 games. The excellence of the Yankees was no accident, but the result of careful planning, first by Ed Barrow, then George Weiss, and a scouting staff that was without parallel. Paul Krichell, Joe Devine, Vinegar Bill Essick and Gene McCann, shrewd practitioners of their trade, scoured the country for the best players they could find.

Raschi's case provides a glimpse at how it worked.

"I was a freshman in high school when McCann found me," Vic said. "He told me the Yankees wanted me to finish my education, but I signed an agreement that when I was finished, I would join the organization. I thought I was going to Manhattan College. In fact, I'd been accepted there, but I was late in registering and ended up at William & Mary."

It was at William & Mary that he had the good fortune to meet Sally Glen, a co-ed from Rochester, who became his wife. Their daughter, Victoria, graduated there and William will be heading that way in September.

For many years in baseball, there was a vague idea that no player of Italian ancestry had succeeded as a pitcher. Then, as if to refute the folklore, there came into the game almost simultaneously Sal Maglie and Raschi. Vic's father, Simon, emigrated from Italy, but instead of joining an urban labor pool as so many of his countrymen did, he went to the woods of Maine and became a lumberjack, a highly individualistic act. Later, however, he went to West Springfield, Mass., to work for the railroad, and there, in 1919, Vic was born.

The Yankees started Vic at Amsterdam in 1941 and elevated him to Norfolk before the Air Force beckoned in World War II. He reached the big club at the end of the 1946 season and recalls how Bill Summers, umpiring at first base, gave him tips in his first appearance.

He appeared in six World Series, every one a winner, and although the loot thus acquired does not put him into the class of Frank Crosetti, who is rumored to own San Francisco's Golden Gate Bridge, it did assure that he would not be wanting for worldly goods. He won five out of eight in World Series play. One of those three defeats, a 1-0 job to Preacher Roe in 1949, still jars him.

"Jackie Robinson was on third with two out," he remembered. "He was dancing up and down the line and it bothered me, so I changed my windup to a stretch position, then got the pitch too far inside to Gil Hodges, and he singled to left for the only run of the game."

It is possible that Raschi might have won 21 games each year indefinitely had it not been for an injury. One day he was the runner on a squeeze play against the Indians. When he tried to score, he crashed into Jim Hegan's shinguards, suffering torn cartilages in his knee. There was the usual operation and, after that, he was unable to run well.

"Casey Stengel used to take me out for a runner after that in close games," he said. That's why my victory total dropped off. I just didn't get as many decisions. But the percentage was still good, as I was 16 and 6 in 1952 and 13 and 6 in 1953."

The Yankees sold his contract to the Cardinals, and he struggled through a National League year in which he won eight and lost nine. Then he called it quits after grabbing four decisions out of ten for Kansas City in 1955.

The Raschis, who have a cottage on the lake in addition to their big place, still see baseball people now and then, and usually take in the Old-Timers' Day festivities at Yankee Stadium. They also like to entertain here such old friends as the Jerry Colemans and the Ed Lopats.

Another friend and occasional visitor from an entirely different milieu is Carl Carmer, author of "Stars Fell on Alabama" and various other works. No matter how you look at it, the view that Vic and Sally have is a pleasant one, whether they glance backward to the Yankee years of glory, or ahead, where the glistening waters of the lake caress their land.

LEGENDS

AUGUST 3, 1968. IT OFTEN HAS OCCURRED TO ME THAT THE essential charm of baseball lies far beyond the box scores in a deep forest of legendry.

Because so many millions have followed the play for more than a century, there has arisen about the game a misty but mighty folklore, a vast memory bank in which has been stored the congealed recollections of six generations.

But we are fallible, memory is faulty, and many tales become confused in the telling. However, even the spurious legends make their contribution to the game's literature, and are no less romantic because they contain only a smidgen of truth.

I was reminded of this again when the morning mail yielded an extremely interesting letter from Alan D. Moyer, managing editor of the Wichita Eagle, a morning journal of considerable circulation throughout Kansas.

It seems that one of Mr. Moyer's reporters, roaming recently in the Flint Hills section, was told by a rancher that there are nine little towns in Kansas strung along the tracks of the Missouri Pacific that were named for the nine players in the batting order of the old Chicago White Stockings of Cap Anson.

This story has been kicking around for years, as elusive as a bar of soap in a bathtub. The names of the whistlestops in question are Miller, Admire, Allen, Bushong, Comiskey, Rapp, Helmick, Wilsey and Delevan.

Looking at those names, Mr. Moyer was shrewd enough to sense that some of them belonged, not to the old Chicago White Stockings, but to the old St. Louis Browns.

"The fact that the Missouri Pacific was headquartered in St. Louis," he wrote, "makes me believe that if the towns were named for players, it must have been for the Browns."

How true! The fact that there exists in Kansas a place called Comiskey and a place called Bushong would certainly indicate that they were named for someone who followed Chris Von der Ahe's Browns of the '80s, a team that won four consecutive flags starting in 1885, a team managed by Comiskey and for which Doc Bushong performed as the catcher.

The only trouble with the legend is that there never have been major league players named Admire, Delevan, Helmick or Wilsey, and the names

Miller, Allen and Rapp are as common as dandelions and could refer to anyone.

One version of the story, published years ago, had a Chicago urchin who idolized the White Stockings growing up in the best manner of Horatio Alger to become an important official of the Missouri Pacific and then bestowing on the hamlets the names of the Chicago players embedded in his unconscious. That such nonsense could persist is a tribute to the theory of the late paperhanger, A. Hitler, that people will swallow anything if it is repeated often enough.

The places in question are in Lyon County far to the northeast of Wichita and north of Emporia. In 1929, Miss Laura M. French authored a book, "History of Emporia and Lyon County," and although she was perhaps not familiar with the legend, she certainly demolished the claim for Chicago by explaining how some of the towns received their names. She pointed out that the Missouri Pacific first crossed that section of Kansas in 1886; demonstrated that Jacob Admire was an Osage City man who worked in the interests of the railroad company to secure the bond issue; stated that Miller was named for Clyde Miller, a Topeka ranch owner; and said that Allen was proud of the fact that it was the direct descendant of Lyon County's first post office, also called Allen.

It is a good guess, however, that Bushong and Comiskey, whose nomenclature Miss French could not explain, were slipped in by a baseball buff in 1886 who was well aware of the St. Louis Browns and the fact that they were the hottest team around. If he had ever been a Chicago urchin, the fact would be irrelevant, as he would have been such no later than the 1860s. No important baseball team was formed in Chicago until 1870. Comiskey did not reach the city until 1890, when he managed the Brotherhood team there, and Bushong never played there.

The fact that in Kansas the legend persists is proof of how deeply rooted a love of baseball is in America. For Kansas, unless I am badly mistaken, does not have in the entire state a single minor league franchise.

Yet, the state provided at Humboldt the birthplace of Walter Johnson and in all has produced 139 players for the majors. In other words, Kansas, which represents 1.2 percent of the population of the United States, has yielded 1.3 percent of the big leaguers, which is certainly holding up its end.

The first Kansan to arrive on the major league scene was William W. Hughes, an outfielder who played with Washington of the Union Association in 1884.

Hughes was born at Leavenworth in 1862 and lived to be 81.

The latest (not the last) is Mike Torrez, a pitcher born at Topeka, from whom the Cardinals expect much, after he concludes his current apprenticeship at Tulsa (Pacific Coast).

So Kansas is doing all right. And if you're ever driving from Wichita to Topeka or vice versa, you can leave the Kansas Turnpike at Exit 7, and search for Bushong and Comiskey, names on the land that indicate the tremendous hold that baseball always will have on the people of America.

THE FIRST BAT CHAMP

AUGUST 31, 1968. IT WAS TIME TO LEAVE FOR THE DAY, BUT the phone rang and the girl said, "There's a Mr. Walter Meyerle here to see you."

"Send him over to the library."

I stood there by the window then and watched him cross Cooper Park, a small man in his sixties with a package under his arm. He was accompanied by a friend.

After shaking hands, we all sat down and Walter opened the package. It contained a scorecard from the home park of the Athletics in 1871 bearing a picture of his great-uncle, Levi Meyerle, on the cover, contracts that the player had signed with various clubs of the '70s and a copy of his release by the Nationals of Washington in 1879.

"That's all he left," Walter said. "We found the things when he moved from one house to another long ago and asked him if he still wanted them. But he said he didn't. Now we want you to have them."

Levi Meyerle was the first batting champion in professional baseball, with an average of .492 with the Athletics of the National Association in 1871. He went on to hit .318 in 1872, .331 for the Philadelphias in 1873, .369 for Chicago in 1874 and .314 for Philadelphia again during the season of 1875.

He was one of the original players of the National League and batted .336 for the Athletics in 1876 and .327 for Cincinnati in 1877.

There has been a tendency in some quarters to downgrade the National Association, but if you want to discover for yourself whether or not it was a major league, the following facts are pertinent. It was the only professional league of its time and the games were played for the championship of the United States. Six of the teams that competed for the pennant in 1875 became charter members of the National League the next season, and most of the players active in its ranks continued their careers as National League performers.

Long Levi he was called, a righthanded batter and thrower who stood one inch over six feet in height in a day when most players were shorter by far.

He weighed 177 pounds. His normal position was at third base, but he could play anywhere and frequently was used at other infield positions and in the outfield.

Most of the professional players of his time were city boys of Irish or German descent and members of the laboring class. So it was with Levi, a German.

When his days on the diamond were done, he remained in Philadelphia and became a lather, a plasterer and a carpenter, a fact learned long ago by tracing him through city directories at the Philadelphia Free Library.

"I'm a lather, too," Walter Meyerle said. "Retired now. In Levi's time, he made wood laths by hand and was paid ten cents a thousand. Now the union wage for lathers is $5.25 an hour."

So it was men like Levi Meyerle who built a century ago the cities in America that are now decaying after years of neglect. In the simple age in which he lived, there were cobblestone streets and sprinkling wagons, with vendors who sold pretzels on almost every corner, four mail deliveries a day and ten daily newspapers. Baseball's first batting champion became a cipher in those streets, moving about from place to place over the years. By thumbing through the directories, you almost became familiar with those streets and you always remembered their names. Levi was born at 1524 Fawn, but he also lived at 1540 Cumberland and 1617 N. Clarion.

As the cities grew to chaotic proportions, it became almost impossible to publish more directories. In the last one available for Philadelphia, in 1935, there was only one Meyerle listed, Frieda, who was shown as a helper at Olney High School. You remembered that Del Ennis attended Olney a few years later, and you wondered if she was still there and their paths ever crossed.

"Frieda was my mother," Walter said.

When Levi died of heart trouble on November 4, 1921, not one Philadelphia newspaper published anything about it on the sports page. He simply had been swallowed up by the city, and his name meant nothing to a generation then more concerned with the fact that the Giants had just beaten the Yankees in the first subway World Series.

But here at the National Baseball Library, an effort is being made to restore the Levi Meyerles of the baseball world to their proper place in history.

The game of 1871 was loosely played, but it was the best of its time, and it was on that primitive base that the entire structure of the major leagues was laid.

How good was Meyerle? When Alfred H. Spink [Editor's note: It was actually A.G. Spalding] published "The National Game" in 1910, he had this to say: "A big, stout fellow was Levi Meyerle, the third baseman of the Athletics of Philadelphia in 1871, when they were the champions.

"Meyerle was a very fair fielder, but his best asset was his ability to hit the ball hard."

I walked to the door with Walter Meyerle and his friend.

"We can make it back to Philly in less than six hours if we want to," Walter said. "But we may stop and have a beer. The Phillies are playing tonight and we can hear it. Maybe that Richie Allen will hit a couple."

It seems that Philadelphia third basemen have been doing that for a century.

INTERLOCKINGS

SEPTEMBER 7, 1968. ONE AFTERNOON 24 YEARS AGO, BILL Lohrman, a sinkerball pitcher with an ailing arm, walked over to his manager, Bill McKechnie, in the Cincinnati clubhouse at Crosley Field and asked, "Did you see how hard I was throwing today?"

McKechnie shot him a puzzled look. Lohrman, that afternoon, had been batted out by the Cardinals in the first after a volley of five runs and the visitors had rolled on to a ridiculous 18-0 triumph.

"Well, that's as hard as I can throw," Lohrman said. "I've had it, you might as well release me right now. I can't do you or the team any good."

A few minutes later, McKechnie entered the press room and repeated the conversation to Warren Giles, then general manager of the Reds. "It was one of the most decent statements I ever heard a player make," he told Giles. "Just imagine," he said. "Lohrman could have gone on drawing salary for the rest of the year. But he's just too honest to do it."

I do not suppose that the pitcher ever knew the effect his statement had on his boss, and he smiled when I told him about it recently.

"Well, it was true," he said. "I couldn't help anybody. I just did what I should have done."

Lohrman today is a successful executive with IBM, charged with administrative work at the company's country club. Before that, he served the firm as manager of plant protection. And his days are bathed with the pleasant memory of nine years in the Big Show, first with the Phillies, and then the Giants, Cardinals, Dodgers and Reds.

He was an extremely effective righthander who kept the ball down. Only two years before the unhappy denouement at Cincinnati, he won 14 and lost five for the Cards and Giants, pitching for Mel Ott on a staff that included Carl Hubbell, Hal Schumacher and Cliff Melton. His earned-run average of 2.47 was the stingiest offered by anyone on the corps.

Then, one day in the 1943 season, Lohrman made a pitch no different than the thousands of pitches he had thrown professionally since 1933. Only this time he heard something snap, and although he did not know it at the time, it was the beginning of the end of his career as a Big-Time pitcher.

Lohrman originally came to the Phillies when Jimmie Wilson managed the team in 1934. He was then too inexperienced for National League play and drifted to Baltimore. When he won 20 and lost 11 for the Orioles in 1937, the Giants grabbed him, and he soon graduated from the rank of a spot pitcher to take his turn in the rotation.

In the constantly shifting sands of baseball fortune, the death of one career is often marked by the birth of another, and it is curious to recall that the box score in which Lohrman made his last appearance was the first in which another pitcher, Joe Nuxhall, appeared. Lohrman allowed the Cardinals their first five runs that day, and Nuxhall, almost two months short of his 16th birthday yielded their last five. Nuxhall, as nervous as the youngest player ever to appear in a major league game should have been, retired two of the first three batters in the ninth, then walked Stan Musial and went all to pieces.

The Reds signed Nuxhall as a result of his showing in a tryout camp. He was 6-3 and weighed 195, and they were astonished to learn he was only 15 years old.

"I'll use him," McKechnie said. "I'm not afraid to throw him in there." But after that one appearance in the Lohrman game, it took Joe eight years to work his way back to the National League and resume what turned out to be a lengthy and successful career.

Now Nuxhall is part of the Cincinnati broadcasting team. Earlier this year in the press box at Wrigley Field, he was recalling his debut. "I got a bonus of $500 and a salary of $175 a month," he said.

"Well, that wasn't bad for a 15 year-old boy," someone told him. "And it turned out all right. You're doing all right today."

So is Bill Lohrman, now 55, a lean, dark man of quiet manner who lives comfortably with his wife of 33 years, the former Alma Pederson. A Brooklyn boy who went to P.S. 181 and Alexander Hamilton High School before hitting the baseball trail, he wouldn't change a thing.

Still another pitcher who appeared for the Reds in the game that was the last for Lohrman and the first for Nuxhall, was a kid from Juniata College named Hank Eisenhart. A big lefthander, Eisenhart finished up for Nuxhall without allowing a run, but it was the only big league contest in which he would ever appear. When last heard from, he was a schoolteacher at Levittown, Pa.

Eisenhart may have been lacking in experience, but he certainly wasn't short on confidence. The Reds had a shortstop a the time, Eddie Miller, who was a master of the position, but in a game one day he misjudged a pop fly, possibly for the first time in ten years.

"What's the matter with you?" Eisenhart asked him at the end of the inning, when Eddie came back to the bench.

One of the questions asked on the questionnaires that the Hall of Fame sends out to former players is, "If you had it all to do over, would you play professional baseball?"

I never have tabulated the number of affirmative answers, but it is safe to say that ninety-nine percent of the players would follow the same profession again.

Most of them settle the question with a simple "yes."

Not Bill Lohrman. Such an answer would not be emphatic enough. "I sure would," he wrote.

SHUTOUTS

SEPTEMBER 14, 1968. STATISTICS ARE THE LIFEBLOOD OF BASE-ball, but many fans find them tedious. For this reason I have always employed them sparingly, like paprika.

But there are certain situations in the game in which it is impossible to prove a point without resorting to figures. For example, it has been widely printed this year that the National League is headed for a record crop of shutouts, and the books assure us that that record is 164, set by the National League in 1908. Before discussing whether or not that mark can be surpassed, a highly technical matter must be pointed out.

Here is how the eight teams made out in shutout play in 1908:

	Chi	NY	Pgh	Pha	Cin	Box	Brk	StL	G	W	L	T
Chi	—	2	5	2	6	3	5	5	43	28	14	1
NY	3	—	2	3	2	6	5	4	35	25	10	0
Pgh	5	2	—	5	4	1	3	4	40	24	16	0
Pha	2	1	2	—	5	2	3	6	45	21	23	1
Cin	1	1	1	6	—	2	3	3	41	17	24	0
Bos	2	1	1	1	3	—	2	4	32	14	18	0
Brk	1	1	4	3	2	2	—	7	44	20	24	0
StL	0	2	1	3	2	2	3	—	46	13	33	0

| Totals | | | | | | | | | | 162 | 162 | 2 |

This table would indicate there were 164 shutout games. Actually, there were 162 shutouts played to a decision and one tie, a scoreless ten-inning joust between the Cubs and Phillies at Philadelphia on September 19 in which Ed Reulbach and Lew Richie went all the way.

Both Reulbach and Richie were credited with shutouts in that game, as well they should have been, but when the statisticians added up the shutouts, they apparently figured out those accomplished by each pitcher in the league instead of adding the number of shutout games. In other words, there were 163 shutout games, but in those games there were 164 shutouts pitched. Admittedly, this is highly technical.

The National League of 1908 had 616 games scheduled, and all were played. There were also six ties. So, of the 622 games, 163 were shutouts, and this figures to be 26 percent.

This year, operating with a schedule of 810 games, the National has seen just one tie. If all scheduled games are played and there are no more ties, 811 games will have been played. Twenty-six percent of that figure is 210, and that is the number of shutouts that will have to be played to surpass the record.

This, in other words, is an asterisk situation because of the increased schedule. It would be ridiculous to claim that 164 shutouts would constitute a record when the scheduling differences are considered. And this is why I feel Ford Frick's decision that Roger Maris did not surpass Babe Ruth's home-run record was eminently wise.

In many ways, 1908 was the most exciting baseball season that the game ever enjoyed. It was the year of Merkle play, for one thing, and the pennant races in both leagues were decided on the final day, the Cubs beating out the Giants by one game, and the Tigers nosing out the Indians by one-half game.

When Fred Merkle failed to touch second base on September 23 at the Polo Grounds, he did not force the National League into a playoff, as many seem to believe. It merely meant that the game in question became a tie game that had to be replayed, and when it was replayed, the Cubs beat the Giants and won the flag.

Christy Mathewson led the National in shutouts in 1908 with 12, Mordecai Brown of the Cubs had nine, and Vic Willis of the Pirates, Hooks Wiltse of the Giants and George McQuillan of the Phillies each had seven.

Reulbach pitched six, as did Nap Rucker and Kaiser Wilhelm of Brooklyn. Joe McGinnity of the Giants, Lefty Leifield of the Pirates, Bugs Raymond of the Cardinals and Andy Coakley of the Reds and Cubs turned in five shutouts apiece.

But my favorite shutout pitcher of that season was Reulbach, a righthander from Notre Dame. One shutout was the tie at Philadelphia already mentioned. Two of the others were pitched on a single day, September 26. Pitching at Brooklyn Reulbach blanked the Superbas, 5-0, in the first of two, beating Kaiser Wilhelm. Time of game: 1:40. He then felt so refreshed that he talked Frank Chance into letting him pitch the second contest, and this time he whitewashed Sunny Jim Pastorius, 3-0. Time of game: 1:15.

Some of the shutouts of that year were slightly strange. At Pittsburgh, for instance, it was decided to hold a "day" for Honus Wagner on July 17, a decision with which it would be difficult to quarrel. But the Pirate fans who turned out to honor the great shortstop hardly enjoyed the afternoon.

Before the game, both teams surrounded the modest and embarrassed Wagner at home plate, and a group of fans presented him with a $700 watch, the Carnegie lodge of Elks added a charm, and a small boy made his way to the field to present Honus with a rooster which he claimed "could lick anything."

But Pittsburgh that day could not lick Boston. Tom McCarthy, who won only seven games in his entire big league career, blanked the Pirates. Boston scored six runs in the eighth inning when a tremendous cloud of dust swept the field, followed by a pounding rain. The home fans, perhaps madder than the now "wet hen" given to Wagner, sat there until the umpires decided further play was impossible. The score reverted to the seventh inning, and Boston won, 4-0.

EDDIE MURPHY

SEPTEMBER 21, 1968. THERE ARE CERTAIN INDIVIDUALS WHO go through life so serenely and with such quiet manners that one would never suspect that they were ever involved in dramatic and turbulent events. But here in Dunmore, Pa., really a suburb of Scranton that follows that larger city around like a persistent lover, I found a man who answers the description exactly.

Eddie Murphy, a widower who will be 77 in October, was shaving when I rang his doorbell shortly after noon on a recent day. But he greeted me warmly, welcomed me in and said, "I'd love to talk to you. I'll finish shaving and then we'll go down to Cooper's Seafood House. You just sit down here a minute."

It was a comfortable house on a shady street, where he has lived since he bought the property in 1916. The first things you notice in his living room are a jar of salted peanuts, a neatly folded copy of The Sporting News, a baseball bat made of cut glass heavier than any ever swung by Ruth and a picture of his lovely daughter, Betty, who keeps house for him.

Soon we were seated at Cooper's, and as I looked at him over a tin of Norwegian sardines, it seemed difficult to believe that such an unobtrusive, soft-spoken man had witnessed some of the most stirring episodes in the history of the game.

Consider that he sat on the bench of the Athletics in 1911 when Home

Run Baker earned his nickname by smashing homers on successive days off Rube Marquard and Christy Mathewson; or that he played right field for the A's in the World Series of 1913, in which he made the final putout, and in 1914, when the Miracle Braves rose up and inexplicably won four straight games; or that he was a member of the Black Sox in the ill-starred set of games in 1919 against the Reds; or that in 1926 he was still on the job with the Pirates during the Carey-Adams-Bigbee insurrection.

This man had seen all these things through his soft blue eyes, but as he talked about them, his conversation was punctuated with no phrase more salty than "My gracious!" I had to smile, seeing such visible evidence of the good influence of Connie Mack.

"That bat you saw in my living room," Eddie said, "it was given me by a glass company at White Mills, Pa., where I played as a kid. That's Mathewson country around there, you know. I was born at Hancock in New York State. My father ran a hotel. I went to high school in White Mills, and then Villanova, and that's where Connie Mack found me. Danny Murphy also was on the Athletics at the time, and he also played the outfield, and people were always getting us mixed up, but we weren't related. My real name is John Edward Murphy, but I dropped the John long ago, and somehow my name got into some record books as Joseph Edward. I don't know how."

Eddie spent most of the 1911 season at Scranton, but he batted .317 for the Athletics in 1912 and won a regular outfield job in 1913, playing right, with Rube Oldring in left and Amos Strunk in center. The A's beat the Giants in five games in the Series that year. In the last game, Eddie was 2-for-3 off Matty and scored what turned out to be the winning run as Eddie Plank won, 3-1.

As everyone knows, Connie Mack broke up his great machine that had won four flags in five years after the unexpected loss to the Braves. Murphy was one of the last to go, not departing until July 16, 1915, under circumstances that were rather strange.

"We were in Chicago that day," Eddie remembers, "and Mr. Mack came to me on the field before the game and said, 'I'd like you to meet Clarence Rowland.' We went under the stands, and when I shook hands with Rowland, who was manager of the White Sox, he said, 'You ought to know I just bought you.' So I just changed suits."

Eddie was a lefthanded hitter, a leadoff man, who had an incredible ability to get on base one way or another. He did not remain a regular at Chicago, but in the tragic year of 1919, he batted .486 in 30 games. Were the Black Sox as gifted as legend has it?

"Oh, yes," he said thoughtfully. "Chick Gandil, at first, was slow, but he was a good target and a good clutch hitter. Buck Weaver was a better third baseman than a shortstop, the best I ever saw outside of Pie Traynor. He was a switch-hitter, and had power righthanded, but hitting left, he used to like to bunt and drag. Joe Jackson, of course, could murder the ball, and Swede Risberg was just coming into his own when the thing happened.

"There were cliques on the club, and the eight who were thrown out always hung around together, even at the batting cage. And there were cliques within cliques. Weaver and Happy Felsch were very close, and Felsch would do anything Weaver wanted. Eddie Cicotte and Lefty Williams were close, and so were their wives. Cicotte was a clean-living fellow who had never been in trouble before."

So went the afternoon, and suddenly Eddie said, "My gracious! It's almost time for me to pick up Betty where she works down at Acme Fast Freight."

"I'll drive you," I said.

Getting into the car, he said, "I have to tell you one about Ira Thomas. You know, Ira caught for the Athletics and then scouted for them, and he was a great story-teller. Once he was addressing a banquet that Ty Cobb attended, and some fellow kept hollering, 'We want Ty Cobb! We want Ty Cobb!' Finally, Ira got tired of it and he pointed out Ty in the first row and said, 'There's Ty Cobb.' 'Oh, no, it isn't,' the fan shouted back, 'that's the fellow who gave me twenty-five cents to shout, "We want Ty Cobb."'

THE SLUGGER OF '03

OCTOBER 5, 1968. HERE IN BOLIVAR, N.Y., THE ROLLING HILL country of western New York, where bowing goldenrod hints of the winter to come, I sat, on the eve of another World Series, with Frank A. Dougherty, 81, a life-long bachelor and retired banker, whose brother, Pat, was a hero of the first World Series played in this country. [**Editor's note: "country" here, of course, should be "century."**]

Patrick Henry Dougherty was a slugging left fielder with the Boston team that we now call the Red Sox. A slashing, lefthanded hitter and leadoff man, he smashed two home runs in the second game of the 1903 World Series against the Pirates, accounting for all the runs as Boston won, 3-0, and then went on to win the important set of games.

"Oh, my! Those were the days!" Frank Dougherty said wistfully. "Later, when Pat was with the Highlanders and White Sox, I used to visit him and work out with the teams. I knew all the players — Jack Chesbro, Wid Conroy, Fred Parent, the wonderful Ed Walsh, Hal Chase, who was then a young, good-looking man...all of them."

Pat's feat of hitting two home runs in a World Series game went unduplicated for a dozen years, or until Harry Hooper, also of Boston, did it against the Phillies in 1915. In Dougherty's case, it was not an isolated fluke.

As a rookie in 1902, he had batted .335. In 1903, he had led the club in hitting at .332.

"He was a very serious player," Frank said, "and a sensitive person."

There is a legend, spurious like so many of them, that Dougherty had gone to high school with Fielder Jones, manager of the Hitless Wonder White Sox of 1906 and other fine clubs, and Frank E. Gannett, founder of a newspaper chain and once a Republican presidential aspirant. Dougherty did attend high school here with Gannett, who was a catcher on the school team, but by that time Jones, who came from Shinglehouse, Pa., was playing professionally in the Oregon State League.

"Jones did discover Pat, though," Dougherty said. "Fielder came home one fall and played for the Shinglehouse town team, and often batted against Pat, who pitched for the Bolivar team. And after looking over Pat, he said, 'Why, that kid's good enough for the Eastern League.'

"So Pat hit the road—Bristol, Olean, Canandaigua, Homestead — and at Bridgeport in 1901 he played in the outfield when he wasn't pitching, just like Ruth later, and led the Connecticut League in batting."

Immediately after that, Pat went to California to play winter ball. With Los Angeles, he led the California League in batting that year, too. Somehow Jimmie Collins, the Boston manager, snared him, and his reputation was made. He was an adept bunter, extremely fast in getting down the line, and pitchers dreaded him.

In 1904, the Boston club was acquired by John I. Taylor, playboy son of the publisher of the Boston Globe, and in June of that year, his infield riddled by injuries, he traded Dougherty to the New York team for Bob Unglaub and a stack of greenbacks. Unglaub didn't work out at all, and the Boston fans were furious, but the deal was noteworthy for an entirely different reason. One newspaper, in reporting the trade, used the headline, DOUGHERTY NOW A YANKEE, the first instance I have ever been able to find of the use of that nickname in New York, although Highlanders remained as the more commonly used designation for the club until the old hilltop grounds were abandoned and the team moved into the Polo Grounds in 1913.

Pat's batting fell off to .263 in 1905 and Clark Griffith offered him a contract for $600 less in 1906. Disgusted, Pat never did sign, but in the haphazard way that business was conducted in that day, he played a dozen games before jumping the team. He went back to Bolivar and thought he would never play again. But, in June, who should show up for an exhibition game at nearby Olean but Fielder Jones and his Hitless Wonders. Jones signed him after straightening out his status with Ban Johnson.

The White Sox soon zoomed to 19 consecutive wins, which is still the American League record (tied by the Yankees in 1947), and went on to the flag and a surprise World Series triumph over the Cubs.

Dougherty remained in the majors through the season of 1911, went home to Bolivar, fiddled around in the oil business for a while, and then went to work at the bank until his death in 1940 from a heart attack. His widow, Florence, followed him in death nine years later.

The Dougherty family is not yet finished demonstrating athletic prowess. Pat had five children, and his older daughter, Helen, married Joe Palone, who coaches soccer and fencing at West Point. They have two sons, Pat and Mike, which almost sounds like the start of an Irish joke.

Mike graduated from West Point last year. He did not play baseball there, but he won an award for making the outstanding contribution to athletics at the historic institution and served as captain of the hockey team.

Frank Dougherty followed me to the door. We shook hands and said good-bye outside. "I'd like to stay longer," I told him, "but I've got to go to Canisteo to see an old friend named Mort Flohr. A strange thing him. He left Duke University to join the Athletics in 1934, and his first big league pitch hit Babe Ruth."

WILD BILL

OCTOBER 12, 1968. IT WAS F. SCOTT FITZGERALD WHO wrote: "The very rich are different from you and me," and Ernest Hemingway, hearing of it, commented, "Sure they are. They have more money."

I thought of this one evening recently when I ran into Bill Hallahan, the old southpaw who was an accomplished World Series pitcher for the Cardinals in 1930 and '31.

It always has seemed to me that lefthanded pitchers "are different from you and me," an observation probably not true, but nevertheless emphatic. Somehow I worry more when a lefthander I am rooting for goes to a 3-and-1 count than I do when a righthander does. And although I do not have a neurotic trauma about the southpaw breed as did John King, the legendary figure of Texas baseball folklore who hated lefthanders with an intensity that bordered on mania, I always feel uneasy when one is in the box, unless, of course, he has the control of a Hubbell, a Pennock, a Spahn or a Koufax.

The Hallahan I remember from his glory days was a pudgy fellow who seemed a little smaller than his five feet, ten and one-half inches, a truculent guy who used to stalk onto the field with his glove jammed into his hip pocket and a big wad of tobacco in his cheek. He was sort of a lefthanded Burleigh Grimes, and vertical lines at the side of his mouth gave him the appearance of a bulldog.

Now the lines have softened, the pugnacious attitude has gone and he looks just like any other pleasant man who is enjoying in retirement the fruits of a lifetime of labor. In 1960, he retired as a supervisor for the General Aniline and Film Co. and at 66 he enjoys a round of golf and watches baseball on TV.

"I'll tell you about that wad of tobacco," he said. "I never chewed off the field or in winter. But, when I reported for Spring Training, into my jaw it went. It was almost like part of my uniform."

There was one play I wanted to ask him about, a play I often had discussed with Jimmie Wilson, his catcher on the day in question. In the second game of the World Series in 1931, Hallahan had the Athletics shut out, 2-0, with two out in the ninth and runners on first and second. Jim Moore came out to bat for George Earnshaw. Hallahan quickly whipped over two strikes, then made a low pitch that struck the ground near the plate and Moore lunged at it and struck out. All Wilson had to do was to tag Moore or to throw to Jim Bottomley at first and the game was over. Instead, he fired the ball to Jake Flowers at third, astonishing everyone present. The throw was wide and Jimmie Foxx slid safely into the bag. Max Bishop then raised a foul fly near the boxes back of first. Bottomley made a nice catch and the shutout was preserved.

When Jimmie used to tell me about the play, he'd wink and say, "I really made a smart play. All Flowers had to do was tag third." But then he'd say, "I pulled an awful rock. A terrible thing. Poor Hallahan was apt to be wild, he'd already walked Foxx and Dykes in the inning, and here I filled the bases for him after the game should have been over. I walked out to the mound and said, 'Bill, I'm sorry,' and Hallahan said, 'Forget it. Who is the next hitter?' I told him Bishop and he said 'I can get him out any time I want to.' But I could have been a real goat."

Hallahan smiled when I told him what Wilson had said. "Well, it turned out all right," he said.

Bill was a real Gashouser and a perfect example of perseverance. For it was not until his sixth trial with the Cardinals that he made it to stay in 1929. Wildness, of course, was his problem, and he worked on it patiently everywhere Branch Rickey could think to send him...Syracuse, Kalamazoo, Fort Smith, Houston.

I'll never know where Rickey found all those wonderful prospects. The word "genius" is terribly overused, but that is what he was when it came to finding and polishing gems.

In the case of Hallahan, he was tipped off to Rickey by Johnny Haddock, an old catcher who became a well-known big league scout. Bill started out in 1923 with the Corona Typewriter team at Groton, N.Y., which Haddock managed. Haddock knew what he had and reported his find to Rickey. Hallahan accomplished the rest himself.

Bill was shunted to the Reds on Decoration Day in 1936, had little left and was passed along to the Phillies in 1938. He worked a few games for Minneapolis of the American Association in 1939 and then called it quits.

But he was a whale of a pitcher in his time, and in four World Series he won three out of four decisions. In 1930, his first year as a regular starter, he led the National League in strikeouts, mixing a good curve with his fast ball.

"Righthanders didn't bother me any," he said. "I'd rather pitch to them than lefthanders." Then he grinned and added, "Except Paul Waner."

He was born in Binghamton, where his father was a railroader, an inspector for the old Delaware and Lackawanna. When he was 18 months old, he was playing on the floor with his sister, Katherine, and when he picked up a rubber ball, she discovered that he was a lefthander. They tried tying his left hand behind him after that, but it didn't work, and it wasn't until he had the liberty of that left arm that he began to make his mark.

But, lefthanders...well, you know. They're different from you and me.

'ORGANIZE THE PIPPIES!'

NOVEMBER 9, 1968. I AM ALL FOR YOUTH. IT SEEMS DOUBTFUL that any generation has made more of a mess of the world than has mine, and that youth is in rebellion is completely understandable to me. But I do not have enough yip left to be a yippie, not enough hair to be a hippie, and my only hope is to organize the Pippies, a group consisting of those who remember Wally Pipp. When I was a kid, pot was something that Ruth's stomach was beginning to show, speed was what Walter Johnson had, and LSD, if it stood for anything at all, stood for Lost in the Second Division. But I dig the scene, and wish I could have been there when Mommie socked it to the Harper Valley PTA.

There was a recent essay in Newsweek by Pete Axthelm which made some valid points and deserves serious study by baseball people. But some of his contentions I think are dubious, particularly his claim that sports fans demand a measure of violence that baseball lacks. This point was also made by Paul Gallico in 1942 in an article which I read on one of the islands in the Aleutians. He said that when the veterans returned from World War II, baseball would be entirely too tame and they would demand more violent games. Well, when the veterans returned from World War II, they found more minor leagues than at any time in history and major league attendance records were set all over the landscape. My hunch is that when the fine young men return from Vietnam, they will be sick and tired of violence and will find baseball a blessed relief.

Mr. Axthelm quotes an anonymous survey to the effect that baseball is having trouble appealing to young adults in the 18-to-32 range. This generalization was not the result of a survey taken in ball parks or at the Hall of Fame, where there has not been a noticeable shortage of fans in the 18-32 range. It would be interesting to know who was surveyed and who did the surveying.

There is enough violence in America and throughout the world today without bringing it into the ball parks. I have never heard of a single fan who attended a game in the hope of seeing another Marichal-Roseboro incident.

There is a sub-teen group that is tremendously interested in baseball, and my desk is flooded with mail from that source. Let me cite one example.

A few months ago, there walked into the library here a 12-year-old boy from Pittsburgh named Dan Ginsburg. His father is a mathematician who works for an atomic power laboratory. "I'd like to look up the heights and weights of players from 1871," he said.

I eyed him suspiciously, but with growing wonder as he took the list I gave him and assiduously copied the data.

A few weeks later, I received a letter from him announcing that he had solved a particularly baffling case. The Thompson-Turkin Official Encyclopedia of Baseball lists a player named Wylie, with no first name shown, an outfielder for Pittsburgh in one game in 1882 and presumably born there. So Dan Ginsburg went to work. He called every Wylie in the Pittsburgh phone book until he located the player's son.

So now it is know that James Renwick Wylie was the player in question, that he was born at Elizabeth, Pa., on December 14, 1861, and lived to be almost 90, dying at Wilkinsburg, Pa., on August 17, 1951. He was a graduate of Geneva College at Beaver Falls, Pa., and it was from that institution that the Alleghenies, as that 1882 Pittsburgh club was called, recruited him.

Later prominent in the real estate and insurance fields, Wylie would have been worth a feature to any Pittsburgh newspaper for a period of years, but it took a 12-year-old boy to locate his data in 1968.

This, of course, is the type of thing that will bore some fans stiff. The persons who go to the parks in anticipation of yelling at the umpires and booing the players would care nothing about Wylie. But there are other lovers of the game, a higher type, who derive pleasure from filling in the game's facts, reducing the unknowable, and looking at the game and its past as an exercise in mathematics. When Edna St. Vincent Millay wrote that "Euclid alone has looked on beauty bare," she might very well have been referring to baseball.

Dan Ginsburg wants to be a baseball writer, and he would certainly appear to be a good prospect. Currently he is trying to get information on other players such as John Abadie, Nathan Berkenstock, Leonard Lovett, William J. Steen, Marty Berghammer and Charles E. Mason.

Mason is a particularly interesting case. He was one of three men who owned the Athletics in 1883, the two others being Billy Sharsig and Lon Knight. They also served as managers of the team, but no one will ever be able to break down their won-and-lost records in that capacity because they took turns sitting on the bench and no newspaper bothered to record which one was on duty for a particular game.

But Dan has already set the record straight concerning one aspect of Mason's career. The old Athletics' manager is shown as having been born in New Orleans, but in response to Dan's persistent prying, he received a person-to-person phone call from Mason's great-nephew in a distant city saying that the old manager was born in Arkansas, and full details of his career and life are on the way.

It seems to me that Dan Ginsburg has the making of a good reporter. It seems to me also that the Dan Ginsburgs represent the best hope of the nation. Perhaps there are not many of his generation so keenly interested in the game as he, but there will be enough who are sufficiently fond of baseball to keep the grandstands full.

And who needs violence?

A STREETCAR NAMED DISASTER

NOVEMBER 16, 1968. THERE REALLY WAS IN OLD NEW ORLEANS a streetcar named Desire, a fact which provided Tennessee Williams with the title of his most widely acclaimed play. But the only streetcar to my knowledge that ever played a part in baseball history was in Louisville, and it should have been named Disaster.

For that is precisely what it spelled out for Lyle Judy, 55, who makes his home in St. Augustine, Fla. now, and who has been able to forget the sorrows of his baseball life as a railroad executive engaged in real estate.

There are still many men active in baseball who remember the Lyle Judy story. Although the game's history is bright with the green fields of accomplishment, there is also a desert strewn with the bones of ruined hopes and the dreams of what might have been. It would be difficult to find a case more representative of the cruelty of destiny than that of Lyle Judy.

During the season of 1935, Judy, a second baseman with Springfield, Mo., of the Western Association, stole 107 bases, batted .337, and was looked upon as one of the brightest prospects in the Cardinal farm chain and the eventual successor to Frankie Frisch. Branch Rickey brought him to St. Louis for a September trial, liked what he saw, and thought he might have unearthed another Pepper Martin.

But then came the streetcar named Disaster. Judy, who originally came out of Lawrenceville, Ill., and obtained his professional start by attending a Cardinal tryout camp, made his home in Louisville. On Election Day that year, a gray, rainy morning, he was driving to work as usual and tried to pass a streetcar. The tracks were wet, of course, and although his front wheels cleared the slippery rails, the rear of his auto skidded sideways with terrible force into the back of the streetcar. They pulled him out of the wreckage and he was unconscious for two days.

Then he awoke to find that he had a fractured skull, a dislocated shoulder and a severely lacerated face. It was questionable that he could ever play again.

Judy had started at Springfield in 1934, on a typical fighting Cardinal farm club that included such familiar names as Bill McGee, Oscar Judd, Joe Orengo and Emmett Mueller. Managed by Mike Ryba, one of the most versatile and interesting figures in the game's history, the team won the pennant for the third straight year. Ryba, who could play anywhere, started the season as the team's catcher. But Judy, the rookie, was also then a catcher, so Mike switched to the mound, won 12 and lost three and batted .327. Judy, meanwhile, caught 68 games, played shortstop in 32 more and hit .315.

Lyle switched to second base, his proper position, for his big sophomore year in 1935 because Springfield introduced another fine young catcher, Mickey Owen. Judy was an instant sensation, teaming up well with his shortstop, Harrison Wickel, who now scouts for the Cardinals. But it was on the paths that he was breathtaking. In addition to stealing 107 bases in 135 games, he added three more in nine playoff games with Ponca City (which Springfield lost), then picked up two more for the Cardinals to give him 112 for the year.

Not long ago, the stolen base was considered a lost art, but such players as George Case, Jackie Robinson, Luis Aparicio, Maury Wills and Lou Brock have restored it to its proper place in the game, a fact which now makes the case of Lyle Judy seem even more poignant.

It has often been observed that almost every important major league record, with the exception of Lou Gehrig's streak of 2,130 consecutive games played, has been surpassed in the minors. And this is true of the seasonal record for steals. Wills' mark of 104 set in 1962 was astonishing, but in the minors the late Ovid Nicholson stole 111 in 123 games for Frankfort, Ky., of the Blue Grass League in 1912. Judy's mark ranks favorably with that.

In the Pacific Coast League, Jimmy Johnston, later a fine all-round performer for the Dodgers, stole 124 over the almost incredible route of 201 games in 1913.

After the accident with the streetcar, Judy retained his speed afoot, but the shoulder injury made it impossible to throw with any degree of accuracy. He never reached the majors again.

The Cardinals tried him at Columbus and Sacramento in 1936, but without much success. Lyle had the shoulder operated on and signed with Baltimore in 1937, then drifted to the lower minors and turned to managing, enjoying a long career. When Rickey found his successor to Frisch, it was first Stu Martin and then Jimmie Brown, who, with some irony, had replaced Judy at Springfield.

The remarkable thing about the Cardinal empire was not that it turned up such exciting players, but that it did so despite losing some of its greatest prizes because of injury and illness. Charlie Gelbert, one of the finest young shortstops to enter the National League, was crippled in a hunting accident after the season of 1932. Then Bill Delancey, the young Gashouse catcher not unlike Tim McCarver in talent, was ravaged by tuberculosis. And then, of course, Lyle Judy.

I thought of him as I watched Brock in the World Series. I thought of him again as I recently drove through his hometown. You might think of him, too, if chance should lead you in the dusk down A1A, where the glittering neon of motels winks a collective welcome. Had it not been for that streetcar named Disaster, he might have been one of the best remembered of them all.

WHO'S FLOYD KROH?

NOVEMBER 30, 1968. IT HAS NOW BEEN MORE THAN 60 YEARS since Fred Merkle failed to touch second base at the Polo Grounds, a thoughtless act that ignited the greatest controversy the game has ever known. One would think that in all that time every aspect of the play had been examined. But several months ago, when a letter addressed to the Hall of Fame asked what had become of Floyd Kroh, I realized that there were still loose fragments remaining to be explored.

Who was Floyd Kroh? In order to answer, it becomes necessary to recall the circumstances surrounding the play itself.

On September 23, 1908, the Giants and Cubs, fighting desperately for first place, had a confrontation at the Polo Grounds. With the score tied,

1-1, and two out in the bottom of the ninth, Moose McCormick was on third and Merkle on first. Al Bridwell lined a single to center, and McCormick loped home with the apparent winning run. Merkle, noting that McCormick had scored, did not bother to continue to second, but ran for the clubhouse in center to escape the fans. This was customary procedure. In such a situation, the umpires never called the forceout at second.

But Johnny Evers, the second baseman for the Cubs, was a student of the rule book. Three weeks previously, in a game between the Cubs and Pirates, Warren Gill, a Pittsburgh runner, had done the same thing that Merkle would do. After the game, Evers screamed at the umpire, Hank O'Day, insisting that no run could cross the plate when a forceout ended the inning. O'Day refused to call Gill out, but after giving the matter much thought, concluded that Evers was right, and that if the play ever came up again, he would make the correct decision under the rules.

As luck would have it, it was O'Day who was umpiring behind the plate, with Bob Emslie on the bases, when the Merkle play came up. After Merkle broke for the clubhouse, Evers called for a ball, touched second with it, and then ran in to confront O'Day. Emslie asked O'Day if Merkle had touched second. Hank replied that he had not, and Emslie then called Merkle out. The crowd was all over the field, and the game was ruled a tie and had to be replayed. When it was, the Cubs won, and the victory gave them the pennant.

Iron Man Joe McGinnity was one of the Giant coaches that afternoon, and when Solly Hofman, the Chicago centerfielder, threw the ball back to Evers, Joe raced out to make certain Evers did not get it. At this point, Kroh, a 22-year-old Cub southpaw who had appeared in only two games that year, charged out of the dugout and wrestled McGinnity for the ball. The Giant pitcher managed to push Kroh aside, grabbed the ball and threw it into the grandstand behind third. Somehow, Evers obtained another baseball and touched second with it.

So that was Floyd's footnote to one of the most dramatic moments in the game's annals. But who was he, and what became of him? The encyclopedias of baseball all tell us that he was born at Friendship, N.Y., in 1883, but show no date of death.

Friendship, with a population of 1,231 is in Allegany County in western New York. I learned that Kroh had never returned there after his baseball days were done, and I could locate no one who knew if he was alive.

It then occurred to me that Kroh, like many players of the time, might have gone into umpiring. Sure enough, when the records were checked, he turned up as an umpire in the Texas League, working for the last time in 1930. His home address was given as Milan Street in New Orleans.

Collin B. Hamer, Jr., of the New Orleans Public Library, then checked old city directories and discovered that Kroh was last listed in 1940.

I turned the matter over to Arthur Schott, the New Orleans baseball historian and one of the game's top authorities. Through an odd coincidence, Schott learned that when he had been 12 years old he had lived only two blocks from Kroh without knowing who he was.

Arthur then visited City Hall and asked for help in locating a possible death certificate. What's more, he found it.

Floyd Myron Kroh was born in Friendship, N.Y., on August 25, 1866. A veteran of World War I, he died at the U.S. Marine Hospital in New Orleans on March 17, 1944, of heart disease.

This is by no means Schott's first contribution to baseball history. It was he who located the headquarters of the first team to go south for Spring Training. That was also a Chicago team, the White Stockings of 1870, organized specifically to defeat the Cincinnati Red Stockings, who had gone undefeated in 1869. Newspapers of the day said that the Chicago players stayed at the Lee House in New Orleans.

Schott investigated and discovered that the name was a euphemism. The Lee House turned out to be "Matilda Lee, furnished rooms, 244 Custom House." By studying old maps, Schott learned that Custom House is now Bienville Street. The centennial of that first Spring Training trip is coming up. There should be a marker at the site.

CARING FOR HEROES

DECEMBER 7, 1968. WHEN MICKEY MANTLE REPORTS TO THE Yankee training camp to see if his weary body can carry him through a 19th American League campaign, he will bring with him the good wishes of fans everywhere.

That the Yankees will offer Mickey a fat contract to do his thing is no surprise. He is still a magnetic player, and his promised presence in the lineup is always a draw, not only at the big stadium on the Harlem, but on the road as well. One does not have to be an astronomer to recognize a super-star. The combination of speed and power and switch-hitting skill that he brought to baseball was rare enough, but even more rare was the stoical courage that enabled him to survive a succession of injuries that would have taxed the patience of a hero in a Greek tragedy.

The fact that the Yankees stand willing to offer him an annual contract in six figures is only justice, but it provides a dramatic demonstration of how greatly baseball has changed. There was a day when the game's most shining players were allowed to grow dim and fade like a cigarette ash in the gloom.

Compare Mantle's situation with that of Honus Wagner, one of the greatest players of them all. Such knowledgeable men as John McGraw and Ed Barrow rated Wagner with Cobb. Eight times he led the National League in batting, he was the finest shortstop of his day and he could also play at first and in the outfield. All around the National League, he was celebrated as the Flying Dutchman, a gentle Teuton who could do anything the game required.

But the difference between the situation that confronted Wagner in 1917 and Mantle in 1969 constitutes a study in eschatology, the theological science of "the end of things." Wagner was 43 when the 1917 season got under way. He had recently married, was overweight, there were rumors that he had invested in oil with Fred Clarke, and there was doubt that he would join the Pirates in their training camp at Columbus, Ga. Barney Dreyfuss had paid him $10,000 annually since 1909, but now the offered stipend was half of that sum. Honus had opportunities to go into real estate and to sell automobiles, and he was uncertain about playing baseball again, although he had been a landmark in Pittsburgh since moving there from Louisville in 1900.

When Wagner finally decided to skip Spring Training, Dreyfuss and Jimmy Callahan, the Pirate manager, announced that his place would be taken by Warren Adams, a rookie who had batted .331 for Winnipeg in the Northern League. Wagner by this time was too slow to take his post at short, and he would be replaced there by Chuck Ward, whose contract had been purchased from Portland. Wagner, who had been counted on at first, would be replaced there by Adams, who suddenly was boosted in the newspaper as a phenom.

The results were disastrous. Warren Adams was a total bust and never got into a major league game. Bill Hinchman, an outfielder, started the season at first.

However, Hinchman was so terrible in the field that he was soon moved back to left and Bunny Brief was brought in from Salt Lake to play first on a 30-day look.

Wagner finally signed and appeared in his first game on June 7. By this time, the season was a shambles. The Pirates were in the cellar and destined to finish there for the first time since 1891. There had to be a goat. Of course, it was the manager, Callahan, who was fired on the morning of June 30.

Much against his better judgment, Honus agreed to replace Callahan, but that experiment lasted for only five games. Pittsburgh won the first, but then dropped four in a row, and Wagner decided managing was not for him.

He was replaced by Hugo Bezdek, a scout whose experience in baseball had been confined to collegiate ranks, but he proved to be a competent leader who soon won the respect of his players.

Wagner, meanwhile, though handicapped by a spiked heel, hobbled to first each day, or sometimes went to third. He appeared for the last time on September 17, finishing up at second for a rookie named Billy Webb.

Everywhere the Pirates went there were "days" for Wagner. Occasionally, grateful fans would present him with something as valuable as a silver service, but he would usually be "honored" with a dozen roses, which he would modestly accept and lavishly praise before the batboy could find a way to dispose of them.

It was a shabby end for a superlative player, but that was the way of the time, and Wagner, at that, was more fortunate than one of his 1917 teammates, Frank Schulte. A former Cub outfield star of the Tinker-Evers-Chance era, Schulte had come to the Pirates along with Bill Fischer for a catcher, Arthur Wilson. But before he reported, his mother died, then one of his brothers was killed, and then his house burned down.

Shortly after joining the team, Schulte engaged in a friendly wrestling match with Duster Mails and fractured a rib. The Pirates then passed him on to the Phillies, and he closed out his career the following year with the Senators.

Mantle will make out better than that. His final game of baseball will be for the Yankees. When it will be, nobody knows, but hopefully it will not be for a while.

FRESCO THOMPSON

DECEMBER 14, 1968. WAITE HOYT, OF THE YANKEES, WHO later delighted his vast radio audience in Cincinnati with his effervescent wit, has always enjoyed telling a mild but whimsical anecdote about Fresco Thompson, general manager of the Dodgers, whose recent death brought sorrow to all in the game who knew and admired him.

Hoyt was serving briefly with the Dodgers in 1932 when Thompson, who had been captain of the Phillies only two years before, was riding the Brooklyn bench. On one occasion, a seldom-used pitcher was about to go to bat for Brooklyn, but a pinch-hitter was employed instead, and when he reached base safely, Fresco was sent in to run for him.

"How do you like that!" Fresco shouted from first base. "From captain of the Phillies to a pinch-runner for a pinch-hitter for a pinch-pitcher!"

Thompson will be recalled mostly for his quips, but they cannot disguise the fact that he was an accomplished player and, later, a hard-working and knowledgeable executive.

Fresco batted .324 for the Phillies in 1929, a mark which any second baseman would settle for today, but the amusing thing is that four members of the team who saw frequent service did better than that. Lefty O'Doul, who played left, batted .398 and led the National League. Chuck Klein, who was in right, finished at .356; Spud Davis, a catcher, hit .342; and Pinky Whitney, at third, sounded off at .327. The entire Philly team, pitchers included, batted .309, yet the club won fewer games than it lost and finished fifth.

Although Fresco as a player is recalled now chiefly for his work with the Phillies, he actually started with the Pirates in 1925. But he spent most of that season with Kansas City and, although recalled in September, he was not eligible for the World Series. Pittsburgh, under Bill McKechnie, won out over Washington in seven games, beating Walter Johnson in a steady drizzle in the finale.

Although Thompson gave early evidence of his smoothness as a fielder and his competence at bat, it will be his destiny to be remembered mostly, as already stated, for his drollery, which caused much merriment. On another occasion at Brooklyn, when Fresco's daily duty was to yell from the bench, Hoyt found him at a washstand in the clubhouse one afternoon before the game, studiously gargling with mouthwash, a ritual that became so prolonged that Waite shouted, "What are you doing, Fresco?" "Just getting in shape for the game!" was the reply.

At the Hall of Fame, we like to list players according to the years in which they first appeared on the big league scene, just as colleges record their alumni according to class. Thompson, therefore, is a member of the Class of 1925, a particularly brilliant group of 116 aspiring players that included such Hall of Famers as Mickey Cochrane, Lefty Grove and Jimmie Foxx.

You could pick an all-rookie team that would show either Fresco or Buddy Myer, the 1935 American League batting champion, at second, Leo Durocher at short, and either Chuck Dressen or Mark Koenig at third. The outfield would be weaker, but you could still select a competent trio from such eligibles as Mule Haas, Sheriff Harris, Jack Rothrock, Earl Webb and Jimmy Welsh. Freddy Fitzsimmons, Bill Hallahan, Ray Benge, George Glaeholder and Walter (Jumbo) Brown could assist Grove with the pitching, and if Cochrane required help behind the plate, there would be Shanty Hogan.

Fresco Thompson, of course, was one of the fortunates who remained in the game and added to its luster, attaining a prominence wide enough to interest a publisher in issuing his autobiography, "Every Diamond Doesn't Sparkle."

As a title, it wasn't bad. Every diamond doesn't sparkle, and neither does every player. But Fresco did!

A TRIP TO A CEMETERY

DECEMBER 21, 1968. ALTHOUGH THIS (LA GRANGE, GA.) IS A thriving textile town of about 30,000 devoted mostly to towel mills and the manufacture of fibers for automobile tires, the dead seem to outnumber the living. There are six cemeteries. On one recent afternoon, I walked around the largest one with the superintendent of all six, Charlie Gibson, who caught a dozen games for the Athletics in 1924.

Charles Griffin Gibson is a jaunty man of 69, a trim figure in a neat red sweater and brown hat with a snap brim. He sells cemetery lots.

Gibson was found during his college days at Auburn by Tom Turner, who did a lot of scouting for Connie Mack, along with another collegian, Ed Sherling, who later owned a bank at Enterprise, Ala., and died there about a year ago. Gibson attended his funeral. The two of them came out of Auburn in 1924, attended the A's training camp at Montgomery, Ala., and remained with the team all year, later returning to college to earn their degrees.

That Charlie did not remain in the American League in 1925 is not remarkable when you consider that the Athletics, already blessed with a superior catcher in Cy Perkins, announced the purchase of Mickey Cochrane's contract from Portland and brought up another kid named Jimmie Foxx.

Gibson joined the A's at an extremely interesting point in that club's history. As almost everyone knows, Connie Mack broke up his great combination that had won four pennants in five years after losing the World Series of 1914 to the Braves, finished dead last for seven years in a row and did not capture the championship again until 1929.

But, in 1924, the team, which had finished seventh in 1922 and sixth in 1923, showed signs of respectability and climbed to fifth. It was an exciting year because Mack had brought up a young center fielder, Paul Strand, who had made 325 hits, including 43 homers, while batting .394 for Salt Lake. But Strand did not find American League pitching to his liking and was hitting .228 in early July when Mack decided he never would hit and shipped him to Toledo, along with pitcher Rollie Naylor, for Good Time Bill Lamar, a rollicking outfielder.

Everything had been expected of Strand, and he had produced little. Nothing was expected of Lamar, but he began to pound the ball so steadily that he became a Shibe Park favorite and ended up at .330, then raised his average to .356 in 1925. Strange to say, you hardly ever hear Lamar's name mentioned today, and Gibson and I wondered about it out loud. When I last heard of Good Time Bill, he was said to be enjoying himself in the

Washington, D.C., area, but I have never been able to get in touch with him.

"We had a pretty fair team," Gibson recalled. "It was Max Bishop's first year, and his tremendous judgment of pitches was apparent from the start. It was the first year for Simmons, too, and there was a lot of speculation about whether he would hit using that foot-in-the-bucket stance, but I always thought he would hit because it was only his foot that he moved, never his butt, and he really tore into the ball. And don't think he couldn't run to first base! Joe Hauser had a good year at first, as did Bing Miller in right. Jimmie Dykes played second and third and Chick Galloway short.

"Pitching was our weakness, but we had Byron Harriss, Ed Rommel with his knuckler, Fritz Heimach, Roy Meeker, Sam Gray and Stan Baumgartner."

I told him that Baumgartner had later become the Philadelphia correspondent of The Sporting News and that Heimach had recently retired as a policeman in Miami Beach and was planning to move to Homosassa, Fla., the place made famous by Dazzy Vance, and that Meeker had died in the training camp of the Reds at Orlando while still an active pitcher in 1929. But these were all things that he knew, and once again I marveled at the way that old ball players know about each other.

Gibson played for Fritz Maisel at Wilkes-Barre in 1925, asked to be traded to a team in the South, and when this was denied him, bought his release for $1,000. He signed with Jacksonville in 1926, Charlotte in 1927, Alexandria in 1928, Spartanburg in 1929 and Baton Rouge for the 1930 season.

He batted .336 in the Cotton States League for Baton Rouge, but the Depression had begun, baseball salaries were low, so he took a good job as cashier for the Duval Spirits Co., which distributed whiskey from Jacksonville to 73 counties.

He came back here in 1935 to become occupied with spirits of a different sort, replacing his father, who had served as superintendent of cemeteries for 29 years.

We walked around the grounds, and I was struck by the sudden realization that almost all the tombstones bore Scotch-Irish names. Another old player who lives here is Ed Levy, who had trials as a first baseman with the Phillies and Yankees at the time of World War II. He works as a golf pro at Hogansville, a few miles north on the road to Newnan.

We went to Levy's house, but he was not in. His daughter apologized for not inviting us in, but said she had the Hong Kong flu. Too bad, for she looked better with it than many girls do without it.

AN ALL NEW-YEAR'S TEAM

JANUARY 4, 1969. WHENEVER THERE OCCURS THE TURNING of another year, my thoughts invariably stray to Wee Willie Keeler, greatest of bunters and one of the most accomplished place-hitters of all time, a star of the old Orioles and Hall of Famer whose often-quoted phrase, "Hit 'em where they ain't," might provide a resourceful philosophy for batters of today.

For Willie died on New Year's Day in 1923. He had been suffering from pneumonia at his home in Brooklyn, and on New Year's Eve a group of his neighbors, in a misguided attempt to cheer him up, paid him a call in his bedroom.

Willie sat up in bed to join the party, but the effort cost him his life, as his heart gave out the next day.

But usually we think of the new year as a time of birth, and it so happens that there have been 38 major league players who were born on the first day of the year. To name them all would be tedious, but you could put together a fair team of New Year babies, including two members of the Hall of Fame: Tim Keefe, a pitcher who won 345 games, most of them for the Giants; and Hank Greenberg, still recalled vividly as a producer of home runs, and one of the most memorable of the Tigers.

Greenberg, more at home at first base, would have to be put in left field on this mythical team, to strengthen an outfield that would show Ethan Allen in center and Hack Miller in right.

Allen this year retired as baseball coach at Yale, and is enjoying life at Chapel Hill, N.C. His powers of observation are as keen as the batting eye that gave him an average of .300 for 13 major league seasons. Last summer when I referred in a column to Bill Lohrman as a sinkerball pitcher, Allen wrote to say, "Lohrman didn't throw a sinker but a sailer." Apparently Ethan kept a book on everything that was thrown to him, and Lohrman later confirmed Allen's judgment of what he threw.

Miller, with the Cubs from 1922 through 1925, is not so well remembered, but he left a lifetime mark of .323, and he was one of the strongest physical specimens who ever took to the diamond. He actually used a bat that weighed 67 ounces, 15 ounces more than the heaviest swung by Babe Ruth.

An infield of players born on New Year's Day would include Earl Torgeson at first; Sherry Robertson of the Senators, at second; Joe Benes of the Cardinals, at short; and Foster Castleman of the Giants, at third. Keefe's catcher could be Dave Zearfoss, who was with the Giants in the '90s, or Randy Bobb, the youngster Leo Durocher presented to the Chicago public in 1968. Other pitchers might include Charlie Devens, Harvard's gift to the Yankees, Carl Scheib of the Athletics, or Bumpus Jones of the Reds.

Jones wandered into the Cincinnati clubhouse on the final day of the season in 1892 and asked Charlie Comiskey, then completing his first year as manager of the Reds, for a trial. Comiskey let him pitch the game that day against the Pirates; Jones then turned in a no-hitter while working on a lineup that included Jake Beckley, George Van Haltren, Foghorn Miller and a young catcher, Connie Mack. But in 1893, he took his lumps, never won another game in the majors, and was passed on to the Giants.

Available to manage the New Year squad would be Bill McGunnigle, who won consecutive pennants for Brooklyn in 1889 and 1890 in two different leagues. He led the Bridegrooms, as his team was then called, to the championship of the American Association, then moved over to the National League to repeat.

McGunnigle was the first of the famous sign stealers, and he anticipated Connie Mack in waving his scorecard to signal his players. But his strangest innovation was never put in use. Not until his retirement did he tell the writers about his plan to put a small metal plate in the batters box, connected by means of an underground wire with a button on the player's bench.

Each batter was supposed to put one foot over the metal plate, and the manager intended to instruct them by electrical shock what kind of ball the pitcher was about to let loose. But electricians told him the idea was impractical, and shock therapy was never applied to the Brooklyns.

The first New Year's baby to reach the majors was Tom Mansell, one of the three ball-playing brothers from Auburn, N.Y. Tom, or Brick, as he was called, joined Syracuse the same season, and John, the youngest, was recruited by the Athletics in 1882. All of the Mansells were outfielders, and long before the Alous were ever heard of, they formed the picket line in an exhibition game at Albany.

There is not one Mansell family listed in the Auburn phonebook today, and unless they left daughters who married, it is unlikely that they can ever be traced.

Tom was probably the best of the trio, and although the oldest, he outlived the others, not dying until 1934. For many years he was well known in Auburn for delivering the mail, and it was vaguely recalled there that he had once played baseball professionally.

The end of his career was hastened by a strange accident. While playing for the Reds in 1883, he entered the lobby of the Grand Hotel one night, walked to the bank of elevators, stepped carefully into an empty shaft and found himself in the basement with a badly wrenched knee.

Everybody makes mistakes.

THE STRATEGY OF HOUK

JANUARY 11, 1969. RALPH HOUK SAT COMFORTABLY IN HIS living room, oblivious to splashing in the swimming pool behind him, and gathered his thoughts in a neat bundle.

"Things look better for the Yankees than they did a year ago," he said. "I'm very happy about the promised return of Bobby Murcer and Jerry Kenney from the military. I've always thought that a good infielder could play the outfield, so it looks like I'll use one of them on third and move the other to the outfield. Then I could keep Tom Tresh at short.

"And I'll tell you something else. The Yankees will be running more. Last year we stole 90 bases, more than any Yankee team since 1944. A lot of people think the lowering of the pitching mound will result in more bases on balls. Well, what's wrong with that? More walks mean more runners, and more runners mean more action and scoring. I think you'll find that more hitters will be going for singles, and that batting averages will rise."

Last year, the Yankees had a team batting mark of .214, and that Houk was able to land his club in fifth spot under such horrendous circumstances is a tribute to his great skill.

Houk is in the peculiar position of not knowing how good a player he himself would have been had he been used regularly. Although he spent eight years with the Yankees, he watched Yogi Berra do almost all the club's catching. In six of those eight years, Ralph appeared in ten games or less.

"You're a good judge of players," I told him. "Suppose you had to hand in a scouting report on Ralph Houk. What would you say about him?"

He thought for a minute and then responded, "I'd have to say I was a good catcher and not a bad hitter, but with no power."

But there is no correlation between major league stardom as a player and later success as a manager. Joe McCarthy, for example, a great Yankee manager, never had played in a major league game.

"I think the fact that I spent so much time in the bullpen helped me when I turned to managing," Ralph said thoughtfully. "I used to sit out there with pitchers who weren't in the starting rotation, and I learned exactly what went through their minds. I think I know how to handle them now to get the most out of them."

In his minor league days, Houk made the all-star team in every circuit he was in. When he joined the Bombers in 1947, he caught whenever the club faced a southpaw, appearing in 41 games. But then Berra started working every day.

Bill Essick spotted him catching for Lawrence, Kan., in the Ban Johnson

League in 1938, the year he finished high school, and signed him to a Joplin contract for $75 a month. They sent him to Neosho of the Arkansas-Missouri League, where he made his debut in 1939, playing for Dennis Burns, a spitball pitcher who had been with the Athletics in 1923 and 1924.

He hit .286, went 2-for-5 on the league's all-star team that met Fayetteville in mid-season, and was the only player in the four-club league that ever rose to the majors.

"I figured I was worth more money when they advanced me to Joplin in 1940," he said with a laugh, "so I held out for $100 a month. They wouldn't give it to me, but they did give me $90. I must say that, ever since that time, the Yankee organization has been good to me."

At first, the climb was slow. At Joplin, he hit .313 and almost had a fist fight after a play at the plate with a young Topeka shortstop, Bill Rigney, a threatened brawl that he and the present manager of the Angels have joked about regularly for the past eight years.

Then Houk advanced to Augusta in 1941, where he first caught such future Yankees as Joe Page and Bill Bevens and was just ripening when the Army called him to action in World War II. He served with valor, rose to the rank of major, then emerged to find himself bunched behind Berra along with such other catchers in the chain as Bill Drescher, Charlie Silvera and Gus Niarhos.

After training with Kansas City, he put in a year at Beaumont before hitting the top.

Houk caught his first game with the Yankees on April 26, 1947, and must have thought that American League pitching was a soft touch as he made three hits in as many trips off Mickey Haefner, Bobo Newsom and Walt Masterson.

He broke into the game on the next day also. It was Babe Ruth Day, and a throng of 58,339 filled Yankee Stadium to pay tribute to the team's folk hero. It was the first time Ralph had met the Bambino and he was properly awed.

One of Houk's greatest attributes as a manager is psychological, his ability to keep his men in the the right frame of mind. His optimism is perpetual. I asked him if this was simply his nature, as it is in the case of Ernie Banks, or whether it is a sort of premeditated, Norman Vincent Peale plan of accenting the positive.

"Look," he said, "some writers have practically challenged me because I thought the Yankees could win a particular game and said so.

"But I always feel that way. If I have a pitcher with a sound arm going, I always figure we have a chance."

There certainly isn't anything wrong with that.

CHAPMAN/CHAPLIN

JANUARY 18, 1969. BERT CHAPMAN AND I SAT ON HIS PRIvate pier on a recent afternoon here in Sanford, Fla., soaking up sun and looking out over Crystal Lake. Near shore you could see algae growing at the bottom and the fringes of the lake were choked with watergrass, but far out it was clear and calm, and beyond you could see groves of pine and oak that gave the landscape a sense of orderliness and peace.

Behind us, on a sun porch of the big house, Mrs. Chapman was giving painting lessons to a pair of lovely teenage girls. One of them was working on abstract designs in oil, the other with more conventional water colors.

"I wonder," Chapman said, "if I'm not the only player in the history of baseball to walk the first four times I batted in the big leagues."

"I don't know," I told him, "It would take a lot of checking. But I wonder if you aren't the first player to take the field against Babe Ruth in your first big league game, and against Ty Cobb in your second major league contest."

Bert Edgar Chapman, a retired celery grower and manufacturer of concrete blocks, was born on a cotton farm near Pelzer, S.C., September 25, 1893.

For three years starting in 1920, he was a third-string catcher for the Red Sox under the name of Chaplin, a circumstance that requires some explanation.

"I was managing Sanford in the Florida State League in 1919," he told me, "and we won the first half easily. During the second half, the other clubs began cheating and using class men. The president of the league was a fellow named Walter Rose. He was an Orlando realtor and partial to the Orlando team, which won the second half.

"Every club in the league was cheating. Bradenton brought in a pitcher from the Virginia League, and we noticed three players from that league playing under assumed names.

"Maybe you think baseball wasn't mean and cutthroat in those days! I remember the day the playoff started between Sanford and Orlando, the Reds and the Black Sox were playing the fixed World Series and we posted the scores at the Sanford park. But our series was every bit as controversial. Rose came up to me before the game and handed me a typewritten list of instructions for the playoff, and one of the rules was against freak deliveries. Well, I had this emery-ball pitcher, Alexander Moore, and I was fixin' to pitch him. So I cussed Rose out, and I told him I'd fill the bleachers with the railroad mechanics who ate umpires live. Anyway, we won four straight after losing the first two games."

"The Spalding Guide says Sanford and Orlando each won three before the series was abandoned because of a dispute," I told him.

"I don't care," he said. "We won four games. You can check it in the Orlando paper. But then I got this telegram from Rose telling me I'd been fined $500 and suspended from Organized Ball. I still don't know what for. So I decided to change my name and play somewhere."

"Everybody called me Chappy, so I changed from Chapman to Chaplin and just joined Carrollton of the Georgia State League. Not a single person in Sanford knew where I had gone, and when the Red Sox bought me from Carrollton, no one knew who I was."

Chapman (Chaplin) made his debut on September 4 in the first game of a double-header with the Yankees, batting for Harry Harper and drawing a walk from Bob Shawkey.

A crowd of 33,027, then a record for Fenway, saw Ruth hit a home run in each game, his 45th and 46th.

Bert didn't appear in another until September 17, a wild game at Navin Field which Detroit won, 14-13, in 12 innings. He went to bat three times as a relief catcher and drew three more walks.

"I had started playing in 1914 with Waycross," Chapman said. "We played the Athletics before the season opened and I hit against Eddie Plank, the first big leaguer I'd ever seen. I bunted, and Eddie Collins picked up the ball and just nipped me. In 1915, I played amateur ball at Miami and a man offered me seven lots for $700 three blocks west of the courthouse.

"They'd be worth three or four million today. The next year I went with Zack Taylor to Eufala, Ala.

"Where do you think I was when we got into the First World War? Just on top of the Washington Monument, that's all. I'd gone there to do some sightseeing, and while I was up there, I heard all this shouting, and steamboats tootin' and everything. So I walked down the steps, and joined the Navy.

"I just wasn't a good enough hitter to play regularly in the majors, but I had a good eye and waited the pitchers out. When Frank Chance came on to manage the Red Sox in 1923, he sent me to Shreveport, and I learned more about baseball under Ira Thomas than I ever learned at Boston. Later I was traded to Mobile for Dutch Henry and Denny Williams, and I stayed in the game until 1929, when I ended up managing Tampa."

We strolled back through the house, as the painters stopped their work and smiled a greeting. Chapman walked out to the car with me.

"I still follow baseball," he said, "and there are some mighty good players around.

"Bill Jacobson has been down to see me — Baby Doll. Remember him?

And Mrs. Roy Ellam. We hear from her. Roy was a shortstop with the Reds and Pirates. He's been dead about 20 years."

FRANCIS THE RED

JANUARY 25, 1969.   I HAD TOLD FRANCIS THE RED BARRETT that I would be at his Leesburg, Fla., Phillips 66 station at 7 a.m. and I was ten minutes early, but at that, I was not the first customer. A dilapidated bus loaded with orange pickers had preceded me and was monopolizing the attention of the proprietor.

First of all, you have to distinguish between Francis The Red Barrett and Charlie The Red Barrett. The Cardinals, who seldom have had a shortage of anything, had no shortage of Red Barretts and employed both.

Charlie The Red, who was also with Cincinnati and Boston in the National League and who was addicted to crooning in night clubs, now runs a warehouse for Sealtest at Wilson, N.C. Francis The Red, a sturdy man of 55, appeared for the Cardinals in 1939, the Red Sox in 1944-45, the Braves in 1946 and the Pirates in 1950. Both Barretts were righthanded pitchers.

Disneyland soon will change the map of this part of Florida. Leesburg is metropolitan enough to have a jelly factory, and mines of kaolin to supply clay for chinaware, but the scarlet poinsettias in full bloom at this time of year give the town a touch of rural beauty. While I was waiting for Red to stuff the dilapidated bus with gasoline, I noticed a sign in the station alerting customers to the fact that they could leave their orders for Apalachicola oysters in any quantity up to a bushel.

Now the thirsty bus was sated and Red was able to relax and talk about his baseball days. In addition to the station, he owns real estate in town and does a lucrative business hauling sand and gravel. The station is on U.S. 41 at the eastern edge of town, the road to Orlando.

"I'm not sure," Barrett said, "but I think I'm the first ball player turned out by South Florida. I was born at Fort Lauderdale in 1913. You'd never believe it looking at that city today, but at the time I was born, there were only 25 families living there. My father had come there about 1906 or 1908. I can remember as a kid seeing a priest, Father Callahan, in a canoe with a couple of Indians, riding down a creek to say Mass."

Thinking about it gave Barrett a wistful look, and as you envisioned the scene he remembered, you thought of William Lamprecht's brilliant painting, "Marquette on the Mississippi." Jacques Marquette, of course, was the Jesuit who, with Louis Joliet, explored the greatest river of this continent as far south as the Arkansas.

"Anyway," Red told me, "I pitched semipro ball around Florida and someone spotted me and wrote a letter to Sid Keener, who was then a baseball writer in St. Louis and later your director at Cooperstown. Keener gave the letter to the Cardinal office, and I heard from Harold Roettger, inviting me to the Rochester training camp at Bartow."

That was in 1935.

"I didn't know if I was good enough to pitch in pro ball or not," Barrett said. "But Joe Sugden — remember him, the old catcher? His fingers were so gnarled, when you shook hands with him it was like shaking hands with a pound of walnuts — Sugden liked me, I heard, because I had a good curve to go with my fast one, and one day Tony Kaufmann came to me and said, 'Kid, you've got it made.'"

But the road to the National League was a long one, with stops at Albany and Columbus in Georgia, Huntington (where he played with Walt Alston and Marty Marion), Union Springs, Ala., Mobile and Houston.

"I got my chance by winning 13 and losing seven at Houston in 1939. What a pitching staff we had there! Harry Brecheen, Ted Wilks, Ernie White, Murry Dickson, Spud Krist, Howard Pollet! Pretty good staff for a minor league team, eh?"

At the end of the season, Barrett reported to the Cardinals, along with Johnny Hopp, among others, a circumstance that provided him with his most vivid big league memory.

"We went over to Cincinnati for a series the last week of the season with a chance to win the pennant," Red said, "but the Reds broke even with us, and that was enough for them to win. But I'll never forget one particular play when Hopp was put in as a pinch-runner on second, and Ernie Lombardi picked him off right away with just about the greatest throw I ever saw a catcher make.

"I never made it as a regular starter with the Cardinals," Barrett added.

"Then, during the war years with the Red Sox, Joe Cronin used me mostly in relief.

"I also had some good years at Columbus, but more important, I met a girl there named Helen Schneemilch. We were married there at St. Mary's Church, the same church where her mother was married. George Trautman, who ran the minor leagues, was at the wedding and so was Bob Hooey, who used to write baseball for the Ohio State Journal."

A panel truck with a bullet hole in the windshield drove up for service. Red waved at the driver, but was in no hurry to attend to him.

"I'd have to say I've had a happy life," he went on. "Helen and I have three kids. JoAnn Frances is married and lives at Fort Lewis, Wash. Michael is in the Navy and just finished his tour of Vietnam. Patricia's only 14 and she's still with us.

"See the bullet hole? Luckiest thing you ever heard of. Some fellow along the highway shooting deer, just missed the driver. Grazed his ear and went out the back."

FOUL-BALL ARTIST

FEBRUARY 1, 1969. "THE STRANGEST THING THAT EVER happened to me in baseball," Walter Kimmick said, "was when I was a shortstop with the Phillies in 1926. This fellow — I'd seen him around the park — came to me under the stands and said, 'Kimmick, can you hit foul balls?' 'Sure I can,' I told him. 'I don't believe it,' he said. 'Well,' I replied, 'I guess I could hit ten in a row. Naturally, I wouldn't try it if there were men on base, but if I come up with nobody on, you just watch.'

"They told me later the fellow made $10,000 betting I would hit fouls," Kimmick said with a laugh. "He'd bet a thousand I'd foul the next pitch and let the money ride.

"I didn't know he was a gambler, so I hit one after another. But I never saw him after that."

Kimmick, a pipe-smoking man with blue eyes and white hair, will be 72 on Memorial Day. A retired industrial worker from Turtle Creek, Pa., a suburb of Pittsburgh, he and his wife occupy a luxury condominium one block from the Atlantic Ocean in Fort Lauderdale. But he wishes he were back in Pennsylvania, a preference that in January makes him virtually unique. On a recent morning we sat in the enormous, almost empty lobby, and over the background noise of a maid's vacuum cleaner, he told me about his baseball life.

"I was just a kid around Pittsburgh," he said, "when I started playing with the Westinghouse Air Brakes. I had this friend named Roy Steele, and he knew Burt Shotton, who was Branch Rickey's Sunday manager and all-round assistant on the Cardinals. This was in 1919. So Roy told Shotton about me, and one day when the Cardinals were in Pittsburgh, they gave me a trial. I guess I looked pretty good, because they told me to report to St. Louis in September. I stopped at a place called the Beers Hotel. On my first turn in batting practice, I hit two balls out of the park.

"'Who is that kid?' Rickey asked, and when they told him he said, 'Well, get that dark suit off him and put a white one on. I wouldn't be afraid to use him in a game.'

"So they let me hit in batting practice. One oldtimer, Fritz Mollwitz, didn't like it. He ordered me out of the cage, but Hornsby told me, 'Don't pay any attention to him.'

"I weighed 190 then, and after Hornsby told Mollwitz I was the amateur heavyweight boxing champion of Pennsylvania, which wasn't true, Mollwitz let me alone.

"The first time I was used, they sent me up to hit for Bill Sherdel against Art Nehf. Boy, was I scared! My knees were knocking together. Bill Klem was the umpire. The first pitch was a strike, and the next was under my chin. Klem dusted off the plate, and said, 'Don't be scared, kid. Take your cut.' Nehf then threw me the prettiest curve you ever saw, right over, and Klem said, 'Ball two.' Frank Snyder was catching, and he yelled, 'What?' 'Ball two,' Klem repeated. 'You remember your first time up in the big league, don't you, Snyder?' Then I hit a line drive to the third baseman.

"The Cardinals must have had 70 kids working out. I don't know where they all came from. So that winter Rickey sent me to the Pirates for the waiver price — $1,500. I guess Pittsburgh figured they could use a hometown boy. But it rained most of the time at Hot Springs and we got in only 12 days of work. I batted only once all spring and struck out. I was so disgusted I jumped to Oil City in that outlaw league that was paying players four times what they'd get in the majors. Why, they gave Jake Pitler a house and a poolroom, and they were paying me a thousand a month.

"But I was young and thought the majors was the place, so I got straightened out with Garry Herrmann's office and joined Waynesboro of the Blue Ridge League. That fall, the Reds bought me.

"I stayed with 'em three years, but seldom got to play since they had Daubert and Fonseca and Bohne and Caveney and Groh and Pinelli in the infield, and finally they sent me to Vernon of the Pacific Coast League, in a deal for Jakie May.

"I hit .315, and the Phillies gave 'em Phil Weinert, a lefthanded pitcher, for me.

"In 1925, I played half the schedule and hit .305 for the Phils, but somehow I hurt my arm, and the next year I had trouble throwing. Boy, was my arm ever sore! I signed with Buffalo, but couldn't throw, and then tried Nashville. And do you know there was a trainer who put something hot on my arm that helped it some? Did it ever burn! I asked him what was in it, and he said, 'Gasoline, whiskey and mothballs.'

"Then I played for Seattle in 1927, managed by Bill Killefer, and we had a fine ball club there, and a great bunch of fellows — Jimmy Hudgens, Pid Purdy, Marty Callaghan, Walter Schmidt, Ed Brandt, Jack Knight.

"I hit .359 that year, but the arm never did come around entirely, and I knew I wasn't going anywhere. I was at Mobile in '28 — I remember Milt Stock and Al Niehaus were there, too — and then finished up at Waterbury and Bridgeport. I led the Eastern League in '29, and someone gave me a silver bat and ball, but they cut my salary from $750 a month to $500."

The maid had finished her vacuum cleaning, and Kimmick sat there puffing on his pipe.

"Well," I said, "if you had it all to do over, would you play professional baseball?"

"Are you kiddin'?" he asked.

THE SAD TALE OF ROY SPENCER

FEBRUARY 8, 1969. TO BE A LUCKLESS FISHERMAN IS SAD enough, but when that circumstance is combined with the flu, chronic insomnia and impecunious old age, the resulting symphony of fate is almost funereal.

Roy Spencer has been a catcher for most of his 69 years, first of baseballs, then of fish. Now he is too old and ill to catch either. When I happened upon him here on a recent day, and he told me about his situation, the irony of the name of this village on Gasparilla Bay (Placida) became almost unbearable. For there is nothing placid about his tortured existence.

"My entire income — and it's from Social Security — is $61 a month," Roy told me. "I have to pay $15 a month to park my trailer and another $5 to the marina for my boat. The weather's been so bad, the fish haven't been biting, and the last time I went out, the only thing I caught was the flu. I used to have a 32-foot boat and live on it and go out for kingfish and grouper. Now I just fish the bay for trout, and by the time I pay for my trailer, I've got $41 a month for food, tobacco and fuel for my boat. I worry about it so much I can't sleep."

Spencer played professionally for two decades starting in 1921, and in his time he caught for the Pirates, Senators, Indians, Giants and Dodgers.

"I grew up at Norfolk, where my father was a shipbuilder," Roy said, "although I was born at Scranton, a little place in North Carolina. When I got out of high school at Norfolk, Detroit wanted to sign me, but I had an older brother, Elmo, who had played some pro ball at Elizabethton in Tennessee, and he told me I'd do better signing with a minor league team, so I went with Raleigh. That was in 1921.

"Well, Detroit still wanted me and bought me. I spent the last month of the season on the Tiger bench. The next spring, they sent me to Denver, but I seldom got into a game, so I wired Frank Navin, 'Send me anywhere; I want to play.' So he shipped me to Omaha.

"The Tigers trained at Augusta in 1923 and I met a girl there I wanted to marry, so I asked to stay there with the Sally League team, and Navin let me. But, that winter, Detroit traded me to Birmingham in a deal for Earl

Whitehill, I think. Anyway, I had a good year at Birmingham, and Pittsburgh bought me."

Roy remained with the Pirates three years, but could not win a regular job with Earl Smith and Johnny Gooch ahead of him. In 1926, however, he broke into 28 games and batted .395. To make room for Rollie Hemsley, Pittsburgh sent Spencer to Indianapolis in 1929, and there he caught 140 games and batted .296. Scouts trailed him all around the American Association.

"I must have been there on some sort of a cover-up deal," he said. "Scouts used to come to me and say, 'I'd like to buy you, but you're not for sale.' Whatever it was, Judge Landis found out about it and made me a free agent. I got $25,000 to sign with Washington, but that included my 1930 salary." At Washington, with Muddy Ruel nearing the end of the line, Roy became a regular. In 1931, he was behind the plate in 145 games, more than any receiver in the American League, but, after the 1932 season, the Senators shipped him to Cleveland for Luke Sewell.

"I put in a full year and part of another with the Indians, then went to the International League. I spent 1934 with Buffalo and 1935 with Baltimore," Spencer added. "Then Bill Terry bought me for the Giants in 1936, and I landed with a pennant-winner. Gus Mancuso did most of the catching and Harry Danning was also ahead of me. I didn't get into the World Series, even as a pinch-hitter, as I'd hurt my arm sliding. Then I was sold to Brooklyn, and drew my last release in 1938. I remember Heinie Manush got his pink slip on the same day, as we both lived in Sarasota.

"Did you know I was with the Dodger champions in 1941?" Roy asked. "Hardly anyone knows that. I stayed out of the game entirely in 1939 and 1940, but in 1941 I was with the Dodgers as an 'in case' catcher. I was to be used only 'in case' someone didn't show up. Charlie Dressen carried a blank release in his pocket at all times — he was coaching there for Durocher — and he could have released any player he wanted and put me on the active list in five minutes. But it never happened, although on Decoration Day Mickey Owen was late reporting to the park, and I thought I was going on the list sure. But, at the last minute, Owen showed up. I caught in the bullpen all year, and they cut me in for $2,500 in World Series money."

He stood there outside his trailer sniffing the wind. The sea is in his weatherbeaten face, and you got the idea that if he only felt better, he could try to fish some more.

"I don't know," he said. "Maybe I could get a job here helping repair boats."

There didn't seem to be any more to say. But if you once knew Roy Spencer and would like to cheer him up, you can reach him at Placida, Fla. He'll get the letter addressed just that way. He isn't going anywhere.

COONEY'S SAGE

FEBRUARY 15, 1969. HERE IN THE SWANK WHITFIELD ESTATES
section of booming Sarasota, Fla., Johnny Cooney, who spent 20 years in the
major leagues and another six in the minors, often has occasion to sit in the
luxury of his trophy-laden living room and think back over the strange
happenings of an unparalleled career.

For the Cooney story has more angles than Euclid ever heard of.

"I think," he told me during a recent visit, "that I'm the only man who ever
played in the National and American Leagues, coached in both of those
leagues, managed in both and umpired in one.

"This is technical, I admit. My career as an American League manager
lasted only one day with the White Sox, when Al Lopez was attending his
mother's funeral, and my career as a National League umpire was for only one
game," Cooney said. "You remember how the umpires used to travel from
New York to Boston by boat? Well, on this day, they were fog-bound, so
Freddy Fitzsimmons, representing the Giants, umpired on the bases and I was
behind the plate, representing the Braves."

But that is only the start of the Cooney saga. It's no wonder that the
scrapbooks kept by his wife, Alice, over the years are bulging.

Here are just a few of the aspects of his baseball life that make Johnny
(Alice always calls him "Jack") virtually unique:

1. He is the son of a ball player and a brother of a ball player. His father,
Jimmy, was a shortstop for Cap Anson with Chicago for three years starting
in 1890. His brother, also Jimmy, was a big league infielder from 1917 to 1928
and once made an unassisted triple play.

2. Johnny was one of that rare breed who batted right and threw left. The
only other players of prominence who did this were Jimmy Ryan, Hal Chase
and Rube Bressler.

3. A fine major league pitcher, he injured his arm severely, turned to the
outfield and became an accomplished star at that position, as a few great ones
like George Van Haltren, Elmer Smith and Smoky Joe Wood had done
before him.

4. When Rogers Hornsby batted for the unbelievable average of .424 for
the Cardinals in 1924, Cooney was the only pitcher in the league to hold him
hitless in three different games.

"And I'll tell you something else," Cooney added, "I could be wrong about
this, but I don't think I am. I honestly don't believe that in 20 years in the
majors I ever struck out twice in the same game."

It all started somewhere, and the somewhere was Willimantic, Conn., in the season of 1920, when Johnny was 19 and a southpaw with a wicked fast ball. There he pitched two no-hit games in semi-pro ranks and also knocked off the Boston Braves in an exhibition.

"What happened was really funny," Cooney chuckled. "Paul Krichell was scouting for the Red Sox and saw me and brought me to Boston to meet Ed Barrow, who then managed the Red Sox. I took my semi-pro manager along and I was supposed to get $500 to sign and $300 a month. Barrow started to write out a check, and my manager yelled, 'No checks. Cash or nothing!'

"Well, you should have seen Barrow. I thought he was going to explode. 'What?'he thundered. 'Do you mean to tell me that a check signed by the Boston Red Sox isn't good enough for you?' So, of course, after that the Red Sox wouldn't sign me at all. I had to go with the Braves, and I got a better deal — $500 to sign and $400 a month. I had beat the Braves, as I said, and also they had this pitcher, Eddie Eayrs — he was from Providence and told them about me, too."

The Braves at the time were owned by George Washington Grant, a New Yorker who was close to Charlie Stoneham, who owned the Giants. It seemed that every time the Giants needed a pitcher, Stoneham would call Grant and come up with an Artie Nehf or a Hugh McQuillan.

In this way, the Giants won four consecutive National League pennants, starting in 1921. But Stoneham and John McGraw never could get Cooney.

"I understand the Giants offered $75,000 for my contract once," Johnny said. "But the Braves wouldn't take it. And, on another occasion, I heard that McGraw offered Bill Terry even up for me."

So Cooney remained with the Braves, and the arm injury was an event of the 1926 season. He does not think it was the result of any particular pitch, but just a soreness that started and grew to terrible proportions. He submitted to an operation, but then paralysis set in, and it appeared unlikely that he would ever play again. Even today his left arm is three or four inches shorter than the right. For him to have come back from such a severe injury is a tremendous tribute to his courage.

He remained with the Braves through the season of 1930, then began a tour of duty in the minors.

It was Casey Stengel who brought him back to the National League as an outfielder with the Dodgers, at the age of 34, in 1935. It was a shrewd judgment, but not surprising when you learn that Stengel rates Cooney with Joe DiMaggio and Edd Roush as a centerfielder.

Johnny remained with the Dodgers until 1938, then went back to the Braves for five years, batting .318 in 1940 and .319 in 1941. Then, after another whirl with the Dodgers, he ended his big league days with the Yankees in 1944. He finished that year at Toronto and closed out his active career in 1945 with Kansas City.

Cooney also came close once to owning a piece of the Braves. He put in $15,000 at a time when the franchise was shaky, but Judge Landis vetoed the deal.

PRINCETON

FEBRUARY 22, 1969. THE SELECTION OF BOWIE KUHN TO RUN baseball is one of the happiest and most radical developments in the history of the game.

He is no figurehead. Do not be misled by your previous unfamiliarity with his name. He is a tireless, intelligent physical giant gifted with imagination, an attorney sympathetic to the nuances of the complex legal situation confronting baseball, a man capable of first restoring order in labor relations and then plunging into a program designed to make baseball get in tune with the times. Best of all, he grew up in a ball park.

He is also a graduate of Princeton, so color him orange and black! Not since the late Arch Murray roamed the press boxes has Old Nassau been prominent in the game's affairs, so the appointment is, in effect, a restoration.

It is noteworthy that the game's five commissioners have attended five different institutions of higher learning. Judge Kenesaw M. Landis never actually attended college, but received his legal training first at the YMCA Law School in Cincinnati and then the Union Law School, which is not part of Northwestern University, in Chicago. A.B. (Happy) Chandler attended Transylvania, Ford C. Frick went to DePauw, and William Eckert, of course, is a graduate of West Point.

Princeton has been prominent in baseball affairs for a century, or ever since Joseph McElroy Mann, along with Ham Avery of Yale, picked up the curve ball from Candy Cummings and used it in collegiate ranks. Mann certainly could have made his mark in the majors, but like Avery and another Yale pitcher, Amos Alonzo Stagg, he spurned professional offers and went into publishing, working for the house of Scribner until his death at Bloomfield, N.J., November, 1919.

So far as I am able to determine, there have been only 17 major league players with Princeton backgounds. By far the most prominent was Moe Berg, the erudite catcher who started as a shortstop with the Dodgers in 1923, and who then worked behind the bat for the White Sox, Senators, Indians and Red Sox in a career that extended through 1939. For sheer intellectual accomplishment, baseball never has seen anyone even vaguely resembling Moe. His thesis on Sanskrit is a valuable reference work at the

Library of Congress, and he speaks English, Latin, Greek, French, Italian, German, Spanish, Russian, Japanese and Hebrew.

Princeton's first gift to baseball was Leonidas Pyrrhus Funkhouser, who played under the name of Lee and appeared in four games for St. Louis of the National League in 1877. He was of Swiss descent and became a physician, serving as head surgeon at St. Mark's Hospital in Chicago. He then abandoned the medical profession, became auditor for the Pacific Express Co. in Omaha and was an executive with banks, utilities and insurance companies before his death at Hendersonville, N.C. in 1912.

Then came Daniel D. Bickham, who left Princeton in 1886 to pitch one game for Cincinnati, which he won, staggering the distance to beat the Athletics, 12-11. Bickman, who became publisher of the Dayton (O.) Journal, lived to be 86, and not long before his death in 1961, I interviewed him at his home, and he told me how he happened to leave the game.

"John Montgomery Ward talked me out of making baseball my profession," he said. "'Look, Bickman,' he told me, 'this is no business for you. I don't mind it because I like to handle myself with my fists, but if I were you, I would go into something else.'"

A really famous Princeton pitcher was Homer Hiller Henry Hillebrand, who could have joined any major league team he chose upon graduating in 1905. He picked the Pirates and remained with them for more than two years, although he was sparingly used. Unless I am greatly mistaken, he is still living in Elsinore, Calif., and will be 90 years old in October.

In two different years, three different Princeton men made their major league debuts. In 1909, Bill Cooney, Fred Cook and Bobby Vaughn appeared, Cooney pitching for the Red Sox, Cook pitching for Cleveland under the name of Winchell, and Vaughn playing second base for the Yankees, then more often called Highlanders. Vaughn later bobbed up in the Federal League as the regular third baseman for Fielder Jones' St. Louis Terriers.

Again, in 1912, a Princeton trio appeared. Roger Salmon, a southpaw, pitched for the Athletics, as did Steve White for the Senators, and Charlie Sterrett was a combination first baseman and outfielder for the Yanks.

The last Princeton player was Dave Sisler, pitching member of that famous baseball family who joined the Red Sox in 1956 and who also saw service with the Tigers, Senators and Reds.

Other Princeton men who reached the big leagues were Hy Gunning, a first baseman with the Red Sox in 1911; Charles B. Lear, a pitcher with the Reds in 1914 who was, of course, nicknamed King; Ralph (Ted) Reed, Bill McKechnie's third baseman with the Newark Federals in 1915; Waddy MacPhee, a Brooklyn boy who joined the Giants in 1922; Tom McNamara, who pinch-hit once for the Pirates in 1922; and John Easton, an outfielder

Bob Carpenter tried with the Phillies in 1955. Easton had been president of his senior class at Princeton.

One of these men — and please do not write to ask me which one — inserted an amusing aside on his Hall of Fame questionnaire. Asked the maiden name of his wife and the date of his marriage, he wrote the following: "It was just a minor league affair, and the details are uninteresting."

GRAVY ON APPLE PIE

MARCH 1, 1969. TOM SWOPE, THE OLD CINCINNATI BASEBALL writer who died recently, was a man of peculiar eating habits who particularly enjoyed putting hot coleslaw on cantaloupe and hot gravy on apple pie.

He also had the most literal mind of any person I have ever encountered. "Tom, do you think it will stop raining?" writers in the press coop used to ask him, putting him on, whenever the heavens released a torrent.

"It always has," he invariably replied.

Actually, it was the subject of rain that got me into difficulty with him during the season of 1928, when I was 13. That year I used to occupy a box seat in the upper deck at Redland Field, which is now called Crosley Field, immediately next to the press box, which was without cover and exposed to the public. Swope always sat in the first press row at the extreme right.

One day during the game, the scoreboard carried all the out-of-town contests except the one at Pittsburgh. This puzzled me somewhat, and merely to make conversation I asked, "Mr. Swope, do you know if it is raining in Pittsburgh?"

"How in the hell would I know if it is raining in Pittsburgh?" he retorted, and after that I approached him with extreme caution.

He used to send me on errands. I remember once that the late Ernie Orsatti of the Cardinals crashed into the center field wall and was carried off the field on a stretcher. Tom asked me to see Doc Weaver in the Cardinal clubhouse, and I hurried down to check on Orsatti, the first reporting I ever did. After that, I used to hope that players would be hurt — not seriously, of course — so that Tom would send me to the clubhouse.

Tom didn't drink, but he traveled with just about the wildest crew of baseball writers ever assembled, unless it was the gang that came out of Chicago a little later. Tom joined the Cincinnati Post in 1915. For the first ten years, he traveled with Jack Ryder of the Enquirer, Bill Phelon with the Times-Star and Bob Newhall of the Commercial Tribune. Curiously enough, the Post, started by E.W. Scripps as a scandal sheet selling for a penny in 1880, came to own the whole town.

Ryder was visited daily by friends all during the prohibition era. He referred to them as his "providers." They brought him bootleg gin and whiskey, which he mixed with lemon pop, or "lemo," as he liked to call it, that was sold by the vendors. He would reward the "providers" by mentioning in the interminable column of notes he wrote daily the fact that they were at the park. Jack also liked to eat hardboiled eggs, shells and all, and his favorite snack was a frankfurter loaded with horseradish. As an afterthought, he would tell the vendor to omit the frankfurter, making it a plain horseradish sandwich which he would wash down with the gin-lemo, meanwhile acting as official scorer.

He also chain-smoked Sweet Caporals and between pitches read such magazines as The American Boy.

Phelon, meanwhile, was accompanied on his daily rounds by a pet monkey, a hygienically careless creature, which had the liberty of the press box.

Newhall, an immaculate dresser, was a strutter who liked to pace up and down all during the game. He liked to insult players in his column with such notes as "Jim Dolan will pitch this afternoon, fans, so if you come to the park, bring your adding machines."

How Swope managed to get his work done daily in such an environment is difficult to understand, but he did.

He was not a gifted writer, but a more accurate one never lived. He loved statistics, kept a thermometer in the press box and noted in his scorebook every day the temperature when play began. In the nine years that Bill McKechnie managed the Reds, he received from Tom at the conclusion of every game a carbon of the box score including an elaborate summary that included the press box temperature. Tom's scorebooks were kept meticulously and in them he had every game played by the Reds from 1915 to the present time. When he stopped traveling, he would pick up the play-by-play from Waite Hoyt's radio description and enter the games in his books.

When I reported to the Reds at Tampa in 1938 to become Gabe Paul's assistant, I still called him "Mr. Swope," mindful of that silly question of mine about the rain in Pittsburgh a decade before. But he said to me, "Lee, I think you're old enough now to call me Tom." And after that I did, although his name was really Edmund, a fact known to only a few.

After that we had only one unpleasant moment. The Reds were playing the Red Sox in Greensboro one day that spring. We ran out of general admission tickets at the ball park, and Gabe sent me back to the Hotel O. Henry for more. I grabbed a cab, had the driver wait, and dashed through the revolving door just as Swope was coming out of it, carrying his typewriter. I didn't see him, and went through the door so fast that Tom was sent flying into the street on the seat of his pants, his typewriter sailing into the gutter.

I thought that surely I would be fired, but Tom got up, assured me he was perfectly all right, and never said a word.

He hated night ball, and he often used to say, "When they start playing more than seven games a year at night, that's when Tom Swope stops writing baseball." He didn't, of course.

PAUL DERRINGER

MARCH 8, 1969. THERE WAS A TIME WHEN PAUL DERRINGER and I were closely associated and met almost daily. But for some reason not entirely clear, it had been more than 18 years since we had seen each other.

When I pulled into his driveway in Tampa recently, he stood on the porch grinning, and when we shook hands, he said, "Long time between visits."

It was indeed. The last time I had seen him, we had appeared on a TV panel together in Cincinnati and then gone our separate ways in the night.

Paul now works for the American Automobile Association as a trouble-shooter concerned with such esoteric matters as bail. The AAA seems to be building an all-star baseball team. Unless I am mistaken, the organization, in addition to Derringer, employs Roy Parmelee in Michigan, Clydell Castleman in Tennessee and Harry Rice in Oregon. Parmelee and Castleman pitched for the Giants in the regime of Bill Terry, and Rice was an outfielder with the Browns, with a .359 average in 1925.

Derringer, who weighed 205 when he started as a rookie with the Cardinals in 1931, ballooned up to 316 after he quit pitching. He is now down to 289, or six pounds less than Jumbo Brown weighed when he was still active with the Giants. But he still can get in uniform, and last summer he worked an inning in an old-timer affair at Shea Stadium in New York and still proudly wears the expensive watch the Mets gave him on that occasion.

"I can't say enough for the Mets," Paul said. "But come on, Jane and I want to take you to a seafood place we like at Clearwater."

As we got into the car, I was reminded again of what a superb pitcher this fellow was when handled carefully, and how much Bill McKechnie got out of him at Cincinnati, as McKechnie had a way of doing with pitchers. Derringer had a record of 25 and 7 for the Reds in 1939, pitching the game that nailed down the National League pennant. In 1940, he won the seventh and deciding contest of the World Series against the Tigers.

"How did you get into baseball, anyway?" I asked him.

"Well," he replied, "you know, it's funny. I might have done all my pitching for Cleveland. This story never has been printed anywhere. The Cardinals had seen me in semi-pro ball around Kentucky in 1926 — I guess it was Frank Rickey, Branch's brother, who spotted me — and I reported to their Florida camp at Avon Park in 1927. The agreement was that I was to get a bonus of $2,500 if they kept me. Well, days passed and I didn't sign anything, and finally Cy Slapnicka, who was scouting for Cleveland, came around and gave me five thousand."

"In cash?"

"In cash. So I went to Clarence Lloyd, secretary of the Cardinals, and he tried to get Branch Rickey on the phone, but couldn't reach him. I told Lloyd the Cardinals hadn't come through with the $2,500 and I was going to go to Cleveland. Just then McKechnie — and he was just a coach at the time — came in the office and he said to Lloyd, 'Clarence, we can't let this fellow get away.' Lloyd explained that he had tried to reach Rickey without success, and meanwhile he was not permitted to write out any check for a ball player in excess of $500.

"'All right,' McKechnie told him, 'you just write out a check to Derringer for $500 and then you write four more just like it and we've kept our agreement with him.' So that is what Lloyd did, and McKechnie turned to me and said, 'Now you give Slapnicka back his money.'"

When Red Ruffing was at Cooperstown last summer, he told me a story about Derringer that I never had heard before. Ruffing beat Derringer, 2-1, in the first game of the 1939 World Series at Yankee Stadium, a thrilling duel not settled until the bottom of the ninth when, with one out, Charlie Keller hit a long fly that Ival Goodman got his hands on, but could not hold, with Keller pulling up at third.

McKechnie then ordered an intentional pass to Joe DiMaggio, chose to pitch to Bill Dickey with the infield halfway in, and Dickey spoiled the strategy with a single over second. It was a heartbreaking loss for Derringer after one of the best pitching battles in World Series history.

"Paul," I said, "Ruffing told me that after the game, you ran down to the umpires' dressing room and asked to see Bill McGowan, who had worked behind the plate. McGowan, of course, knew you must be furious after losing such a close game, and he had no particular desire to see you at that point, but he finally poked his head out, asked what you wanted, and you said, 'Bill, I just want to tell you that's the greatest job of calling balls and strikes I've ever seen. You didn't miss a single call all afternoon.' And McGowan, of course, told Ruffing later he never had heard of such a thing and it gave him a very warm feeling."

"Well, it was true," Derringer said. "It happened the way Ruffing heard it."

The seafood was every bit as good as Derringer claimed and during the evening there were many more stories. Then, two days later, back in Boca Raton, the phone rang, and it was the big trouble-shooter for the AAA.

"Heh," he said. "What do you know? I've got to fly to Palm Beach today. How about meeting me at the airport there?"

As he got off the plane, he was grinning again.

"Short time between visits," he said.

A STORY BEHIND EVERY NAME

MARCH 15, 1969. EDEN, FLA. IT WAS DOROTHY PARKER, FAMED for her acid wit, who replied to a question seeking her opinion of a particularly atrocious play she had just witnessed by saying, "I think there's less to it than meets the eye."

In baseball, the opposite is true. There is so much more to it than meets the eye. You can, for example, thumb through one of the encyclopedias of the game without the slightest hint of the personalities of the men behind the names. What is needed is a dictionary of baseball biography. But such a work would require many volumes, commercially it would be impractical, and it seems doubtful that any person of means could be found to subsidize such a worthwhile undertaking.

But a list of names that gives demographic data and playing statistics is not sufficient. Suppose, for example, you come upon the name of Leven Lawrence Shreve, a pitcher with Indianapolis back in the 1880's.

There is no way to tell from any published work that there was a Shreve who was a law partner of Thomas Jefferson, and a Shreve who was the first president of the Louisville and Nashville railroad, and a famous chemical engineer, Norris Shreve, now at Purdue and listed in Who's Who. All were or are related to the pitcher.

Or take George Henry Keerl, a second baseman with Chicago of the National Association in 1875. The Keerls were Bavarians. Jorg Heinrich Keerl, a surgeon general in the Hessian army, remained here at the close of our Revolution and became one of the charter doctors of Johns Hopkins.

Every name in the record books represents a story of this kind, but no person will ever live long enough to hear and remember them all. What brought me here, for instance, is a question that has puzzled me for many years. John Albert Rothfuss was a first baseman who hit .348 for the Pirates in 1897 and never played in another major league game.

For the life of me, I could not figure out how a player capable of batting .348 and pushing as competent a performer as Harry Davis off first base, as Rothfuss did, was not invited back.

At odd moments over the years, the matter bothered me, but I never was able to do anything about it until recently when Joe Simenic of the Cleveland Plain Dealer, so often helpful to this column, unearthed the address of the player's son, R.M. Rothfuss.

To reach Eden, Fla., just a speck on the Atlantic three miles north of Jensen Beach, one has to drive through cypress swamps along the Indian River and look for a hill called Pineapple Ridge, where Mr. Rothfuss makes his home.

I found him to be a pleasant, ruddy-faced man of middle years, an artist who lives with his wife in a house he built of cypress. In fact, he built six of the houses here, and rents out the five others for the season, an experiment in real Florida living far in spirit though not in distance from the luxury appointments of the Gold Coast and the outstretched palm of the condominium doorman.

"What I want to know right away," I told him, "is how your father could hit .348 for Pittsburgh and not go back."

"Ah! But he did go back," Mr. Rothfuss replied. "What happened was this. Dysentery. The drinking water of Pittsburgh gave him dysentery when he played there in 1897, and when he went to the training camp and the same thing happened in 1898, he quit the big league scene for good.

"For years after that he played in smaller leagues, and he made out all right, financially, too.

"This used to be one of the few places in the United States where pineapples were grown for commercial use," Mr. Rothfuss told me. "But then they found Cuban pineapples were better, so they aren't grown any more.

"Since Castro, we get pineapples from South America, Mexico and, of course, Hawaii."

The cypress used in constructing the houses also supplies the surface on which Mr. Rothfuss paints.

"These cypress trees are wonderful," he said. "Some of them are 3,000 years old. It takes about a thousand years until worms kill them, and after that they often topple dead into streams and the water preserves them. I use casein paint on them, and you can leave the paintings out in any kind of weather and the paint will never run."

Some of his paintings are now on exhibition, and they enjoy a lively sale.

"It's too bad you can't meet my mother," he said. "She could talk to you all day about Ed Barrow and Honus Wagner and baseball around New Jersey. Dad was originally from Newark, and he died at Basking Ridge, which is really a suburb of Morristown, in 1947. Mother's in a nursing home at Fort Pierce and she'll be 90 in November. I was a salesman for a mattress company for a long time. I came down here 20 years ago and built these houses, but I still go back to Jersey in the summers."

"How's the drinking water here?" I asked him.

"Great," he said. "No dysentery."

On the way home, it seemed a strange environment in which to disinter the reason why his father had a lifetime .348 confined to a single season. On either side of the road, the ascending branches of cypress, bearded with Spanish moss, looked patriarchal in the late afternoon.

They were far older than the 72-year-old mystery that had just been solved, a beautiful mottled gray, carrying their great height with dignity and majesty.

SATCHEL

MARCH 29, 1969. HENRY AARON LAY ON HIS BACK ON THE rubbing table in the clubhouse of the Braves. An errant pitch from the arm of Pete Mikkelsen had hit him on the right knee his last time up the day before.

Three feet away, Satchel Paige sat in great dignity. The morning was cool, and a windbreaker covered his lean frame. A neat mustache graced his upper lip, and Satch looked out at the world through shell-rimmed glasses.

A writer came in, nodded to Satch and smiled at Aaron. "How's the knee?"

"Okay," Hank said. "No bones broken. I'm all right."

"It scared me," the writer said, "but not as much as that story about you on the wire this spring, saying it might be your last year." Aaron smiled.

"You can't quit when you get 3,000 hits," the writer went on. "That's when your life will start to get interesting. Most players who get to that total limp there, but you'll take 3,000 hits in stride."

Aaron didn't say anything, but looked pleased.

"There are a lot of records within your grasp you ought to know about," the writer told him. "You could beat some of Musial's records. You might even go to bat more times than Cobb did. How many times up do you need now for 9,000?"

"About a hundred," Aaron said.

"Well, give it four more years, five more, and you can pass Cobb. And you won't even be 40 at the end of the 1973 season. Cobb played when he was 41."

"Let me ask you something," said Satch, who knows what it is to play when you're 41. "You've seen Koufax?"

"Of course."

"Tell me something," Satchel said again. "How does Koufax's fastball compare with some of the others' like Diz and Feller?"

"I don't think I'm qualified to answer that," the writer said. "You could answer that a lot better than I."

"You know what you saw, don't you?" Satch asked. "You said you saw him."

"Right. But from the grandstand or press box it's hard to tell. You'd have to hit against him, or at least see him from the field. How do you think his fast ball compares?"

"I don't think he was quite as fast as Diz or Bobby," Satch said.

"I don't know," Aaron said, sitting up. "He looked plenty fast to me. Of course, when I hit against Feller, he was using breaking stuff and change-ups."

"Koufax had a great curve ball," Satch said.

"I know," Aaron replied. "But I remember one day Sandy pitched against us and had a blister and couldn't use his curve. We knew nothing but fast balls were coming, but I think he beat us, 2-1, in 13 innings. Something like that."

"What about Diz, was he fast?" Paige asked the writer, knowing the answer.

"Certainly he was fast. And so was Bob Grove. Funny thing, though. Feller was with a group of pitchers who had their speed tested by one of those machines. And I think Atley Donald of the Yankees threw the ball faster than Feller."

"Bobby was a hundred-mile-an-hour pitcher," Satch replied.

Aaron looked at the writer, nodded to Satch and asked, "How old is he?"

"Satch?" the writer asked. "Sixty-two."

"That's right," Satch agreed. "All that mystery stuff about my age, that's all Bill Veeck's doings. He'd go up to the press box 20 years ago when I was pitching and shake his head and say to the writers, 'Isn't Paige remarkable? I wouldn't be surprised if he was 75 years old.' But I saw in a magazine where you went to the health department of the city of Mobile and got my birth certificate."

"That's right," the writer said. "And you were born on July 7, 1906."

"Correct," Satch said. "The Braves know how old I am, too. They just don't say anything about it."

You left, and you wondered if part of the charm of baseball wasn't that all the generations pass on their legends to the next, and all the records are made to be broken, and all the time you're trying to compare the incomparable and know the unknowable. Grove, or Dean, or Feller or Koufax — who was the fastest?

How can anyone tell?

You remembered that they had this argument when Walter Johnson came up in 1907, and players and fans wondered if he was as fast as Rube

Waddell, and whether Waddell had been as fast as Amos Rusie.

And you remembered a story of how they took Walter Johnson to see Feller pitch shortly before Johnson's death in 1946, when Feller was at his absolute peak. And after the game Johnson didn't say anything, but his friends kept after him and asked him, "Is Feller as fast as you were?"

Johnson smiled. A humble, modest man, he didn't want to have to say. But his friends insisted. "Walter," they said, "is Feller as fast as you were?"

Finally Johnson said, almost whispering, as if he was ashamed to say it, "Feller isn't quite as fast as I was."

Come to think of it, how fast was Satchel Paige? There are so many things in baseball you cannot know, so many things you cannot find out.

THE LITHUANIAN ALL-STARS

APRIL 5, 1969. ONE OF THE HOT SPOTS HERE IN BOCA RATON that I hit regularly is an ice cream parlor that features 33 flavors. To show you how mod the place is, the proprietors, Jack and Marilynn Neal, this month are pushing hazelnut krunch, pineapple cheesecake and banana split ice cream, all of which are groovy.

With such an abundance of flavors to choose from, the decision is often harrowing, and the exercise involved in standing on tiptoe to gaze into 33 separate containers provides more than enough exertion for one devoted to the Robert Benchley theory of exercise ("When I feel the urge to exercise, I lie down until the feeling goes away").

When I hesitated in making a selection the other day, before finally settling on hazelnut krunch, Mr. Neal said to me:

"I have a theory that you can tell a person's politics from his choice of ice cream. There's a girl I know who's an ultra conservative.

"Every time she comes in, she carefully looks over every flavor and finally ends up by taking vanilla. She's just cautious, that's all. Really square. But the members of the New Left aren't afraid to try licorice or Italian lemonade."

It seems to me that a similar situation exists in regard to the ancestry of ball players. Baseball today really reflects the melting pot tradition of America. For many years, the Irish and the Germans dominated the game; they were the vanilla, chocolate and strawberry of the profession. But in the complex world we have at the start of baseball's second century, the Yankees exhibit such exotics as Tony Solaita, a Samoan and the game's first Polynesian, and Mike Kekich, who is Irish and Montenegran. The Braves, meanwhile, present Mike Lum, who is Hawaiian-Chinese; and the Red Sox can call on Joe Lahoud, who is Lebanese.

Bill Sudakis, the fine young third baseman of the Dodgers, told me recently that he is Norwegian and Lithuanian. This was tremendously pleasant news because it enables him to cinch the third base job on my all-time Lithuanian team, displacing Tony Malinoski of the 1937 Dodgers.

Lithuania, of course, is one of the three Baltic nations swallowed by Stalin, the others being Latvia and Estonia. I never had heard of a Latvian in the major leagues, and the only current Estonian I know of is Wally Bunker of the Kansas City Royals. So I'd match my Lithuanians against their immediate neighbors and might even pit them against the Finns.

Johnny Podres, who won the deciding game for the Dodges against the Yankees in the 1955 World Series, is the starting pitcher, and his catcher is Walt Hriniak of the Braves. Should Podres run into any difficulty, he could be relieved byVito Tamulis, Joe Krakauskas, Johnny Broaca, Dick Rusteck, Bruce Howard, George Piktuzis, Nelson King, Stan Ferens, Alex Mustaikis, Ed Cole, Uete Naktenis, Whitey Wistert, Joe Zapustas or Joe Samuels.

Eddie Waitkus of the championship Phillies of 1950 is at first; Bob Boken of the pennant-winning Senators of 1933 at second; Eddie Miksis of the Dodgers at short, and Sudakis of course, at third.

The outfield shows Frank Thomas in left, Barney McCosky in center and Morrie Arnovich in right.

But the team's secret weapon is bench strength. Ready to step in at any moment are Pete Gray, the one-armed outfielder of the Browns, and Eddie Gaedel, Bill Veeck's celebrated midget.

This is a remarkable combination when you consider that Lithuanians are very recent arrivals on the big league scene. The first one I know of was Simon Pauxtis, a catcher who joined the Reds in 1909. A product of the coal region around Pittston, Pa., Pauxtis, who died in Philadelphia in 1961, was an ambitious young man who attended both the University of Pennsylvania and Lebanon Valley College.

He appeared in only four National League games, and there was not another Lithuanian to follow until 1926, when Adam Comorosky, who also had Polish blood in his veins, joined the Pirates as an outfielder. Comorosky later drifted to the Reds and played left field for two years during Larry MacPhail's regime. John McDonald was MacPhail's traveling secretary, and sometimes in winter he helped out in the sale of opening game tickets.

When the tickets arrived, McDonald always pulled out the seats that were behind the poles and put them aside. Believe it or not, there were people who asked for these locations because they preferred to sit behind poles.

One day McDonald was behind the counter. The supply of pole seats was exhausted, and the only tickets were field seats on the terrace in left, a temporary structure. When a customer asked for a seat behind a pole, McDonald said to him, "I can give you a seat behind a pole — Comorosky."

When Whitey Wistert left the University of Michigan in 1934 to join the Reds, giving the team two Lithuanians, he appeared only three times, but his only big league start was unforgettable. Pitching in September at Wrigley Field, he lost his game, 1-0, when another boy making his first appearance at the age of 17, hit a home run. That boy was Phil Cavarretta, and he stayed around until 1955.

So far there have been 28 Lithuanians mentioned in this piece, and there are five others who deserve to be named also: Charles F. (Cotton) Nash, the University of Kentucky marvel who joined the White Sox as a first baseman in 1967; Stan Andrews, a catcher with the Braves, Dodgers and Phillies from 1939 to 1945; Johnny Dickshot, outfielder with the Pirates, Giants and White Sox from 1936 to 1945; Al Reiss, a shortstop with the 1932 Athletics, and Bill Karlon, an outfielder with the 1930 Yankees.

TURN, TURN, TURN

APRIL 12, 1969. ECCLESIASTES SAID IT BEST OF ALL.

"To everything there is a season, and a time to every purpose under the heaven: A time to be born, and a time to die; a time to plant and a time to pluck up that which is planted; a time to kill, and a time to heal; a time to break down, and a time to build up; a time to weep, and a time to laugh; a time to mourn, and a time to dance."

So the season is here again, and in this city where the professional game began a century ago, another team, the 85th to represent Cincinnati in the National League, wears its proud red stockings on the friendly and familiar field.

In the training season just concluded, it was a time to laugh and a time to weep, a time to cheer and a time to mourn. The period began under the pall of a threatened player strike, then a succession of overcast days gave Florida its gloomiest aspect in many and many a year.

The talent was thinly spread over four more expansion clubs, and the beckoning military posed its usual threat.

But the strike was averted, the weather cleared, and if there were borderline major leaguers assured of jobs, the excitement generated by divisional play more than made up for it. Besides, who is there who can sit in the stands and tell the difference between a major league game and a Triple-A encounter?

The differences in class are so slight as to be scarcely visible in a single game.

There was also the shot of adrenalin given the game by forceful actions of a confident new commissioner, Bowie Kuhn, and the pleasure radiating throughout baseball by the return to the wars of an old hero, Ted Williams, in his surprising role as manager of the Senators.

So often dreary in the past, the Washington club now finds itself a cynosure.

The political vocabulary of the nation now will pervade the language of baseball so that games will be called confrontations, teams will be said to be viable, and a few players will be said to have charisma. And as the promise of spring fades in the heavy heat of summer, some club spokesmen will have their credibility called to question.

Cincinnati always has been an extraordinary opening-day city, with a full park assured. This tradition was carefully built by Frank C. Bancroft, who came here as the team's business manager in 1891 and remained until his death in 1921. Bancroft reserved every seat in the park and usually sold them out before Christmas. After his death, the custom was so deeply imbedded in the city's consciousness that it continued without requiring any stimulus.

Now a new ball park is arising a mile away on the north bank of the Ohio, as the Reds hopefully anticipate their second century of existence. The storied one here at Findlay and Western Avenues has been in use since 1884, and the present grandstand dates back to 1912. At first, the plant was called simply League Park, but upon being rebuilt after a disastrous fire in 1901, Ren Mulford, local writer, named it Redland Field. It was known that way until 1934 when Powel Crosley, who had a radio and refrigerator business to promote, bought the club and put his name upon the club's real estate.

When the present grandstand was built in 1912, it was not thought likely that a home run ever would be hit over the fences. The ball then used was dead, and it was 360 feet to the barrier in left, 420 in center and 385 in right. More than nine years passed before a fair ball left the lot.

Then Pat Duncan, the Reds' leftfielder, hit one over the fence in left on June 2, 1921, off Ferdie Schupp of the Cardinals. The first visiting player to clobber one was George Kelly of the Giants, off Dolf Luque, on July 20 of that same year.

Now the field is a chummy one, 328 feet to left, 387 to center and 368 to right, and home runs fly off the bat in monotonous procession. And yet Pete Rose, the most exciting player on the present team, hopes to earn $100,000 annually by lining out singles.

You sit back now to watch the groundskeepers manicure the infield, and when two of them delineate with whitewash the contours of the batter's box, you are reminded that this again provided the Reds with a "first."

For the groundskeeper of the Red Stockings of 1869 was William Wing, and it was his idea to mark the foul lines with a chalky substance. Before that, they were made by digging a furrow with a plow.

The batter's box is perfect now, and the game and the century are about to start.

Will the Reds have charisma? Will they survive their confrontations and be viable? It seems credible.

But win or lose, the Reds, like other aggregations, will contribute to the drama as the plot of the season unfolds. Baseball is numerous things; a sport, a business, a source of civic pride. It is also a release from the terrible tensions of the nuclear age. When the assassination of Archduke Ferdinand of Sarajevo set off World War I at a time when the tariff on wool was a domestic issue in the United States, the Philadelphia Ledger observed the following in an editorial:

"Who cares about Montenegro or wool when three are on and Baker's at bat?" Today's problems are worse, but the ball park at least offers a brief escape from the agonies of Vietnam and the urban crises.

HAPPY AND SAMMY

APRIL 26, 1969. THE LATEST WITH HAPPY CHANDLER IS THIS thing with Sammy Davis, Jr., about fried chicken.

The game's second commissioner and the great entertainer have combined efforts in forming a company, Daniel Boone Fried Chicken, Inc. Several locations here in Kentucky are open and when the company goes public in several months 1,000 franchises will become available. Happy is serving as chairman of the board and has a handsome office, in which soft carpeting blends with soft background music. Appropriately enough, the vocalist is Sammy, a principal stockholder in the firm.

Now 70, but as trim and spry as ever, Happy also maintains his law practice, representing three major railroads. His thinning hair now presents a salt and pepper effect, but he's in perfect health, vigorous and dapper.

He and Mrs. Chandler, his wife of more than 43 years and a former school teacher, now live in Versailles, Ky., in an eight-room house of early Colonial brick, which they share with Wyatt Earp, a French poodle from Alsace-Lorraine. They have four children, three of whom live near here, and 12 grandchildren.

The older daughter, Marcella, is Mrs. Thomas Davis Miller, Jr., of Wilson, N. C., but the three other children live in Kentucky. Mimi, a former movie actress, is the wife of James L. Lewis, a farmer and engineer, and they occupy

400 acres of Blue Grass. Albert B., Jr., is publisher of the Woodford Sun, and Joseph Daniel, a broker, also lives in Versailles.

The Blue Grass, attractive at any time, takes on an aura of almost unbearable beauty at this time of the year. The day of my visit coincided with the opening of Keeneland, and the lawns of the great estates were manicured perfectly and surrounded by fences as gaily painted as peppermints.

But what sets the Chandler house apart from those of the neighbors is the contents. Landscapes by Howard Chandler Christy, a relative, dominate the first floor, but the real treasures are in the basement, where the proud acquisitions of his days in baseball — books and autographed balls and pictures — find themselves in the company of souvenirs from his years in the Senate and his two terms as governor.

The briefest tour of the premises reveals a picture autographed by Mahatma Gandhi, a Bible signed by Ben Gurion, a telegram from Winston Churchill and autographed pictures of Franklin Roosevelt, Douglas MacArthur and Harry Truman. But one of his proudest possessions is a silver tray presented him by Ralph Kiner, Allie Reynolds, Fred Hutchinson and Danny Litwhiler that bears the legend, "In sincere appreciation for services rendered to the players of the major leagues."

"People are always saying we should have a baseball man as commissioner," Happy said. "Well, I was a baseball man. I played in high school and college (Transylvania) and professionally in the Blue Grass and Red River Valley leagues. I never had any trouble with the ball players, and I think my trouble with the owners all started with Lou Perini, when he became angry over the Lucky Lohrke case. Lohrke was a farmhand of the Braves and they left him unprotected in the draft. He had been playing on option at San Diego, but Boston failed to exercise the option by October 1 as the rules required.

"At the draft meeting, Perini asked if he could say a few words to the group and I said, 'Sure, go ahead.' He then begged everyone not to draft Lohrke. But when the roll was called, Lohrke, picked by Horace Stoneham of the Giants, was the first player selected."

Lohrke acquired his nickname by twice escaping fatal rides. Once he just missed boarding a plane that crashed and killed all aboard. And he was a member of the Spokane club when the team's bus crashed and nine of the players were killed and six others seriously injured. But he had left the bus at Ellensburg, Wash., to arrange to report to San Diego.

Lohrke, however, was not so lucky in the majors, batting .242 in 354 games with the Giants and Phillies over a period of seven years.

Happy's years in baseball were turbulent ones in the noisy prosperity that followed World War II. Although he is often remembered best for his actions in such thorny problems as the Leo Durocher case and that of the Mexican League jumpers, he also was involved in less spectacular but important matters as negotiating contracts for the broadcasting and telecasting of the World Series and the birth pangs of the pension plan.

"The pension plan originated with Larry MacPhail," Chandler said, "and he should get full credit for it."

We walked from the main house out through the yard in back to another building where Happy has guest quarters and another office. "It was in this building that Branch Rickey came to see me just before he brought up Jackie Robinson," Chandler told me. "He came to me and said he was ready to bring up Jackie, but that he knew there was opposition to it and that he'd have to have me stand by him. 'That's just what I'll do,' I told him."

As the former commissioner and I walked to my car, he said, "Now, in regard to the Mexican League thing, you see, if I'd put the boys out for only a year, it wouldn't have stopped them from jumping. But making it five years gave them something to think about."

Later that afternoon, driving through the sun of Tennessee, I was surprised to learn by billboards that Colonel Sanders is now serving roast beef. Could it be that he anticipates a threat of competition from the chairman of the board of Daniel Boone Fried Chicken, Inc.?

DEATHS IN THE AIR

MAY 3, 1969. EARLIER THIS YEAR AT MARACAIBO, VENEZUELA, when the worst crash in aviation history claimed 155 lives, The Sporting News was the only paper to my knowledge to mention that among the victims was Nestor Chavez, a pitcher who worked five innings for the Giants in 1967 and who was en route to Tucson to join the Phoenix club of the Pacific Coast League.

Shortly afterward, a greasy postcard bearing an undecipherable signature and mailed at Dallas asked me how many major league players have been killed in air disasters.

There have been eight that I know of, counting the unfortunate Señor Chavez, but the possibility always exists that there have been some that escaped public notice.

The first such case involved Marvin Goodwin, a righthanded spitball pitcher with the Senators, Cardinals and Reds from 1916 to 1925. Goodwin had started the 1925 season as a combination pitcher and manager for Houston of the Texas League. By mid-August he had won 21 and lost 9, and the Reds purchased his contract. He lost his only two decisions in the six weeks that remained in the National League, then went back to Texas.

Goodwin had been a flying instructor in World War I and remained a lieutenant in the Air Corps Reserve. At Ellington Field near Houston, he took off on October 18, 1925, in the company of a mechanic, and his plane crashed after achieving an altitude of only 200 feet. The mechanic was not seriously injured, but Goodwin suffered fractures of both legs and internal injuries, and died three days later. His body was removed to Gordonville, Va. for burial.

If I am not mistaken, Goodwin, at the time, was involved in a dispute similar to the recent Staub-Clendenon affair. Branch Rickey had either had the Houston club sell Goodwin's contract to Syracuse, or Cincinnati had sold it to Syracuse. Warren Giles would remember, as he was general manager of the Syracuse club at the time. And Goodwin's death raised the question of whether his club was owed a player to replace him.

Ten years later, the strange case of Leonard Koenecke occurred. An outfielder and lefthanded hitter, Koenecke enjoyed a superlative year at Indianapolis in 1931, batting .353, and the Giants purchased his contract. He was the last player personally scouted by John McGraw. But he never quite cut it with the Giants and drifted to Jersey City and Buffalo before earning another trial with the Dodgers in 1934. He was a streaky player and enjoyed enough hot spells in 1934 to bat .320. But in 1935, he slumped somewhat and became extremely moody. His mates had no idea he was on the verge of serious mental trouble.

In September, Casey Stengel, who managed the Dodgers that year, sent him back to New York from St. Louis to await his release or assignment to another club. Koenecke started the trip by train, but at Detroit he chartered a small plane to take him to New York. In the air, he suddenly ran amuck, and the pilot, attacked by Koenecke and fighting for his life, beat Len to death with a fire extinguisher when the plane was over Toronto.

Tommy Holmes, the New York writer, has often recalled how morose the Dodgers were upon hearing of the tragedy while still in St. Louis, and how Van Mungo, who had been particularly close to the outfielder, peeled off bill after bill, requesting the band leader at the Chase roof to play "My Buddy" again and again.

Elmer Gedeon, an outfielder with the Senators in 1939, was an air casualty of World War II. A graduate of the University of Michigan, where he had been a track star, he passed up a chance in the Olympic Games to concentrate on baseball. Gedeon entered the Air Corps and died in combat when his plane was shot down over France.

For the only time in baseball history, two players died in planes in the same year — 1956 — within ten weeks of each other, Tom Gastall, a rookie catcher with the Orioles, and Charlie Peete, an outfield recruit with the Cardinals, were the victims.

Gastall, a bonus boy, was flying his private plane, taking off from Harbor field, near Baltimore, on September 20. He landed at Easton, then took off again for the return flight over Chesapeake Bay, and crashed. Five days later, his body was found floating in the water off Riviera Beach.

Peete was one of a group of 25 that included his wife and three children who died when a four-engined Constellation they had boarded at Idlewild crashed into a mountain peak near Caracas, Venezuela, November 27.

Bill McAfee, a righthanded pitcher who had trials with the Cubs, Braves, Senators and Browns from 1930 to 1934, was, like Gedeon, a graduate of the University of Michigan. He prospered in business, and at the time of his death, July 8, 1958, was serving as mayor of Albany, Ga. He had taken three companions in a private plane to the All-Star Game at Baltimore, and on the return trip, their craft was downed in a heavy storm near Culpeper, Va.

Finally, there was the tragic death of Ken Hubbs, the young second base star of the Cubs. In his first full National League season in 1962, he established two all-time fielding records by going through 78 consecutive games and 418 chances without an error. Flying with a companion in his own light plane, he plunged into Utah Lake, five miles from Provo, in a snowstorm, February 13, 1964.

Selected as National League Rookie of the Year in 1962, he had obtained his pilot's license only two weeks before his death.

DE WITT ON RICKEY

MAY 24, 1969. BILL DEWITT PUSHED A TENTATIVE SPOON INTO his raspberry sherbet and leaned back in the chair on the porch of his country club, then had this to say about Branch Rickey:

"I'd say," he began, "that Rickey's greatest ability was his tremendous judgment of players. I don't think I've ever seen it printed anywhere, but in this he patterned himself after Barney Dreyfuss, the owner of the Pirates. He often told me that Dreyfuss was the best judge of players he had ever seen, and that John McGraw was the best he had ever seen in running a team on the field. So Rickey tried to copy Dreyfuss in the office, and manage his men like McGraw on the field."

DeWitt should know. He started as Rickey's office boy with the Browns in 1916, followed him to the Cardinals, and rose through the ranks to become business manager and eventually treasurer. In his early days, he operated the scoreboard at Sportsman's Park and sold tickets. After leaving Rickey, he went on to become president of the Browns, Tigers and Reds, and one year he served as coordinator of funds supplied to the minor leagues. He also was an executive with the Yankees. It was J.G. Taylor Spink, publisher of The Sporting News, who recommended him to John Fetzer at Detroit.

In one capacity or another, he has been associated with nine teams that won pennants: The Cardinals in 1926, 1928, 1930, 1931, and 1934; the Browns in 1944; the Yankees in 1955 and 1956, whom he served as assistant general manager under George Weiss, and the Reds in 1961. He thinks that Weiss, now a director of the Mets, is the only living executive who has been with more winners.

Now 67 and theoretically eligible for Medicare, DeWitt is not sure whether he will return to the game.

"I wouldn't care to run the show again," he insisted, "but I wouldn't mind being part of a syndicate that bought a club. I still have as much enthusiasm for the game as ever."

Bill now makes his permanent residence in Cincinnati but, with what seems to be admirable wisdom, spends his winters at Palm Beach.

"Rickey was a terrific influence in my early life," he went on. "When I was his office boy, he insisted that I go on with my education. As a result, I had two years of commerce and finance at St. Louis University, a year at Washington University, and three years in law school. I'm licensed to practice law in Missouri, but never have.

"The greatest change that has come to baseball in my time," he said, "has been its growth. When we won the pennant at St. Louis in 1926, there were exactly five of us in the office: Rickey and Sam Breadon, Clarence Lloyd, who handled business arrangements on the road, a girl stenographer and me."

There is a stereotyped belief in baseball that Rickey was a failure as a manager, that his blackboard theories were over the heads of his players, and that the Cardinals were not able to head for a pennant until Rogers Hornsby replaced him on Decoration Day in 1925. How does DeWitt feel about that?

"Rickey might be a better field manager today than he was then," Bill replied, "but that would be because the intelligence quotient of the players is higher. But what's wrong with blackboard talks? Football teams use them. Besides, Rickey was more than a theorist. He had been a major league player, and his knowledge of the game's techniques was unsurpassed.

"Breadon wanted to fire him even before he did, at Stockton, Calif., in 1925. Rickey actually cried when he got the news. But for some reason Sam changed his mind and let him start the season, then replaced him with Hornsby that day in Pittsburgh."

Rickey then sold his stock in the Cardinals to Hornsby and moved into the front office. But he had a deal that was more profitable than if he had been a stockholder.

"Branch's contract provided that he get ten percent of the profits,"

DeWitt recalled. "And later this was increased to 20 percent. In addition, he got a percentage of the sales price when the surplus of the Cardinal farm system was disposed of to other teams. So he did all right without stock."

When the Cardinals roared to a pennant in 1934 with the team that became known as the Gashouse Gang, DeWitt took on an additional and curious duty, serving as manager of the Dean brothers, Diz and Paul, handling the commercial propositions that came their way.

"Diz earned $7,500 from the Cardinals in 1934," Bill said. "And Paul got $3,000. But during the two years I handled them, 1934 and 1935, they made $8,000 from outside activities."

The conversation always seemed to get back to Rickey.

"One thing you have to understand," DeWitt said, "is what a great innovator he was. He was the first to use a batting cage, at Orange, or maybe it was Brownsville, Tex., in 1920. And that business of his — using strings on poles to indicate the strike zone — that wasn't something he started at Brooklyn.

"I remember him doing that in 1920 to teach the strike zone to Ferdie Schupp."

There was one more chestnut to dispose of. Rickey, well known as a Sabbatarian, supposedly never attended a game on Sunday during his years at St. Louis. But there are cynics who have said that on such days he used to watch the action from a YMCA across the street from Sportsman's Park.

"Not a bit of truth to it," Bill said. "But I must confess that there were Sundays when I used to phone him the scores."

MYTHOLOGY

MAY 31, 1969. MOST OF THESE COLUMNS DWELL AT LENGTH on a single subject, but this one contains, like the hash at Mrs. Murphy's boarding house, a little bit of everything, including such matters as the Kentucky Derby, an exercise in Greek mythology and the ancestry of a famous catcher.

There is a mystery about the Derby. All week before the event, the news media informed us that President Nixon would become the first President to attend the Run for the Roses since Rutherford B. Hayes watched the race in 1879. Immediately afterward, it was announced that Nixon, rooting happily for Majestic Prince, had been the first president ever to watch the race.

Why the sudden downgrading of Hayes? Has it been discovered that Rutherford was not actually present? If he was there, he saw Lord Murphy, with Shauer up, beat out Falsetto and Strathmore. Make what you want of it ideologically. I prefer to believe that Hayes watched the proceedings.

Now for the Greek business. Back in 1921, and again briefly in 1925, the Reds had a catcher whose name appeared in the records as Astyanax Douglas. It turns out that his surname is actually spelled Douglass. But it was the strange first name that always fascinated me, and without thinking about it seriously, I couldn't account for it.

Douglass was a batterymate of Pete Donohue at Texas Christian, and Boyd Chambers signed the pair for the Reds. Donohue, of course, stepped right into the starting rotation, and won 20 or more games in a season three times. For years after his retirement, he owned a chain of dry-cleaning establishments in Fort Worth and lived the good life, playing golf almost daily.

Douglass was less memorable, appearing in only 11 games in his two seasons but I have never been able to forget his first name, which, incidentally, is pronounced as if it were A-sty-an-axe, with the accent on the second syllable. For many years I thought of him often but never did anything about it. Finally, I wrote to Texas Christian and discovered that he is living in El Paso.

It turns out that he prospered in the furniture business and now, at 71, is free to do just about as he pleases. He recently went to Covington, Tex., his place of birth, to cut up old touches and stopped off at Fort Worth for a pleasant reunion with Donohue. Later this summer, he and his wife, the former Catherine Bell Storm, are going to visit Alaska.

"The name Astyanax," Douglass wrote me, "is of Greek mythological origin. You will find it in any large dictionary. I have never met or heard of anyone bearing this name other than our immediate family. My great-grandfather Douglass was the first to carry the name. It was passed on to my grandfather and to my father. Since I'm the last in this line of Douglasses and I have no children, the foolishness will end on my passing."

This sent me rushing — rather sheepishly — to my dictionary, and sure enough it says: "Astyanax. Son of Hector and Andromache, hurled by the Greeks from the walls of Troy, that he might not restore the kingdom as predicted."

How strange it is that so much time must pass before we learn the obvious. For example, when Douglass caught for the Reds under Jack Hendricks, the team had a coach long famous in the minors, Derby Day Bill Clymer. He had been a shortstop with the Athletics as far back as 1891.

I remember him batting fungoes to the outfield in 1925, a paunchy man with a florid face. And I wondered often how he came to be known as "Derby Day." It finally occurred to me to ask Joe McCarthy, who knows virtually everything, and the great manager of the Yankees said, "Do you remember Clymer's cap? It had a long peak like the cap of a jockey. That is why he was called 'Derby Day.'" And you could easily imagine how players might have yelled:

"Hey Clymer! What do you think it is, Derby Day?"

The ancestry of the catcher involves the question of whether Johnny Kling, one of the most gifted receivers in the game's history, was Jewish. This became a matter of extreme importance a few years ago to Roy Silver of NBC, who was writing his authoritative "Encyclopedia of Jews in Sports." I was unable to tell him, although it was widely believed in baseball that Kling was Jewish.

An old trainer for the Cubs of the Kling era (1900-11) stopped in my office at the Hall of Fame one afternoon and I asked him. "I think he was Jewish," the trainer said. "I remember that Joe Tinker always called him by a Yiddish name."

But that was hardly evidence, and the truth had to wait until I located Mrs. Kling, who is, I am happy to say, still going strong in Kansas City. She told me that she is Jewish, but that Johnny was not, that he was a German Lutheran.

She also explained the middle initial "G" that appears in Kling's name in the record books, saying that he had no middle name at birth, but decided to adopt a middle initial to distinguish himself from other John Klings. Her maiden name was Lillian Gradwohl, so Johnny borrowed the "G" as his.

Now, if we could only find out if Rutherford B. Hayes attended the 1879 Derby! It would be too much to hope for to discover that Derby Day Bill Clymer was there, too. He was only six, and it seems unlikely that Churchill Downs was that permissive about juveniles.

INDEX

INDEX